# NOT SO
# FREE TO CHOOSE

# NOT SO
# FREE TO CHOOSE

## The Political Economy of Milton Friedman and Ronald Reagan

ELTON RAYACK

PRAEGER

New York
Westport, Connecticut
London

**Library of Congress Cataloging-in-Publication Data**

Rayack, Elton.
    Not so free to choose.

    1. Chicago school of economics. 2. Friedman,
Milton, 1912–    . 3. Laissez-faire. 4. Free trade
and protection. 5. United States—Economic policy—
1981–    . 6. Reagan, Ronald. I. Title.
HB98.3.R39 1986             330               86-21276
ISBN 0-275-92363-0 (alk. paper)

Library of Congress Catalog Card Number: 86-21276
ISBN: 0-275-92363-0 (alk. paper)

First published in 1987

Praeger Publishers, 521 Fifth Avenue, New York, NY 10175
A division of Greenwood Press, Inc.

Printed in the United States of America

The paper used in this book complies with the Permanent
Paper Standard issued by the National Information Standards
Organization (Z39.48-1984).

10  9  8  7  6  5  4  3  2  1

For Amy and Wendy with much love and respect.
May they always remember a simple fact —
in law and economics, as in human physiology,
both the head and the heart are indispensable.

# CONTENTS

# LIST OF TABLES AND FIGURES

## TABLE

**FIGURE**

# ACKNOWLEDGMENTS

My wife Jean patiently read the manuscript during its period of seemingly endless gestation. She made numerous suggestions which improved its clarity and style and corrected some of my interpretations of black history. All this while carrying the heavy load of a career as a social studies teacher, wife, mother, and keeper of the homestead. In brief, she assumed all the burdens commonly borne by "liberated" women who, despite their long struggle, remain not so free to choose.

A special word of thanks must go to my department's secretary, Ms. Colleen Kology. Her intelligence, patience, accuracy, and legerdemain with the word processor were of incalculable assistance in bringing the project to completion.

# NOT SO
# FREE TO CHOOSE

# 1

# INTRODUCTION

The ideas of economists and political philosophers, both
when they are right and when they are wrong, are more
powerful than is commonly understood. Indeed the world is
ruled by little else. Practical men, who believe themselves
to be quite exempt from any intellectual influences, are
usually the slaves of some defunct economist.

Keynes: *The General Theory of Employment,
Interest, and Money*

Nobel Laureate Milton Friedman clearly cannot be characterized as a
"defunct economist." Nor can President Ronald Reagan be depicted as
his "slave." Nevertheless, Friedman's ideas have been extraordinarily
influential in shaping the ideology, rhetoric, and policies of the president
and his administration.

Milton Friedman is said to be Ronald Reagan's favorite economist,
and for more than a decade the president has been Friedman's favorite
politician. Their mutual respect and admiration go back to 1970 when
Friedman, while spending a semester at the University of California at
Los Angeles as a visiting professor, first met then-Governor Reagan.
Friedman was "very favorably impressed," found him a "very serious,
thoughtful person — interested in the principles," and found that he
"researched them by thinking them through and by reading."[1]

The week following Reagan's election to the presidency, Friedman
wrote of the new president,

His long-held philosophical commitment is to individual freedom and limited government. The basic planks of his economic programs, his record as governor of California, his pioneering role in sponsoring constitutional limits on government spending, the record of his associates, advisers and main supporters — all these are far more basic than election rhetoric. Governor Reagan's election would demonstrate to members of the House and Senate — as probably nothing else can — that it has finally become politically profitable to end the inflation of both government and prices. In that way it could open the road to a renaissance of freedom and prosperity.[2]

On his part, Reagan claimed Friedman as one of his closest and most-trusted economic advisers and wrote a highly laudatory blurb for the dust jacket of Friedman's best seller, *Free to Choose*.[3] Although Friedman has never accepted a political appointment to a government job, he did agree to serve on a nongovernmental panel established to advise the president on economic policy at President Reagan's request.

In addition to playing an influential role in establishing the general direction of the Reagan administration, Friedman has in recent years been an adviser to many foreign governments. It was not always thus. Before reaching national and international prominence, he had to travel a long and rather lonely road as the leading exponent of laissez-faire (free-market) capitalism in the United States.

Born to poor immigrant parents in 1912 (his mother worked as a seamstress in a sweatshop and his father ran a small dry goods store), he won a state scholarship at age 15 to Rutgers University, where he graduated in 1932 with a double major in mathematics and economics. Encouraged by his economics professors at Rutgers, he went on to graduate study at the University of Chicago. The economics department at Chicago, under the intellectual leadership of the brilliant theorist Frank Knight, was then one of the very few remaining bastions of laissez-faire economics in U.S. universities. Although lack of funds and an inadequate tuition scholarship forced him to leave after his initial academic year, the experience at Chicago left an indelible impression on his mind.

Friedman went on to Coumbia University, where he was offered a much more substantial fellowship. He completed work on his doctorate at Columbia in 1941, but his dissertation was not accepted until 1946 because his evaluators objected to his attack on physicians — Friedman had demonstrated that organized medicine had restricted entry into the field to protect and enhance the incomes of those in the medical profession.

During the depressed 1930s and during World War II, Friedman was employed by various government agencies. His work for those agencies was purely technical and did not involve him in any policy-making efforts. After the war, he spent one year as an associate professor at the University of Minnesota before joining the faculty at Chicago, where he remained for 30 years.

At Chicago during the 1950s and 1960s, Friedman quickly became the intellectual leader of a small band of economists, "the Chicago school." Staunch defenders of the free market and vigorous opponents of government intervention in the economy, they were scorned by most economists as atavistic defenders of decadent nineteenth-century laissez-faire capitalism. Not only were Friedman and his followers outside the pale of modern mainstream academic economics, they were virtually ignored in the determination of governmental policy.[4]

The mainstream belonged to liberal Keynesians, who reached their pinnacle of power and influence during the Kennedy-Johnson years. Pre-Keynesian neoclassical economics had developed two fundamental ideas: (1) that a free market economy, if left to operate without government intervention, would always tend toward full employment and stable prices and (2) that the market forces of supply and demand would allocate resources to their most efficient uses, where they would produce what consumers desire. The first idea was shattered in the 1930s by the Great Depression and the devastating attack on its central tenets by John Maynard Keynes in his seminal work *The General Theory of Employment, Interest, and Money,* while the second survived as it was integrated into mainstream economics. Paul Samuelson, the United States's chief Keynesian guru, in the 1961 edition of his text *Economics,* jubilantly proclaimed that the science of economics had achieved a "grand neoclassical synthesis," an integration of Keynesian and neoclassical economic theory: while the judicious use of Keynesian fiscal and monetary policy would guarantee that the economy approximated full employment with reasonably stable prices, the product markets could then be permitted to operate and allocate resources in response to the market forces of supply and demand as described by the neoclassicals. The government would be the deus ex machina that would periodically apply the appropriate spending, taxing, and monetary policies to achieve a stable and growing economy.[5]

While Samuelson himself did not join the Kennedy administration, Kennedy's Council of Economic Advisers was comprised entirely of solid Keynesians. Walter Heller, the council's influential chairman, soon brought the young president into the Keynesian fold. In a major speech before the Yale graduating class in 1962, Kennedy became the first U.S. president to publicly and explicitly embrace Keynesian fiscal policy when he asserted that in order to stimulate the economy, it may be desirable to engage in deficit spending. He attacked the "myth [that] Federal deficits create inflation and budget surpluses prevent it."[6]

After the assassination of Kennedy in November 1963 and the assumption of the presidency by Lyndon Johnson, substantial tax reductions were enacted in February 1964, despite the fact that the budget was then in deficit. In the two years following the reduction in taxes, real gross national product (GNP) increased by 5.1 and then 6.5 percent, the unemployment rate declined from 5.2 to 3.8 percent, and prices and interest rates remained relatively stable. Walter Heller hailed the tax cut as having "ushered in a new era in which the vowed and active use of tax, budget and monetary instruments would keep the economy operating in the vicinity of full employment."[7] Mainstream economics with its "grand neoclassical synthesis" was triumphant — at least for the moment.

Adding to the euphoria of liberals during those years was the passage of a host of progressive legislation: comprehensive civil rights laws; the Great Society programs, directed toward improving conditions in urban areas and eradicating poverty; Medicare for the aged; and Medicaid for the needy. President Johnson's landslide victory over arch-conservative Barry Goldwater, along with the election of an overwhelmingly liberal Congress in 1964, seemed to hammer the last nail into the conservative coffin.

With the memories of the Great Depression still fresh in the national psyche in the decade following World War II and with mainstream Keynesian liberalism delivering on its promises of prosperity and price stability in the second decade, the period did not provide a milieu conducive to the spread of an economic philosophy advocating a return to laissez-faire capitalism.

Nevertheless, throughout those years Professor Friedman continued to vigorously sow his conservative field. Most of his scholarly work during this period was devoted to the development and dissemination of "monetarism," a framework of analysis that runs sharply counter to the liberal Keynesian paradigm both with respect to its explanation of why the economy behaves as it does and with respect to its major policy implications. For monetarists, the money supply is the dominant factor (in some of Friedman's writings it is seen as the sole factor) affecting the nation's gross national product. To achieve high levels of national output, stable prices, and minimal unemployment, Friedman has a simple prescription: tie the growth rate in the money supply to the real average annual growth rate in the GNP, between 3 percent and 5 percent. Fiscal policy (the manipulation of tax and expenditure programs by the federal government) and monetary policy (the manipulation of the money supply by the Federal Reserve monetary authorities), the two basic tools of liberal Keynesians, the monetarists see at best as ineffective and at worst as decidedly counterproductive. Thus, in his major treatise *A Monetary History of the United States, 1867–1960,* coauthored with Anna J. Schwartz, Friedman argued forcefully that the Great Depression was not a product of an inherently unstable capitalistic system as the Keynesians argued, but rather could have been avoided if the Federal Reserve had not made egregious blunders in manipulating the money supply. But, with the Keynesian successes of the 1960s, relatively little attention was paid to Friedman's policy prescriptions.

With the decade of the 1970s came a marked change in the economic and political climate. Price increases generated by the financing of the disastrous and unpopular war in Vietnam, the Organization of Petroleum Exporting Countries (OPEC) induced oil shocks (which seriously aggravated existing inflationary pressures), and persistent stagflation (the simultaneous occurrence of rising prices, high levels of unemployment, and low growth rates in real output) all blended with a rising tide of opposition to increased taxation and the welfare programs of the Great Society. The coalescence of these factors fostered the spread of skepticism concerning the ability of the government to manage the economy. The ebullient references to the "grand neoclassical synthesis" that first appeared in the editions of Samuelson's text in the 1960s — the triumphant years of liberal Keynesianism — were unceremoniously dropped in the revised editions of the pessimistic 1970s, not rating so much as a footnote. The economics profession, along with the economy, was in disarray. The climate was ripe for the growth in influence of the economic philosophy of Milton Friedman.

Thirty years ago, a very small minority of economists shared Friedman's monetarist beliefs. Today, largely as a result of his teaching and writing and the general reaction to the developments in the 1970s, monetarists now hold prominent positions in numerous universities, in businesses, in government, and even in Friedman's bête noire, the Federal Reserve system.

The growth in Friedman's influence was not limited to the spread of the monetarist gospel among academics and other professionals.

Probably of even greater significance in explaining his rise to national prominence were his writings in the popular press, his appearance as a television personality, and two best-selling books in which he set forth his highly controversial ideas. In 1962 he wrote *Capitalism and Freedom,* a popular volume that established him as a leading spokesman of the nascent conservative movement. For 18 years, starting in 1966, he was a regular columnist with *Newsweek,* commenting on current events from his laissez-faire perspective. In 1980, in the midst of a presidential election year, Friedman starred in his own television series, *Free to Choose.* Financed by a host of large corporations, the series in effect gave him a national classroom for disseminating the principles he had taught for three decades within the cloistered walls of the University of Chicago. Those programs became the basis for his national best seller *Free to Choose,* written with his wife, Rose Friedman.[8]

Friedman's first significant foray into national politics came in 1964 as the major economic adviser of presidential candidate Barry Goldwater. He again entered the political arena in 1968, this time in support of Richard Nixon's successful campaign for the presidency. Friedman parted ways with Nixon in August 1971 when the president, despite repeated assertions that he would never institute wage-price controls, reversed himself, announced "I am now a Keynesian," and froze wages and prices.[9]

Friedman's first association with a major political victory consistent with his economic philosophy came with the enactment of California's Proposition 13. The statute imposed severe restraints on state and local tax increases, particularly with respect to taxes on property. Friedman played a key role in its passage, as he appeared in an influential television commercial in support of the cap on taxes. Proposition 13 not only touched off a tax revolt that spread to a number of other states, it also contributed to the political momentum of Ronald Reagan.[10]

The primary focus in this volume is an analysis of some of the major themes in the substantial body of popular writings by Milton Friedman. These include some 300 columns he has written for *Newsweek*; his two best-selling volumes directed toward the general public, *Capitalism and Freedom* and *Free to Choose*; and several interviews and essays appearing in other publications also meant for a general audience. There are several important reasons for concentrating on Friedman's popular writings rather than on his technical articles and books written for the consumption of professional economists.

First of all, it has been largely through the widespread dissemination of his ideas through the popular media that he has exerted a powerful influence on the ideology, rhetoric, and policies of the Reagan administration. This is not to say that Reagan has slavishly followed the advice of Friedman on all policy matters. On some important issues the president has taken positions diametrically opposed to Friedman's recommendations. Nevertheless, in many areas Reagan has moved in the general direction pointed by Friedman, and the ideology of the president as revealed in his rhetoric indicates that he will continue to march along that route.

Knowing where Reagan has not followed the path laid out by Friedman is also of considerable interest. By examining which Reagan policy proposals deviated from Friedman's laissez-faire line, we can gain greater insight into the president's real goals as distinct from the goals enunciated in his free-market rhetoric. In addition, the pattern and nature of the deviations reveal what may be the primary function of an economic adviser: the provision of an intellectual rationale, ex post, for whatever program has already been determined by the president.

Beyond the impact of his thought on the Reagan administration, it is important to analyze Friedman's popular writings because his ideas as expressed therein are likely to have a long-term influence in the ongoing debates over social and economic policy. That long-term impact is ensured by the fact that many of his former students and other adherents of his philosophy now hold key positions in a large number of universities, in business organizations, and in the burgeoning U.S. conservative movement.

Furthermore, since his popular writings are overwhelmingly policy oriented and essentially polemical in nature, they yield a more accurate picture of Friedman's real values and goals (and those of his adherents) than can be obtained by reading his esoteric articles in professional journals.

In *Bright Promises, Dismal Performance: An Economist's Protest,* largely a collection of 70 columns written by Milton Friedman for *Newsweek,* the editor, economist William R. Allen, comments,

> Essays which are very brief, self-contained, and intended for a diverse audience, but which responsibly provide genuine economic analysis, are an extraordinarily difficult art form. One cannot look to such essays for definitive scientific treatments. Still, the reader of the Friedman commentaries will be impressed that he is observing an economist — not an ideologue or a poet — employing his craft.[11]

True, Friedman is not a poet. He is an economist, a brilliant economist. Contrary to Allen's assessment, however, Friedman is also an ideologue, an ideologue in defense of the free market. This will be evident from the analysis of his popular books and essays intended for a diverse audience. Stripped of the technical jargon and careful analysis found in his professional journal articles, the popular writings reveal Friedman the ideologue — often simplistic in his presentation of economic analysis, frequently cavalier in his treatment of history, citing data that tend to confirm a hypothesis he is defending while conveniently ignoring other data that are obviously inconsistent with his analysis.

## NOTES

1.   Boston *Globe* Magazine, April 3, 1983.
2.   *Newsweek*, November 10, 1980, p. 94.
3.   Boston *Globe* Magazine, April 3, 1983.
4.   Leonard Silk, *The Economists* (New York: Basic Books, 1976), pp. 47–93.
5.   Paul Samuelson, *Economics* (New York: McGraw-Hill, 1961), pp. 403–4.
6.   Walter W. Heller, *New Dimensions of Political Economy* (New York: W. W. Norton, 1967), pp. 29–37, as reported in the New York *Times*, June 12, 1982, p. 20.
7.   Milton Friedman and Walter W. Heller, *Monetary vs. Fiscal Policy* (New York: W. W. Norton, 1969), p. 33.
8.   Boston *Globe* Magazine, April 3, 1983.
9.   Ibid.
10.   Ibid.
11.   Milton Friedman, *Bright Promises, Dismal Performance: An Economist's Protest*, ed. William R. Allen (New York: Harcourt, Brace, Jovanovich, 1983), p. 3.

# 2

# FRIEDMAN, REAGAN, AND THE ROLE OF GOVERNMENT: SOME GENERAL PRINCIPLES

Friedman's fame as an economist stems primarily from his development of monetarism. He received the Nobel Prize in Economic Science for his research stressing monetary conditions as the crucial economic factor in business fluctuations and for his influence upon monetary policies. In addition to being the modern monetarist's guru, he is the leading contemporary exponent of Smithian laissez-faire. As we shall see, the two roles are not unrelated, as monetarism also implies a severely limited role for government.

To fully understand not only monetarism but Friedman's ideas on other areas of economic policy and economic analysis, it is necessary to have a clear picture of Friedman's conception of the general principles that determine what he views as the proper role of government.

This chapter has a twofold purpose: (1) to outline the general principles that, according to Friedman, determine the proper role of government and (2) to reveal the striking similarity between Friedman's economic philosophy and that of President Reagan and his administration, as revealed in quotations from the president's first *Economic Report* to the nation.

Professor Friedman's political economy is in essence a restatement of the classical liberalism of the eighteenth and nineteenth century. His defense of a laissez-faire economy and his belief that the scope of government should be limited differs little from the economic philosophy expounded by Adam Smith in the *Wealth of Nations,* published in 1776.

For Friedman, "economic freedom is an indispensable means toward the achievement of political freedom."[1] Although he sees government as a necessary instrumentality for protecting freedom, he also holds that "by concentrating power in political hands, [government] is also a threat to freedom."[2] He could find "no example in time or place of a society that has been marked by a large measure of political freedom, and that has not also used something comparable to a free market to organize the bulk of economic activity."[3]

Now compare the above statements by Friedman with the following quotations from the president's *Economic Report*:

> Political freedom and economic freedom are closely related. . . . All nations which have broad-based representative government and civil liberties have most of their economic activity organized by the market. . . . The evidence is striking. No nation in which the government has the dominant economic role . . . has maintained broad political freedom.[4]

To achieve the benefits from the promise of government while avoiding the threat it poses to freedom, Friedman recommends that we be guided by two broad principles that, he asserts, are embodied in our constitution. First the scope of the government must be limited, with its functions restricted primarily to national defense, preserving domestic law and order, enforcing contracts, and fostering competitive markets. Second, "government power must be dispersed." In those cases where it is deemed necessary to exercise government power, it is better that it be done "in the county than in the state, better in the state than in Washington." If individuals do not like what is done by their local government, they can move to another county. If they object to the actions of their state, they "can move to another." The mere possibility of such a move acts as a check on government behavior. But when the power is centralized in Washington, the individual has "few alternatives in this world of jealous nations."[5]

Again, compare Friedman's statements in the above paragraph with the following quotations from the *Economic Report of the President*:

> A reduced role for the Federal Government means an enhanced role for State and local governments. . . . We should use the level of government closest to the community involved for all the functions it can handle. . . . Federal Government action should be reserved for those needed functions that only the national government can undertake. . . . Chief among these is a strong national defense. . . . Our system of government is a Federal system, one in which certain powers have been granted to the Federal Government while other powers have been granted to the States. . . . One constraint on the power of any government to impose costs on its citizens is the ability of

those citizens to move elsewhere. Thus, one argument for reliance on State government is essentially the argument that it restricts the power of government, since any State which passed laws which were sufficiently inefficient would probably find itself losing residents. . . . Another argument for Federalism is that State and local governments are more likely to choose the amount and quality of governmental services preferred by their voters, whose preferences and resources vary greatly.[6]

Given the restricted role Friedman assigns to the government, how would the economic activities of literally millions of individuals and business firms be coordinated? Through "voluntary exchange [in a] free enterprise exchange economy — competitive capitalism" is Friedman's answer. As long as freedom of exchange is maintained, "the consumer is protected from coercion by the seller because of the presence of other sellers with whom he can deal." Similarly, "the seller is protected from coercion by the consumer because of other consumers to whom he can sell," and the "employee is protected from coercion by the employer because of other employers for whom he can work, and so on. And the market does this impersonally and without centralized authority."[7]

Let us turn again to the president's *Economic Report* to see its similarity to the views expressed by Friedman.

We should leave to private initiative all the functions that individuals can perform privately. . . . Everyone would prefer higher prices for goods sold and lower prices for goods bought. Since the farmer's wheat is the consumer's bread, however, both parties cannot achieve all they want. The most fundamental difference among economic systems is how these conflicting preferences are resolved. A market system resolves these conflicts by allowing the seller to get the highest price at which others will buy and the buyer to get the lowest price at which others will sell, by consensual exchanges that are expected to benefit both parties. Any attempt by one party to improve his outcome relative to the market outcome requires a coercive activity at the expense of some other party. . . . A competitive economy can be shown to lead to general economic efficiency. . . . Each person in such an economy is considered to be concerned primarily with his own welfare. Since there is no central authority directing the course of this economy, whatever results occur are the unintended consequences of millions of individual actions. . . . Such a system relies on the ability of people to trade freely with each other, for a bargain entered into voluntarily by two individuals is expected by both of them to make both of them better off.[8]

Within this laissez-faire framework, Friedman sees the role of the government as being akin to that of a rule maker and umpire in a game.

For the millions of participants engaged in economic activity, the government not only establishes the rules of the competitive game but also provides a mechanism whereby the rules can be modified, mediates differences over the meaning of the rules, and enforces compliance with the rules on the part of the few potential rule breakers.[9]

Beyond government's important role as a rule maker and umpire, Friedman recognizes the possible need for government intervention in the market where strictly voluntary exchange is either exceedingly costly or impossible. Monopoly and similar market imperfections is one class of cases where voluntary exchange breaks down. "When technical conditions make a monopoly the natural outcome of competitive market forces," Friedman notes, "there are only three alternatives that seem available: private monopoly, public monopoly, or public regulation." In such a situation, "public regulation or ownership may be a lesser evil."[10]

On the same subject, the *Economic Report* states, "Sometimes technical and cost conditions in an industry are such that there will be room for one or a few firms. Two approaches have been taken in the United States to this problem . . . direct government regulation or ownership."[11]

A second class of cases cited by Friedman in which strictly voluntary exchange is impossible arises when there are "neighborhood effects," that is, when actions impose costs or benefits on others than the producers or consumers of a product. Pollution is a classic example. If a firm dumps waste into a nearby stream, it imposes costs on those who may be using the stream for recreational, fishing, or other purposes. Since the stream is free, there is nothing in the market that will provide the firm with an incentive to curb its pollution-generating activities. Therefore, when there are neighborhood effects, there may be a justification for government intervention. But in each case of proposed intervention, Friedman argues we should carefully weigh "both the benefits and costs of proposed government interventions," and in particular, "we should give considerable weight to the neighborhood effect of the threat to freedom resulting from government intervention."[12]

On neighborhood effects, the *Economic Report* states,

An externality is said to exist where an economic agent (be it producer or consumer) either does not bear the full . . . costs of an economic action or does not gain its full . . . benefits. . . . The standard example of an activity that imposes external costs is manufacturing that results in pollution. . . . Those who live near the factory will suffer the costs of the pollution, but the

# 3

# THE POLITICAL CASE
# FOR FREE TRADE:
# FREE MARKETS AND PEACE

The period of history that Professor Friedman finds most to his liking is roughly the 100 years between 1815 and 1914, a century that saw the development of "limited government and free market societies" in Great Britain and the United States. While Adam Smith's *Wealth of Nations* (published in 1776) "was one of the early blows in the battle to end government restrictions on industry and trade," the "final victory" in that battle did not come until 1846 with the repeal of the Corn Laws that had imposed tariffs and other restrictions on the importation of grains into Britain. "Britain's repeal of the Corn Laws," writes Friedman, "ushered in three-quarters of a century of complete free trade lasting until the outbreak of World War I and completed a transition that had begun decades earlier to a highly-limited government." He also cites the United States as another "striking" nineteenth-century example of a free market with limited government. Although there were tariffs, "they were modest, by modern standards, and few other government restrictions impeded free trade at home or abroad."[1]

Friedman argues that free trade "fosters harmonious relations among nations that differ in culture and institutions just as free trade at home fosters harmonious relations among individuals who differ in beliefs, attitudes and interests." Since "transactions will not take place unless all parties will benefit from it — cooperation, not conflict, is the rule." On the other hand, when a government intervenes, businesses seek subsidies or tariffs or other restrictions on trade to give them a competitive advantage. Countermeasures are then taken by competing businesses in other countries through their own governments. Trade negotiations factory owner will not consider these costs in deciding how much to produce. . . . Hence, too much of the good, and too much pollution will probably be produced. . . . The Administration is also making a major effort to emphasize the use of benefit-cost analysis in regulation. . . . Even if used as well as possible, however, benefit-cost analysis is only the second best solution. The best solution is to respect the judgment of the private market whenever it is available.[13]

The comparison of the economic philosophy of the Reagan administration with that of Milton Friedman indicates a striking similarity. This is true not only with reference to the particular views expressed, but even with respect to the rhetoric employed. So much so that the *Economic Report,* in its discussion of the proper role of government, reads as if it were a paraphrased edition of Friedman's *Capitalism and Freedom.*

An amusing and revealing postscript to this chapter is a report that appeared in the New York *Times* in March 1981, shortly after President Reagan's inauguration. If there are any doubts about the economic proclivities of the Reagan administration, the *Times* story should lay them to rest. The *Times* reported that neckties embroidered with the profile of Adam Smith, the eighteenth-century political economist, are "all the rage in the White House," and "Friedman and Simon and all those guys have them," according to the secretary to Martin Anderson, domestic policy adviser to the president. Edwin Meese, counselor to the president, owns at least two, and wears them "for all public photos." The mail order house that distributes them sold many to the Executive Office of the President at $14 to $20 per tie. The firm also sells Milton Friedman T-shirts.[14]

## NOTES

1.   Milton Friedman, *Capitalism and Freedom* (Chicago: University of Chicago Press, 1962), p. 8.

2.   Ibid., p. 2.

3.   Ibid., p. 9.

4.   *Economic Report of the President, February 1982* (Washington, D.C.: Government Printing Office, 1982), p. 27.

5.   Friedman, *Capitalism,* pp. 2–3.

6.   *Economic Report, 1982,* pp. 5–6, 36.

7.   Friedman, *Capitalism,* pp. 13–15.

8.   *Economic Report, 1982,* pp. 9, 27, 29–30.

9.   Friedman, *Capitalism*, p. 25.
10.  Ibid., pp. 27–29.
11.  *Economic Report, 1982*, pp. 31–32.
12.  Friedman, *Capitalism*, pp. 30–32.
13.  *Economic Report, 1982*, pp. 30, 43.
14.  The New York *Times*, March 29, 1981, sect. 3, p. 19.

become a political matter. "Frictions develop" and "conflict, not cooperation" becomes the rule.[2]

In support of his thesis, Friedman points to the century from Waterloo to World War I as

> a striking example of the beneficial effects of free trade on the relations among nations. Britain was the leading nation of the world and during the whole of that century it had nearly complete free trade. Other nations, particularly Western nations, including the United States, adopted a similar policy. . . . People were in the main free to buy and sell goods from and to anyone, wherever he lived, whether in the same or a different country. And they were relatively free to travel, to emigrate, and to enter a foreign country and become citizens.[3]

In a key conclusion, Friedman asserts,

> As a result, the century from Waterloo to the First World War was one of the most peaceful in human history among Western nations, marred only by some minor wars — the Crimean War and the Franco-Prussian Wars are the most memorable — and, of course, a major Civil War within the United States, which itself was a result of the major respect — slavery — in which the United States departed from economic and political freedom. In the modern world, tariffs and similar restrictions on trade have been one source of friction among nations. But a far more troublesome source has been the far-reaching intervention of the state into the economy in such collectivist states as Hitler's Germany, Mussolini's Italy, and Franco's Spain, and especially the communist countries, from Russia and its satellites to China.[4]

Friedman's analysis of his favorite century reveals Friedman the ideologue — extraordinarily cavalier in his treatment of history, selecting data that seem to support his hypothesis while ignoring massive amounts of other data that are inconsistent with that hypothesis.

## A CENTURY OF PEACE?

In the paragraph quoted above, he contrasts the century from 1815 to 1914, when free trade and limited government purportedly brought relative peace, with the modern world since 1914, when the collectivist states with their far-reaching intervention into the economy were a source of friction among nations. But the collectivist states that he cites as the cause of friction among nations — Hitler's Germany, Mussolini's Italy, Franco's Spain, and the Communist USSR and People's Republic of

China — could not have contributed to the frictions that led to World War I, since they were not even in existence at the time.

Why then, does he arbitrarily end his favorite century in 1914 before the appearance of the collectivist states and include World War I in the "modern world"? The answer seems clear. The nations participating in World War I were overwhelmingly those same Western nations that Friedman cites as having been adhering to a policy of free trade. To have included World War I as part of his favorite century would have played havoc with his thesis that it was free trade and limited government that brought peace among nations. Rather than deal with this most glaring inconsistency, Friedman develops his own calendar with respect to when a century ends and another begins. By this rather crude analytical legerdemain, World War I and the factors leading up to the war conveniently disappear from Friedman's data bank for his favorite century and, just as conveniently, appear in the era of the modern collectivist world he finds so distasteful.

Let us take a closer look at Friedman's century of relative peace based on free trade, the years from 1815 to 1914, a century that he states was marred only by some minor wars and a major civil war within the United States.

It is accurate to say that there was no general European war and no war involving more than two great powers between 1815 and 1914. But to suggest, as Friedman does, that those years were relatively peaceful and that the relative peace was a product of free trade policies followed by the Western nations and the United States is an assertion that has no basis in historical reality.

The year 1815 was not only the year of the defeat of Napoleon at Waterloo, it was also the year of the ascendancy of the counter-revolutionary forces. It was the year of Metternich's Congress of Vienna, where the leaders of the coalition against Napoleon "re-established the European balance of power and repudiated the revolutionary principles that had shattered the eighteenth century balance."[5] In the words of historian George Rude, the objectives of the powers

which met in Vienna were to restore the old pre-revolutionary dynasties — the Hohenzollerns, Hapsburgs, Bourbons and German secular princes — to their ancestral domains; and to re-establish something like the old balance of power . . . haunted by the fears of revolution, the powers pledged themselves to a twenty-year agreement termed the "Concert of Europe," whose purposes were both to settle disputes without recourse to war . . . and to maintain by force their political settlement against all efforts by Bonapartist pretenders, liberals democrats or nationalists to upset it.[6]

Castlereagh, the British spokesman at the congress, made the issues patently clear when he stated:

> The existing concert (of the Powers) is their only perfect security against the revolutionary embers more or less existing in every state of Europe; and . . . true wisdom is to keep down the petty contentions of ordinary times, and to stand together in support of the established principles of social order.[7]

No words of free trade and limited government here, nor even of freedom. On the contrary, a major goal was, in essence, the suppression of freedom. While there were no general wars of the scale of World War I or World War II, the century following Waterloo was marked by a continuum of wars — wars against workers, peasants, democrats, and liberal nationalists seeking self-determination.

Liberal revolutions begun in 1820 were crushed in Spain (by the French in 1823) and in Naples (by the Austrians in 1821). In 1833, Russia defeated a Polish nationalist independence movement, and liberals and nationalists saw their revolutionary movements quashed by Metternich in the early 1830s. In 1848, revolutionary movements of bourgeois moderates, working-class radicals, peasants, and nationalists broke out in almost all of Europe: France, Italy, Germany, and among the numerous nationalities in the Hapsburg (Austrian) Empire. The widespread revolutionary movements were smashed as the counterrevolutionary powers cooperated to maintain the status quo.[8]

Despite the hope of the powers to avoid wars between nations and thereby prevent any discord that might give rise to revolutionary movements, there were numerous wars of nation against nation during Friedman's "peaceful" century. In addition to the three mentioned by Friedman, there were the Chilean (1817–18) and Bolivian (1823–25) wars of independence against Spain, the long Greek war of independence (1821–31), the Mexican War (1846–48), the Italian war of independence against Austria (1859), Polish revolutions against Russia (1863–64), the Bulgarian revolution against Turkey (1875–78), the Russian-Afghan conflict (1885), the Italo-Ethiopian War (1895–96), the Spanish-American War (1898), the Boer War (1899–1902), the Russo-Japanese War (1904–5), the conflict between Italy and Turkey (1911–12), and a number of others.[9]

Not only does Friedman ignore the revolutions and numerous wars of nation against nation, but even more incredible, he makes no reference to the age of imperialism, an era that covers almost the entire latter half of his century of free-trade-induced peace. In the years from 1871 to 1914, European powers — Britain, France, Germany, and Belgium — in a relentless drive colonized almost all of Africa, with only Liberia and Ethiopia remaining independent. Not free trade and peace but imperial conquest and colonial oppression dominated western Europe's relationship with Africa. And the oppression was often brutal: the genocidal campaign by the Germans against the Herero people, the unrivaled barbarism of Belgium's rule in the Congo, the forced-labor policies and savage repression by the French in French Equatorial Africa, to cite a few examples.

Colonial expansion was not limited to Africa. The British and French annexed territory in Southeast Asia. The Spanish-American War left the United States with control of the remnants of the Spanish empire in America and in the Pacific (the Philippines, Guam, and Puerto Rico), and in 1898 the United States also acquired Hawaii and parts of the Samoan Islands. In the Central and South Pacific, Britain and Germany established sovereignty over various groups of islands. Copying European techniques, the Japanese expanded at the cost of its neighbors, China and Korea.

As a result of imperialistic expansion, by the beginning of World War I more than 500 million people — about one-third of the world's population — were living under colonial rule. In Friedman's century of "free trade" and "peace," one-third of the world's population was not "free to choose."[10]

One must conclude that Friedman's contention that the 1815–1914 period was an era of peace and freedom borders on pure fiction. Rather than historical analysis of the relevant and readily accessible data, he arrives at his assessment by a highly selective choice of bits of information that support his position, while ignoring the massive evidence that would remove the props from under his artificial construction.

## A CENTURY OF FREE TRADE?

Similarly deficient in historical analysis is Friedman's characterization of the century as one in which Britain and the Western nations, including the United States, pursued policies of "nearly complete free trade." In this context, it must again be emphasized that, as a result of the spread of imperialism between 1871 and 1914, about one-third of the world's population was under colonial rule. For them, free trade was little more than mythology. Furthermore, with respect to the Western nations, contrary to Friedman's assertion, the century was not one of free trade either. At best it is reasonable to say that among those nations it lasted for a period of about 35 years, roughly between 1846, when Britain abolished its Corn Laws, and 1880.

For the nineteenth century English advocates of free trade (as for Friedman today), its justification represented "absolute and eternal wisdom for all times and places." However, as Joseph Schumpeter observed,

> As has been pointed out many times, England's individual historical situation in which a free-trade policy was clearly indicated had probably more to do with her conversion than had the element of general truth in the free-trade argument. . . . The superiority of England's industry in 1840 was unchallengeable for the calculable future. And this superiority had everything to gain from cheaper raw materials and food stuffs.[11]

Britain could then legitimately be referred to as the workshop of the world, and it was Britain that took the leadership role in the advancement of free trade. Initially, other countries in western Europe complied with Britain's free-trade policy, since they were in their early stages of industrialization and could benefit from the "unique supply of capital, machinery, and technical skill of Britain."[12] But this did not last. As economic historian Hobsbawm has written,

> National economists in the U.S.A. and Germany never had much doubt about the value of protection and industrialists in fields competitive with the British had even less. Firm believers in Free Trade like John Stuart Mill accepted the legitimacy of discriminating in favour of "infant industries." Once a local economy was on its feet, its need of Britain diminished rapidly. There was only one comparatively brief historical period when both developed and underdeveloped sectors of the world had an equal interest in working with and not against the British economy — the decades between the abolition of the Corn Laws in 1846 and the outbreak of the Great Depression in 1873. After 1873, the situation of the "advanced" world was one of rivalry between developed countries; and what is more, countries of whom only Britain had a built-in interest in total freedom of trade. The free flow of goods was the first to be inhibited by the tariff barriers and other discriminatory measures which were erected with increasing frequency after 1880.[13]

Thus by 1875, in France the movement against free trade "had taken on the character of a nation-wide reaction, and within a decade thereafter the country swung back definitely to protectionism."[14] Germany, which had in essence pursued free trade policies for about a quarter of a century after 1850, under Bismark's leadership "entered upon a new epoch of protectionism" with the enactment of the tariff law of July 7, 1879.[15]

In the United States the system of high protective tariffs dates from the Civil War. The Morrill Act of 1861 inaugurated the subsequent high tariff system, and wholesale advances in tariff rates were made in 1862 and 1864. Of this last act, F. W. Taussig, in his classic study of U.S. tariffs stated, "It established protective duties more extreme than had been ventured on in any previous tariff act in our country's history. [An act] which was in its effects one of the most important financial measures ever passed in the United States, bringing the average level of duties up to 47 percent."[16] Except for a few downward revisions, the general trend of U.S. tariffs was strongly upward. The McKinley Tariff of 1890 raised the average duties to 49.5 percent and, to propitiate the farmer, tariffs were imposed on agricultural products. Tariffs were raised to an average of 57 percent with the passage of the Dingley Bill in 1897, which remained in force for 12 years.[17] Charles Beard, in writing of the period since the Civil War, states that advocates of a high protective tariff were able "to push through measure after measure and to fasten their system upon the nation so tightly that it was not even shaken for nearly half a century."[18]

Despite the record of imperialism and protectionism in western Europe and in the United States, Friedman writes of his chosen century as one characterized by "nearly complete free trade" policies. Despite the suppression of revolutionary movements for freedom, despite the numerous wars of nation against nation, despite the history of imperial conquest and colonial oppression of one-third of the world's population, Friedman finds the century one of the most peaceful in history because nations adhered to free-trade policies.

## NOTES

1. Milton Friedman and Rose Friedman, *Free to Choose* (New York: Avon, 1981), pp. 26, 27.
2. Ibid., p. 43.
3. Ibid., p. 44.

4.  Ibid.

5.  Crane Brinton, *A History of Civilization* (New York: Prentice-Hall, 1955), p. 148.

6.  George Rude, *Revolutionary Europe, 1783–1815* (London: Collins, 1967), pp. 284–85.

7.  E. J. Hobsbawm, *The Age of Revolution, 1789–1848* (New York: New American Library, 1964), p. 126.

8.  Brinton, *A History*, pp. 165–90.

9.  William Langer, ed., *An Encyclopedia of World History* (Boston: Houghton Mifflin, 1948). The list of wars was selected from a number of pages in this volume.

10.  Brinton, *A History*, pp. 375–401. On the slaughter of the Herero people by the Germans and the brutality of Belgium, see Basil Davidson, *Africa in History* (New York: Collier Books, 1974), pp. 247–49, 253–54.

11.  Joseph Schumpeter, *History of Economic Analysis* (New York: Oxford University Press, 1954), p. 397.

12.  E. J. Hobsbawm, *Industry and Empire* (New York: Pantheon Books, 1968), pp. 110–13.

13.  Ibid., pp. 113–15.

14.  Frederic Austin Ogg and Walter Rice Sharp, *Economic Development of Modern Europe* (New York: Macmillan, 1930), p. 272.

15.  Ibid., p. 292.

16.  F. W. Taussig, *The Tariff History of the United States* (New York: G. P. Putnam's Sons, 1892), p. 167.

17.  Harold U. Faulkner, *American Economic History*, 7th ed. rev. (New York: Harper and Brothers, 1954), pp. 548–51.

18.  Charles A. Beard and Mary R. Beard, *The Rise of American Civilization* (New York: Macmillan, 1930) 2:108.

# 4

# FREE MARKETS AND CENTRAL ECONOMIC PLANNING: A CONTROLLED EXPERIMENT

In a comparison of the evils of central economic planning and the virtues of the free market, Friedman cites what he refers to as "an especially illuminating example, worth discussing in detail": India during the first 30 years after it achieved independence in 1947 and Japan during the first 30 years after the Meiji Restoration in 1867.[1] "In these two experiences with economic development," asserts Friedman, "we have something very close to a controlled experiment that we can use to test the importance of the difference in methods of economic organization."[2]

The following is Friedman's description of the results of those two approaches to economic development:

Despite the similar circumstances of Japan in 1867 and India in 1947, the outcome was vastly different. Japan dismantled its feudal structure and extended social and economic opportunity to all its citizens. The lot of the ordinary man improved rapidly, even though population exploded. Japan became a power to be reckoned with on the international scene. It did not achieve full individual human and political freedom, but it made great progress in that direction.

India paid lip service to the elimination of caste barriers yet made little progress in practice. Differences in income and wealth between the few and the many grew wider not narrower. Population exploded, as it did in Japan eight decades earlier, but economic output per capita did not. It remained nearly stationary. Indeed, the standard of life of the poorest third of the population has probably declined. In the aftermath of British rule, India prided itself on being the largest democracy in the world, but it lapsed for a time into dictatorship that restricted freedom of speech and press. It is in danger of doing so again.[3]

"What accounts for the different results?" asks Friedman. His unequivocal answer: The Meiji leaders "adopted a liberal economic policy," whereas those who took charge in India opted for a "collectivist economic policy. . . . The Japanese adopted the policies of Adam Smith. The Indians adopted [the collectivist economic policies] of [the British Socialist intellectual] Harold Laski."[4]

As Friedman notes, "The Meiji leaders who took charge in Japan in 1867 were directed primarily to strengthening the power and the glory of their country."[5] With respect to the specifics of their program, Friedman writes,

> The Meiji government did intervene in many ways and played a key role in the process of development. It sent many Japanese abroad for technical training. It imported foreign experts. It established pilot plants in many industries and gave numerous subsidies to others. But at no time did it try to control the total amount or direction of investment. The state maintained a large interest only in shipbuilding and iron and steel industries that it thought necessary for military power. It retained these industries because they were not attractive to private enterprise.[6]

On the basis of Friedman's own description of the interventionist policies of the Meiji leaders, it is difficult to understand his assertion that they adopted the policies of Adam Smith. Moreover, Friedman's account so significantly understates the actual role of the Japanese government as to be thoroughly misleading and, in essence, erroneous. Rather than adopting the laissez-faire policies of Adam Smith, the government assumed paramount importance as the stimulant to growth. Benjamin Higgins, an authority on economic development, has rendered a succinct and accurate description of the role of the Japanese government during the 30 years after the Meiji Restoration.

> Cited today as a prime example of the successful private enterprise economy, nevertheless private enterprise Japan was launched into economic growth by vigorous government action. . . . The capital needed to effect modernization of the economy was provided mainly by the Japanese themselves, since they did not want to risk borrowing from foreigners. Land taxes were the mainstay of government finances, enabling the government to take the lead in making investments in new industries. Important industrial concerns were nationalized; all facilities for manufacturing arms and ships were taken over and managed by the central government, as well as all mining and engineering facilities. Telegraph lines, iron foundries, and factories for producing cement, paper and glass all came in for government investment. Railroad building and shipping were helped with subsidies. . . . A long-range plan completed in

1884 ... included a review of the Japanese economy, a program of economic development, targets for a ten-year span, and a set of recommended policies. The planning function of the government was stressed, and the need to establish clear objectives. ... A group of strategic products was selected for encouragement (such as raw silk, tea, rice, tobacco, wax, lacquerware, metal products, weaving).[7]

Thus, contrary to Friedman's description, nationalization and government planning and intervention in industry were substantially more extensive than he indicates. Furthermore, his statement that at no time did the government try to control the amount or direction of investment is contradicted by the fact that fully half the investment in the economy was not simply directed but actually undertaken by the government.[8] Public investment generally exceeded the level of private investment in the Meiji period and up until World War I. Also contrary to Friedman's statement, the government's ten-year plan adopted in 1884 explicitly enumerated a series of products selected for encouragement by the government.

In yet another major departure from laissez-faire policies, the Meiji leaders in 1872 established a system of universal military service.[9] That Friedman does not mention this development defies understanding, since he regards conscription as fundamentally inconsistent with the operation of a market economy and with the basic values of a free society. So important is the issue in his view that he devoted fully ten columns to it in *Newsweek* between 1966 and 1980. In those articles he attacked conscription as a "tragedy," "an unfair tax imposed on a small minority [the conscripts]," "inconsistent with a free society because it exacts compulsory service," and "a barbarous custom."[10]

Friedman states (as noted above) that the Meiji leaders "made great progress" in the direction of achieving full individual human and political freedom. That quote is from his 1981 publication *Free to Choose.* Evidently he has forgotten what he wrote about Japan in his previous best-selling volume *Capitalism and Freedom,* published in 1962. In that book, pre-World War I Japan, the Japan produced by the Meiji Restoration, is classified by Friedman with Fascist Italy, Fascist Spain, and Nazi Germany as "societies that cannot conceivably be described as politically free."[11]

What then, was the true nature of the Meiji Restoration period and what did it achieve? As described by distinguished historian Nathaniel Peffer,

Since the state was controlled by a small group at the top and industry and finance were controlled at the top, favorable opportunities were opened from the very beginning to those affiliated with ruling groups. Generous subsidies could be won for new ventures by those in the know or with influence with those who had connections. And later, when the pilot enterprises had served their purposes and there were enough men who had learned to conduct modern industry, the state began to withdraw from industry and sell its holdings. It sold them at tempting prices and those with connections had the first chance at the bonanza profits that followed. This was the foundation of the system of gigantic holding company trusts owned by a few families and their associates — the Zaibatsu, they are called — that held the whole Japanese economy in an unbreakable oligarchic grip. This was the system, too, that not only provided the power for the Japanese war machine, but made it easy for the Japanese militarists to bend the economy to their use. The beginning of Japan's modernization was a prodigious feat and also a dangerous feat — dangerous, as it turned out, for Japan itself even more than for the rest of the world.[12]

Let us now turn to India's experiences with economic development, the other part of Friedman's "controlled experiment."

Friedman's assertion that Japan in 1867 and India in 1947 began their development programs under similar circumstances and that "almost all differences favored India rather than Japan" is a gross distortion of history. Rather than starting out under similar circumstances, India and Japan differed profoundly with respect to demography, internal language barriers, social constraints on change, the structure of the state, economically significant religious taboos, and major sources of civil strife.

## POPULATION AND LITERACY

Friedman writes that the population exploded in both countries during the periods under examination and notes that while in Japan the lot of the ordinary man improved rapidly, in India output per capita did not. However, the population growths in the two countries are far from comparable. What he does not mention is the fact that India's population stood at 350 million, 11 times that of Japan. Moreover, while it is true that Japan's population grew rapidly in the 30 years after the Meiji Restoration (from 30 to 46 million), that growth was virtually a trickle when compared with what happened in India in the 30 years after it achieved independence.[13] India's population then grew by 293 million, more than 18 times the increase of 16 million in Japan. Viewed another way, the growth alone was over 6 times greater in India than Japan's entire population after its 30 years of growth. Furthermore, in the single decade prior to its year of independence, India had already increased its population by an amount equal to the size of Japan's population during the period of the Meiji Restoration.

The large size of the Indian population upon achieving independence in 1947 and the big population growth rates both before and after that date persistently threatened malnutrition and starvation in a country with low agricultural productivity. Even more significant, those demographic conditions generated what development economists refer to as a high dependency ratio (persons not working to persons working). A growing population has a relatively greater percentage in lower age groups than is present in populations that are growing less rapidly. As a result, a nation with high population growth rates requires relatively greater investment in schools, health facilities, urban infrastructure, and other areas just to supply new arrivals with the per capita benefits the present population enjoys.

An International Labor Office study has estimated that in a typical developing country, 4 percent of national income must be spent for every 1 percent of population growth just to maintain the status quo.[14] On the basis of these estimates, with India's population growth rate somewhat more than 2 percent, investment of about 9 percent of gross national product (GNP) would be required — more than half of the nation's savings — just to prevent a decline in living standards.

To state, as does Friedman, that India's population exploded as it did in Japan is a gross distortion of reality. Clearly, the population problem was much more severe for India than it was for Japan. In terms of both absolute size of the population and growth rates, the experiences of the two nations are simply not comparable.

India's massive population at independence was also a serious disadvantage because of extraordinarily high levels of illiteracy, a major barrier to economic development. Only 17 percent of the people were literate.[15] By contrast, education had long been valued in Japan, perhaps because of Confucian traditions, so that by the time of the Meiji Restoration, 40 to 50 percent of all males had some formal education.[16]

## LANGUAGE BARRIERS

In India there never was a common language except the English of the intelligentsia, who made up only about 1 percent of the population. The nation embraces over 1,600 different languages and dialects. India's republican form of government embraces 22 states that are delineated by major linguistic groups.[17] Efforts to promote Hindi as the nation's sole official language have met with great difficulty in execution. The structure of linguistic states came into existence following independence after much strife and some bloodshed. As Myrdal has observed,

> In the absence of a generally accepted all-Indian language as a unifying force, the Union's division into states along linguistic lines invites and strengthens the tendencies toward narrow sectionalism, inimical to national consolidation. The language situation in India is especially complicated and hazardous for national consolidation and development.[18]

None of these barriers to development were present in Japan prior to the Meiji Restoration. Japan was a small country, its people were culturally united, sharing common traditions and customs and speaking the same language. Any change could be made known and put into effect in a short time.[19] Rosovsky and Ohkawa, authorities on Japanese economic development, describe the pre-Meiji Restoration period as one with "high standards of education, . . . [a] good road system by 19th century standards . . . housing well-designed and well-engineered, [and with a governmental structure] effective at both central and local levels." They conclude that "in Tokugawa Japan, the gap between economic and 'other' backwardness was unusually large, and this made the prospect of modern growth all the more promising."[20]

## RELIGION AND POLITICAL CONFLICT

Immediately upon achieving independence, India was beset with major religious and political conflicts such that the first four years of the new nation was devoted primarily to establishing law and order and solving political problems.

Prior to independence there were about 300 million Hindus and 100 million Moslems in India. When the United Kingdom put into effect the Indian Independence Act on August 15, 1947, the subcontinent was divided into two sovereign states: India, which was predominantly

Hindu, and Pakistan, which was predominantly Moslem. Over 40 million Moslems remained in India, where they constituted more than 10 percent of the population.

The partition set the stage for confrontation between the two new nations over accession of various princely states, including the still-disputed Jammu and Kashmir. For a year, India and Pakistan were involved in armed conflict over Kashmir. The centuries-old rivalry based on mutual suspicion between Hindus and Moslems erupted into terrible violence. The first couple of years of independence was marked by massive forced migration, plunder, persecution, and mass murder by frenzied mobs of Moslems, Hindus, and Sikhs. The cost in lives alone is estimated to range from 200,000 to just under 1 million. "Within six months of independence, partition created at least 10 million refugees and possibly many more; in fact, it was responsible for the most extensive and miserable uprooting of human beings in modern history."[21]

By contrast, the Meiji Restoration and its fundamental reforms were carried out with relative ease and remarkably little conflict. The two and a half centuries prior to the restoration of the emperor in 1968 was a long period of unbroken peace under the leadership of the Tokugawa shogunate. The shogun was in essence the supreme military commander. The daimyos (feudal lords) accepted Tokugawa supremacy because they were unable to resist, but were left in substantial autonomy with a tight system of checks designed to keep them submissive. Below the daimyo were the knightly military retainers, the samurai.[22]

Despite the samurai origins of many of its leaders, the Meiji government acted resolutely to abolish the shogunate, reinstate the emperor as supreme ruler, and uproot the old feudal class system. Since the Meiji leaders saw the latter as an obstacle to modernization, their first moves were designed to reduce the feudal han to civil provinces under the direct control of the authorities in Tokyo. The daimyo voluntarily agreed to surrender their traditional rights and privileges. They acted partly out of a desire to stand well with the new government and were well compensated by the state for their losses.[23]

Historian Nathaniel Peffer succinctly summarizes the manner in which the Meiji Restoration and its reforms were adopted: "It was by fiat handed down from above, and though it made the sharpest break with the past ever made by a people, it was accepted with only scattered traces of resistance. It had been decreed that the Japanese people change their way of life, so they changed it."[24]

## RELIGIOUS TABOOS

Because of the Hindu taboo on killing animals, a religious taboo that has been given legislative sanction in a number of Indian states, India is estimated to have more than half as many cattle as human beings and, in fact, one-fourth of all the cattle in the world. The attorney general of India has ruled that legislation on cattle slaughter is not within the competence of the central government but lies within the jurisdiction of the state governments.[25] Numerous riots between Hindus and Moslems have been touched off by incidents arising from their contrary views of cow slaughter.[26]

A U.S. team of agricultural experts concluded that "at least one-third and perhaps as many as one-half of India's cattle population may be regarded as surplus in relation to the feed supply."[27] Many of them are destructive and almost all have a very low productivity. They wander across fields, lie in the streets, and rummage hungrily among piles of food in the bazaars. Myrdal has concluded that the costs of the ban on cow slaughter to modernization goals are very high, though never calculated.[28] Similar religious taboos apply to the killing of monkeys and rodents. With poor storage, losses in grains because of these taboos may run as high as 15 to 20 percent.[29]

## COLLECTIVISM IN INDIA

Friedman's assertions that India, since independence, has adopted a collectivist approach to economic policy, relied on central economic planning, and adopted the policies of Harold Laski are based on an extraordinarily simplistic analysis with as little relationship to reality as his claim that the Meiji leaders followed a laissez-faire program. In order to determine the true nature of India's approach to economic development, it is necessary to distinguish between the rhetoric of its leaders and the actual policies they instituted.

The Congress party has governed India almost continuously since the nation won its independence from the United Kingdom. Much of the party's power and almost all of its financial support came and still comes from the professional, industrial, and commercial upper classes in the more modern sectors of the Indian economy. Nevertheless, radical intellectuals in the Congress party, with the support and inspiration of Pandit Nehru, were able to commit in solemn resolutions to a program of economic and social reform. At its 1955 session, the party postulated as its fundamental aim the creation of a "socialist pattern of society."[30] Since 1951, the Indian government, under Congress party leadership, has promulgated a series of five-year plans aimed at promoting economic development. All this seems consistent with Friedman's view that India has followed a collectivist economic policy.

However, when we look at the reality behind the plans and behind the radical rhetoric, a sharply different picture emerges. Rather than collectivist economic policy, what we find, as Gunnar Myrdal so aptly observed, is "bold radicalism in principle and extreme conservatism in practice . . . a vast separation between resolutions and their implementation."[31] While the plans often discuss at length policies to induce fundamental alterations in institutions and attitudes, "operational controls, and the way in which they should be handled, are usually not discussed at all."[32]

Friedman states that the Indian leaders "regard capitalism as synonymous with imperialism" and that "they embarked on a series of Russian-type five-year plans that outlined detailed programs of investment."[33] Here again Friedman has permitted his ideological rhetoric to run away with his analysis. In the USSR, private enterprise is negligible, whereas in India some 85 percent of production is in private hands.[34] The output of government enterprise in India increased from only 3 percent in 1951 to about 7 percent of national product by the middle of the fourth five-year plan in 1970, shares not significantly different from those in the United States and in the capitalistic countries of Western Europe. Over the same period, the Indian government's total contribution to net national product increased from 7.6 percent to 14.8 percent. In the United States, government controls nearly twice this proportion of income, and in Western European countries the proportions are even greater. Government consumption in India, as a percent of gross domestic product, was 7 percent in 1960 and 10 percent in 1978. The corresponding figures for the United States (17 and 18 percent) and for the Western European countries were about double those for India.[35] India's rate of taxation has been one of the lowest in the world, with taxes taking only 8 percent of national income in 1951, 10.2 percent in 1960, and 16.7 percent in 1972. These percentages were only about half those in most developed countries.[36] Obviously, India has not moved very far down the socialist road.

Friedman is clearly accurate when he cites India's detailed and extensive exchange controls, attempts at regulating investment, subsidies, black markets, and various wage-price controls. But rather than being a product of "collectivist economic planning" of the "Russian type," as Friedman contends, they were the product of a plethora of ad hoc discretionary administrative controls in a society that is basically democratic, with productive facilities overwhelmingly in private hands. The plans are little more than targets. The measures taken to implement the plans are improvised in an ad hoc fashion in response to the play of vested interests in a democratic framework.[37] As Benjamin Higgins observed,

> The main evidence of failure to complete the planning process is the absence of firm recommendations in the Plan for the policy measures and regulations needed to implement it. Statements of targets and broad outlines of the sources of finance are not enough in what is still overwhelmingly a free enterprise economy.[38]

Further, Higgins says elsewhere,

> It is important to distinguish between the announced social philosophy, and the degree of state control. Despite the emphasis on planning and the announced socialist philosophy (which in India means social welfare philosophy), India is one of the least regulated [societies] in the world.[39]

## THE OUTCOME

In comparing the outcome of the Japanese and Indian approaches to economic development, Friedman is grossly unfair to India. He overstates Japanese achievements during the 30 years following the Meiji Restoration and understates India's achievements during the 30 years after it achieved independence. Most important of all, he completely ignores the enormous problems India encountered after independence, problems that were not a result of its approach to development but that clearly had a profound adverse effect on its progress.

That the lot of the ordinary man improved rapidly during the Meiji era, as Friedman asserts, is highly questionable. Between 70 and 75 percent of the population at the time of the Restoration engaged in agriculture, and the lot of the peasant was a difficult one. It is widely accepted that Japanese peasants paid much of the price of their country's industrialization.[40] With about three-fourths of the population engaged in agriculture, it was inevitable that they would provide the main source of primary capital accumulation. Peffer's description of the economic conditions of the peasantry after the Restoration is in sharp contrast with Friedman's characterization of the lot of the ordinary man.

> The passing of the shogunate and later of feudalism brought no amelioration in the lot of the peasants. If anything, it was worse than before. The rice tribute paid to feudal lords became taxes paid to the central government and was probably more onerous under the central government, since the government needed more revenue. One way or another the peasant was lucky if he could keep a third of his crop for his own consumption. Not until 1876 was there any reduction in the peasant's taxes, and between 1868 and that year there were nearly two hundred outbreaks of one dimension or another in different parts of the country, some of them being serious.[41]

Often unable to pay their taxes, they were compelled to sell their land to well-to-do landowners. Those who lost their land became tenant farmers, renting the plots they tilled. Tenant farming under trying conditions persisted until the end of World War II when, as a result of the pressure of U.S. occupation officials, a major land-reform program was carried out, and "practically overnight Japan became a land of small landowners."[42]

The ordinary man in industry fared little better than his peasant compatriot. Labor unions were suppressed. Factories were often little more than prisons where employees lived under guard to prevent their escaping before their contracts expired. Personal behavior was supervised paternalistically, to the last detail. Commenting on labor conditions in Meiji Japan, Loeher and Powelson state, "At least two generations of workers were thus sacrificed to slave-like conditions, and for this reason we do not tout the Japanese model as example for the world to follow holistically."[43]

While the Japanese of the Meiji era dismantled the feudal structure, as Friedman states, nevertheless the social and political position of the daimyo and the top ranks of the samurai remained essentially unimpaired. It was from their class that the highest officials of the new regime were chosen. Furthermore, their economic status was raised by the liberal compensation they received from the government when, in 1871, the feudal system of land ownership and clan rule was abolished. As a result of the grants, the daimyo were able, along with the rising merchant princes, "to get in on the ground floor of the new industrialism and rise as it rose. Japan may have had a revolution, but it was a revolution from the top and by decree, one that left those at the apex of the pyramidal society still at the apex."[44]

Friedman argues that at independence, India started out with a more favorable position than did Japan at the beginning of the Meiji era. India, he writes, "enjoyed substantial economic growth before World War I. That growth was converted into stagnation between the two World Wars by the struggle for independence from Britain, but was not reversed. . . . [In the 30 years after independence] output per capita . . . remained nearly stationary."[45] Here again, we find Friedman making loose and baseless generalizations in order to support his case for laissez-faire. Let us look at the relevant data.

In the first 50 years of this century, with all but the last three years under British rule, India had meager per capita growth rates in income, 0.25 percent per year.[46] Between 1951 and 1957, growth rates in per capita income were 1.6 percent per year,[47] and from 1960 to 1978 1.4 percent per year.[48] Thus the growth rates after independence were about five times greater than during the period of British rule in the first half of this century.

When Friedman writes of stagnation in India between the two world wars, he attributes it to India's struggle for independence, completely ignoring the impact of the great worldwide depression of the 1930s. Then, when he turns to independent India, he attributes its "stagnation" to its "collectivist" economic policies. Aside from the fact that it was not stagnant, as we have just noted, Friedman completely ignores the impact on India's economy of two wars with Pakistan, a war with China in 1961, massive internal religious strife, the inheritance of a nation divided along numerous linguistic lines, religious taboos that constrained the development of agriculture, and the need to absorb some 20 million refugees of the wars with Pakistan.

Finally, Friedman writes glowingly of the "great progress" Japan made after the Meiji Restoration in achieving "individual and human freedom," whereas he refers deprecatingly to the danger of India lapsing into dictatorship. The fact is that Japan became a totalitarian, militaristic, and aggressively imperialistic society, whereas India, despite enormous problems, remains fundamentally the world's largest democracy.

# NOTES

1. Milton Friedman and Rose Friedman, *Free to Choose* (New York: Avon, 1981), p. 49.
2. Ibid.
3. Ibid., p. 51.
4. Ibid., p. 273.
5. Ibid.
6. Ibid., p. 53.
7. Benjamin Higgins and Jean Downing Higgins, *Economic Development of a Small Planet* (New York: W. W. Norton, 1979), pp. 79–80.
8. Angus Maddison, *Economic Progress and Policy in Developing Countries* (New York: W. W. Norton, 1970), p. 20; William McCord, "The Japanese Model," in *The Political Economy of Development and Underdevelopment*, ed. Charles K. Wilbur (New York: Random House, 1973), p. 279.
9. Hyman Kublin, *Japan* (Boston: Houghton Mifflin, 1969), p. 129.
10. *Newsweek,* December 19, 1966, p. 100; March 11, 1968, p. 82; December 30, 1968, p. 44; July 7, 1969, p. 78; March 16, 1970, p. 90; September 6, 1971, p. 9; February 11, 1974, p. 82; April 16, 1979, p. 76; May 14, 1979, p. 101; September 29, 1980, p. 74.
11. Milton Friedman, *Capitalism and Freedom* (Chicago: University of Chicago Press, 1962), p. 10.
12. Nathaniel Peffer, *The Far East* (Ann Arbor: University of Michigan Press, 1958), p. 137.
13. Kublin, *Japan*, p. 136.
14. William Loeher and John P. Powelson, *The Economics of Development and Distribution* (New York: Harcourt, Brace, Jovanovich, 1981), pp. 194–205.
15. Clair Wilcox et al., *Economies of the World Today,* 3rd ed. (New York: Harcourt, Brace, Jovanovich, 1976), p. 62.
16. Kazushi Ohkawa and Henry Rosovsky, "Capital Formation in Japan," in *The Cambridge Economic History of Europe,* (Cambridge: Cambridge University Press, 1978), Vol. 7, Pt 2, p. 141.
17. Arthur S. Banks, ed., *Political Handbook of the World, 1979* (New York: McGraw-Hill, 1979), p. 213.
18. Gunnar Myrdal, *Asian Drama* (New York: Pantheon, 1968) 1:83–87.
19. Kublin, *Japan*, p. 126.
20. Ohkawa and Rosovsky, "Capital Formation," p. 141.
21. Myrdal, *Asian Drama*, 1:234–41.
22. Peffer, *The Far East*, pp. 33–34.
23. Kublin, *Japan*, pp. 128–29.
24. Peffer, *The Far East*, p. 37.
25. Myrdal, *Asian Drama*, 2:1273.
26. Ibid., 1:92.
27. Ibid., 2:1273.
28. Ibid., 1:89–93.

29.    Maddison, *Economic Progress*, pp. 141–42; Ernest Dunbar, "India: Angry, Hungry, Stubborn and Proud," in *20th Century Asia*, ed. John U. Michaelis and Robin James McKeown (New York: McGraw-Hill, 1969), p. 20.

30.    Myrdal, *Asian Drama*, 1:260–62, 276.

31.    Ibid., p. 261.

32.    Ibid., 2:902.

33.    Friedman and Friedman, *Free to Choose*, pp. 53, 54.

34.    Clair Wilcox et al., *Economies*, p. 74.

35.    World Bank, *World Development Report, 1980* (Washington, D.C.: The World Bank, August 1980), pp. 118–19.

36.    Clair Wilcox et al., *Economies*, p. 74.

37.    Myrdal, *Asian Drama*, 2:926–33.

38.    Benjamin Higgins, *Economic Development* (New York: Norton, 1959), p. 729.

39.    Higgins and Higgins, *Economic Development of a Small Planet*, p. 258.

40.    Kublin, *Japan*, pp. 135–36.

41.    Peffer, *The Far East*, p. 136.

42.    Kublin, *Japan*, pp. 136, 187–88.

43.    Loeher and Powelson, *Economics of Development*, p. 394.

44.    Peffer, *The Far East*, pp. 128–33.

45.    Friedman and Friedman, *Free to Choose*, pp. 50–51.

46.    C. T. Kurien, *India's Economic Crisis* (Bombay: Asia, 1969), p. 2.

47.    Lawrence A. Viet, *India's Second Revolution* (New York: McGraw-Hill, 1976), p. 70.

48.    World Bank, *Development Report, 1980*, p. 110.

# 5

# THE CHILEAN MIRACLE: THE TRIUMPH AND TRAGEDY OF IDEOLOGY

Military juntas in other South American countries have been as authoritarian in the economic sphere as they have been in politics. . . . However, to the best of my knowledge, none, with the exception of Chile, has supported a fully free-market economy as a matter of principle. Chile is an economic miracle. . . . Chile is an even more amazing political miracle. A military regime has supported reforms that sharply reduce the role of the state and replace control from the top with control from the bottom.[1]

So wrote Nobel Laureate Milton Friedman in January 1982 with respect to the Friedmanesque policy prescriptions rigorously followed by the Chilean military junta since its overthrow of Allende in 1973.

Despite Chile's limited strategic and economic significance in world affairs, the economic experiment carried out in that relatively small country has attracted worldwide interest and stirred bitter controversy. Several factors explain the international attention devoted to Chile: (1) interest in the social and economic effects of the draconian measures instituted by the junta in establishing a laissez-faire market economy; (2) the revelations in the 1970s of extensive involvement by the U.S. Central Intelligence Agency (CIA) in the internal affairs of Chile; and (3) the fact that the economic rhetoric invoked by the Chilean junta — anti-Keynesian monetarism, severe limitations on the role of the government, and reliance on "free" markets — is strikingly similar to that enunciated by the United Kingdom's Margaret Thatcher and President Ronald Reagan.

Rarely, if ever, has an economist had the opportunity to provide a lab test for theories as Friedman has had in Chile. Perhaps even more remarkable is that the test of this economist's ideas was performed in a country other than his or her own.

Throughout most of its history, Chile has been a constitutional democracy with a remarkable continuity in civilian democratic rule. From 1818, the year that it attained independence, until the military coup d'état of September 1973, Chile experienced only three brief interruptions of its strong democratic tradition. Constitutional rule was unbroken from 1932 until the overthrow of President Salvador Allende and his Popular Unity government by the military in 1973.[2] The coup was brutal, with few parallels in Latin America. Followers of the parties that had constituted the Popular Unity government were arrested, tortured, and killed, and countless others were driven into exile.[3] "The military junta named Army Commander General Augusto Pinochet as President, dissolved the Chilean Congress, declared all Marxist parties illegal, placed all other political parties in indefinite recess, and established press censorship and detention facilities for opponents of the new regime."[4] In 1980, the seventh year of the junta's rule, a new constitution was ratified by a plebiscite, enabling Pinochet to continue as president for another eight years.[5]

Professor Friedman's relationship with the regime established by the military junta aroused a storm of protest. When in 1976 he was named winner of the Nobel Memorial Prize for Economic Science, demonstrators in Stockholm chanted and marched in the street protesting the award. In letters to the New York *Times*, four Nobel laureates — George Wald, Linus Pauling, David Baltimore, and S. E. Luria — attacked the "deplorable insensitivity" of the Nobel Committee in awarding the prize to Friedman. Baltimore and Luria, based on what they said they had read in the *Times* and elsewhere that "Professor Friedman has been a major economic adviser and supporter of the Chilean junta" concluded

> that the Swedish committee should have chosen to honor Professor Friedman at this time is an insult to the people of Chile, burdened by the reactionary economic measures sponsored by Professor Friedman, and especially to those Chileans who are in jail or in exile as a result of the policies of the military government.[6]

In an interview with a New York *Times* reporter, Friedman complained that demonstrators followed him almost everywhere and that "it's a frightening experience to see — the madness on their faces." On receiving the Nobel prize in Stockholm he reacted to the demonstrations against him with the statement that "the stench of Nazism is in the air."[7]

What was the precise nature of the Friedman-junta connection that aroused such bitter controversy? Was there any justification for the passionate moral outcry by Friedman's critics? What were the policies instituted by the junta? How were those policies related to Friedman's economic and political philosophy? Most important of all, is there any validity to Friedman's highly laudatory characterization of the Chilean junta's free-market experiment as an "economic miracle"? In order to answer these questions it is first necessary to trace the political and economic developments in Chile since the period just prior to the election of President Allende in 1970.

## THE REVOLUTION IN LIBERTY: 1964–70

Under the leadership of President Edwardo Frei, between 1964 and 1970, the moderate Christian Democratic government carried out what it called the Revolution in Liberty. A major component of the program was a substantial movement in the direction of state ownership of major shares in the country's foreign owned mining industries, which normally accounted for about 80 percent of Chile's exports. Chileanization, to use Frei's term, resulted in the government's acquisition of 51 percent of the stock of the Chilean subsidiaries of Anaconda Copper, Kennecott Copper, and the nitrate mining subsidiaries of Anglo-Lautaro — all U.S. firms. Chileanization also involved substantial tax concessions to U.S. firms in return for their agreement to expand their investments in Chile. While giving the government a significant role in the decision-making process of foreign owned firms, the program stopped considerably short of outright nationalization.[8]

In addition to Chileanization, Frei's Revolution in Liberty included agrarian, education, and tax reforms. Labor legislation was enacted favorable to the organization of unions of agricultural workers and their engaging in collective bargaining. Rural workers, for the first time, could protect their own interests through the administrative mechanisms of the government or through direct action, the strike. Furthermore, the unions provided the peasants with a potential power base for political activity. An agrarian reform law placed limitations on the size of the property that a single proprietor might hold and led to the expropriation of about 8.75 million acres. Over a period of three to five years, the expropriated land was to be given to individual peasant families or cooperatives formed by peasants. A crash program in education more than doubled the number of school buildings in three years and increased the primary school population by 30 percent. While taxes were increased substantially during the Frei years, they were reduced for low income groups, making the tax structure somewhat more progressive.[9]

President Frei's Revolution in Liberty began to come apart midway through his administration and Chilean society became increasingly polarized. In the year prior to the Christian Democratic's assumption of power in 1964, consumer prices had risen about 46 percent. Halfway through Frei's term in office the rate of inflation was brought down to 17 percent, but in 1967 prices began to rise more sharply, so that by the time of the 1970 presidential election, the inflation rate was running at 35 percent per year. (See Table 5.1.) Few wage earners were able to keep up with the inflation, and some middle class elements (white collar workers and small business people) who had supported the Christian Democrats in 1964 were dismayed by the acceleration of prices and began to desert the party.[10]

Compounding the difficulties resulting from its inability to deal with inflation, the Christian Democratic party's appeal was also weakened by attacks on its key programs by political parties from the right and the left. The right depicted Frei as a Chilean Kerensky who was preparing the way for a communist takeover, denounced the substantial tax increases and moderate income redistribution measures imposed by the Christian Democrats, and deprecated the agrarian reforms as expensive and inefficient.[11] The left accused Frei of selling out to U.S. capitalists by providing excessively generous terms for U.S. firms in his Chileanization program, deplored the slow pace of agrarian reform, and in general attacked the Christian Democrats as mere reformists who had adopted a policy of dependence on the United States.[12]

Although the Frei reforms were impressive, they fell far short of what he had promised. Lacking a majority in the Chilean Congress, opposed by both the right and the left, Frei was forced to compromise on substantial aspects of his original program, thereby alienating many of his early supporters. The steady erosion of support for the Christian Democrats was reflected in the declining vote they received in congressional elections, from 42 percent in 1965 to 30 percent in 1969 — a development that did not bode well for the party's chances in the 1970 presidential election.[13]

# TABLE 5.1
## Key Economic Indicators
## (in percentages)

| | Increase in Consumer Price Index | Annual Aveage Growth Rate in Gross Domestic | | Unemployment Rate | Minimum Employment Plan | Real Wages (1970=100) |
|---|---|---|---|---|---|---|
| | | Chile | Latin America | | | |
| 1960–70 | — | 4.5 | — | — | — | — |
| 1960 | 11.6 | — | — | — | — | — |
| 1961 | 7.7 | 4.8 | — | — | — | — |
| 1962 | 13.9 | 4.7 | — | — | — | — |
| 1963 | 44.3 | 2.2 | — | — | — | — |
| 1964 | 46.0 | 2.2 | — | — | — | — |
| 1965 | 28.8 | 0.8 | — | — | — | — |
| 1966 | 22.9 | 11.2 | 4.5 | — | — | — |
| 1967 | 18.1 | 3.2 | 6.9 | 4.7 | — | — |
| 1968 | 26.6 | 3.6 | 7.1 | 4.9 | — | — |
| 1969 | 32.5 | 3.7 | 6.8 | 5.0 | — | — |
| 1970 | 34.9 | 2.1 | 6.7 | 6.1 | — | 100.0 |
| 1971 | 22.1 | 9.0 | 6.8 | 3.8 | — | — |
| 1972 | 163.4 | −1.2 | 7.0 | 3.1 | — | — |
| 1973 | 508.1 | −5.6 | 8.3 | 4.8 | — | — |
| 1974 | 375.9 | 1.0 | 7.0 | 9.2 | — | 65.0 |
| 1975 | 340.7 | −12.9 | 3.8 | 14.5 | 2.4 | 62.9 |
| 1976 | 174.3 | 3.5 | 5.4 | 14.8 | 5.0 | 64.9 |
| 1977 | 63.5 | 9.9 | 4.8 | 12.7 | 3.8 | 71.4 |
| 1978 | 30.3 | 8.2 | 5.1 | 13.6 | 4.3 | 76.0 |
| 1979 | 38.9 | 8.3 | 6.5 | 12.5 | 3.9 | 82.3 |
| 1980 | 31.2 | 7.8 | 5.9 | 11.8 | 5.4 | 89.3 |
| 1981 | 9.5[a] | 5.7 | 1.5 | 9.0 | 4.8 | 97.3 |
| 1982 | 20.7[a] | −14.3 | −0.9 | 20.3 | 12.0 | 96.9 |
| 1983 | 23.1[a] | −0.8 | — | 14.6[a] | 13.0[a] | 86.7 |
| 1984 | — | — | — | 15.0[b] | 9.6[a] | — |

[a]End-of-year values.
[b]Average for three months ending February 1984.

*Sources:* For increase in consumer prices from 1960–69, Barbara Stallings, *Class Conflict and Economic Development in Chile,* 1958–1973, Stanford University Press, Stanford, 1978, p. 243; for 1970–80, *CEPAL Review,* United Nations Economic Commission for Latin America, Santiago, Chile, April 1983, p. 16; for 1981–83, *Foreign Economic Trends and Their Implications for the United States,* Chile, U.S. Dept. of Commerce, International Trade Administration, Washington, D.C., p. 2. For growth rates in gross domestic product in Chile from 1960–70, *World Development Report,*

## THE 1970 PRESIDENTIAL ELECTION

There were three presidential candidates in the 1970 election. With Frei unable to succeed himself according to the Chilean constitution, the Christian Democrats chose Radomiro Tomic as their candidate. Jorge Alessandri, an arch-conservative who was strongly probusiness and heavily backed by U.S. corporations, was the candidate of the right-wing Partido Nacional. The third candidate, Salvador Allende, the leader of the Socialist party, was the nominee of the Unidad Popular (UP), a coalition of the large socialist and communist parties and four minor political parties.

The Alessandri program emphasized "the need to reduce government expenditures and to release the energies of private enterprise, without abandoning the mixed economy that Chile had been developing over many years." The road to economic development was seen as being achieved through efficiency in public and private enterprise, and "too rapid" income redistribution was attacked as an impediment to economic growth.[14]

During the campaign, the Chilean Road to Socialism became the rallying cry of Allende and the Unidad Popular. The program called for full nationalization of the copper mining, nitrates, iodine, and iron and steel industries; banking and insurance; foreign trade; the strategic industrial monopolies; and large firms and monopolies in the field of

---

1980, The World Bank, Washington, D.C., August 1980, p. 111; for 1961–1971, Roberto Zahler, "Recent Southern Cone Liberalization Reforms and Stabilization Policies," *Journal of Interamerican Studies and World Affairs*, Vol. 25, No. 4, November, 1983, p. 538; for 1972–82, *Latest Information on National Accounts of Developing Countries*, OECD, Paris, November 1983, No. 16, p. 17; for 1983, "Foreign Economic Trends and Their Implications for the United States," *op. cit.*, p. 2. For growth rates in Latin America, *CEPAL Review*, United Nations Economic Commission for Latin America, Santiago, Chile, various issues. For unemployment from 1967–69, Alec Nove, "The Political Economy of the Allende Regime," in *Allende's Chile*, edited by Phillip J. O'Brien, Praeger Publishers, New York, 1976, p. 53; from 1970–73, Lawrence Whitehead, "Inflation and Stabilization in Chile, 1970–77, in *Inflation and Stabilization in Latin America*, edited by Rosemary Thorp and Lawrence Whitehead, Holms and Meier Publishers, New York, 1979, p. 96; for 1975–82, *Economic Survey of Latin America*, 1980, CEPAL; for 1983–84, "Foreign Economic Trends and Their Implications for the United States," *op. cit.*, pp. 2 and 12. For PEM from 1975–81, Roberto Zahler, *op. cit.*, p. 541; for 1982–84, "Foreign Economic Trends and Their Implications for the United States," *op. cit.*, p. 2. For real wage index, Roberto Zahler, *op. cit.*, 1970 and 1974–81; for 1983, "Foreign Economic Trends and Their Implications for the United States," *op. cit.*, p. 2.

distribution. Agrarian reforms would be advanced much more aggressively than under the Christian Democrats, with an emphasis on expansion of the cooperative system. In the area of education, an extensive school building program and the provision of scholarships for students with the elimination of class privileges would open the universities to the children of workers. Rapid and decentralized growth would be fostered and every Chilean of working age would be guaranteed adequately paid employment. The export sector would be diversified to reduce Chile's heavy dependence on copper in international trade. The foreign policy plank denounced the Organization of American States as "an instrument and agency of North American imperialism," called for a special regional organization of Latin American countries, and expressed strong solidarity with Cuba.[15]

The results of the popular vote were extraordinarily close. Allende received 36.3 percent to Alessandri's 34.9 percent, a margin of 39,000 out of 3 million votes. Tomic, the Christian Democratic candidate, ran a poor third with 27.8 percent.[16]

Since no candidate received a majority of the popular vote, the Chilean constitution required that the two houses of Congress meet together to make a decision between the two candidates with the most popular votes. Although precedent dictated that the candidate with the most popular votes would be elected, the outcome was by no means certain. The Christian Democrats held the balance of power in Congress and could cast their votes in favor of either of the two top candidates.

The Christian Democrats, many of whom were sympathetic to much of the Allende program, entered into extensive negotiations with members of the Allende coalition, negotiations that resulted in a Statute of Democratic Guarantees. The statute was "an attempt to bind Allende publicly and explicitly to what he had always supported verbally, the maintenance of the norms of a pluralistic democracy."[17] The guarantees included the maintenance of a free press, education independent of all official ideological orientation, freedom for political parties, and autonomy for the three branches of government — executive, legislative, and judicial. In his last speech to the Chilean Senate, a body of which he had been a member for 25 years, Allende described the guarantees as "not only constitutional principles, but a moral commitment to our consciences and to history." As a result of the agreement on the statute and its passage by a joint session of Congress, with the votes of the deputies and senators of the Christian Democratic party and of the parties making up the Unidad Popular, Allende was elected constitutional president of Chile and was inaugurated on November 3, 1970.[18]

## THE ALLENDE REGIME: 1970–73

In the last three years of the Frei regime, inflation rates rose, industrial output showed little upward trend, and unemployment increased. (See Table 5.1.) Frei's Chileanization of the copper mines (the acquisition of 51 percent of the shareholding by the government) was carried out under terms of agreement that proved highly favorable to the copper companies. In the years following Chileanization, the companies made and remitted unusually high profits.[19] Agrarian reform, despite great promises, moved ahead at a relatively slow pace. Over a decade an already highly unequal distribution of income moved sharply toward even greater inequality. In 1959, the bottom 30 percent of the population received 8.5 percent of the total income, but by 1970 its share fell to 5.6 percent. Over the same period the share going to the top 10 percent of the population rose sharply, from 36.1 percent to 46.9 percent.[20] Such were the conditions inherited by Allende's Unidad Popular coalition.

Allende's Chilean Road to Socialism was in essence an attempt, within a democratic framework, to drastically alter the distribution of income, wealth, and political power. In the words of the *Basic Program of Government of the Unidad Popular,*

> The popular revolutionary forces have not united to fight for the simple substitution of one President of the Republic for another, nor to replace one governing party with others — but to realize the profound changes the national situation requires, based on the transfer of power from the old ruling groups to the workers, peasants, and progressive middle sectors, urban and rural.[21]

The Chilean economy performed surprisingly well during 1971, the first year of the Allende regime. As a result of highly expansionary government policies, the gross domestic product rose 9 percent, about twice the average annual growth rates of the previous decade.[22] The share of national income received by wage and salary earners increased from 53.7 percent in 1970 to 59 percent in 1971. The increase was largely owing to the rise in the average wage rate by 25 percent and the fall in the unemployment rate from 8.3 percent in December 1970 to 3.8 percent in December 1971. Retail price inflation fell from 34.9 to 22.1

percent, despite a dramatic 13 percent increase in consumption. The decline in the rate of inflation was achieved primarily through price controls backed by the threat of nationalization and a system of multiple exchange rates under which many favored categories of imports were supplied at fixed and artificially favorable exchange rates.[23]

The Allende regime also moved ahead with its nationalization program. In July of 1971, a joint session of the Chilean Congress passed a constitutional amendment permitting the nationalization of the mining industry — copper, nitrates, iron, and coal. The widespread popular support for government takeover of the mines is evident from the fact that although the Unidad Popular coalition had only 20 out of 50 senators in the upper house and 60 deputies out of 150 in the Chamber of Deputies, the amendment was passed unanimously with little debate.[24]

The nationalization of the banking system was carried out entirely by administrative action. The process of buying out private banks went forward rapidly, so that by March 1972 only three banks remained in private hands. The Allende government also bought out or purchased controlling interest in a number of private firms, mostly foreign owned, in the manufacturing sector of the economy.[25]

Expropriation of large landholdings, provided for in the Agrarian Reform Law passed during the Frei administration, was rapidly completed under Allende. Within a few months about 50 percent of all the irrigated land in the country had been expropriated.[26]

By mid-1972, however, the Allende program began to unravel at an accelerating pace, leading ultimately to the military takeover of the Chilean government on September 11, 1973. Several factors coalesced to generate rapidly deteriorating conditions in Chilean society and the final downfall of Allende: (1) the unsound economic policies of the Unidad Popular, (2) the anti-Allende activities of the United States, and (3) the alienation of the petty bourgeoisie.

## The Unsound Policies of the Unidad Popular

As noted above, the government took over the mining industry by constitutional amendment and firms in other industries by buying them out or purchasing a controlling interest, actions that generally received widespread support. In addition to those approaches, use was made of a 1932 law that gave the government the power to requisition temporarily industries or firms not operating in a vaguely defined public interest. The law also authorized "intervention" (temporary takeover of management) of industries not functioning because of labor disputes.[27] By December 1972 there were 99 requisitioned and intervened enterprises, and they accounted for 8.5 percent of production. In a number of cases, often encouraged by one or more of the UP parties, workers occupied factories and demanded that the government take over control from the owners. These methods

> caused not only bitterness, but also confusion and uncertainty. Bitterness because they were seen as a way of evading legislative opposition to nationalization. Confusion because there was uncertainty about who might be nationalized or "intervened" next. . . . Business nervousness increased, paralyzing private investment and causing many conflicts with particular firms, who used the press and commercial radio to lambaste the real or alleged efforts of the government to nationalize them. . . . At the other end of the scale, the nervousness of owner-drivers about alleged plans to nationalize road transport contributed to the mobilization of these key petty bourgeois against the government in 1972, with deplorable results.[28]

Between 1970 and 1972 private investment almost evaporated, declining by an estimated 85 percent.[29]

Land reform also ran into serious difficulties. Under the Frei land reform law, owners were allowed to remove their assets, and this meant the loss of equipment and in some cases, livestock. In addition, the fate of the redistributed land was uncertain. There was differing opinion as to whether there would be private ownership or collective or cooperative farming and great unclarity over how the collectives would be run, how the peasants were to work them, how the produce would be disposed of, and how the income would be distributed. As a result, the system of incentives was so greatly confused that output and marketing fell short of expectations. Compounding the problems of land reform, the extreme left encouraged illegal land seizures by peasants. Fearful of offending either the extreme left or the center, the government compromised by repressing some illegal seizures and tolerating others, thereby antagonizing both groups.[30]

The Allende government's wage-price policies, which at first seemed quite successful, ultimately turned out to be a major factor moving the economy down the road to disaster. The formulation of wage policy involved three levels. First, tripartite arbitration boards responsible for resolving collective bargaining wage disputes tended to back the workers' demands. Second, the administration granted cost-of-living adjustments equal to the previous year's rate of inflation. This meant a substantial increase in real wages, since the 1970 inflation rate of 35 percent was significantly higher than the 22 percent of 1971. Third, public sector wages were increased by the same amount as those in the private sector to maintain the loyalty of bureaucrats and skilled state workers.[31] As a result of these policies, money wages and salaries rose 51.9 percent between October 1970 and October 1971; the decline in the inflation rate of 16.5 percent over the same period meant a very large increase in real wages, about 30 percent.[32]

The increased purchasing power of the workers, under conditions of underemployment, stimulated a 12 percent rise in industrial production in 1971. However, the bulk of the increased demand went for food. Agricultural output was not sufficient to meet it, hence, food had to be imported in quantities increasing an estimated 150 percent between 1970 and 1972. Over the same period total imports rose 26 percent, while exports, largely as a result of a severe drop in copper prices, declined about 25 percent. With a highly unfavorable balance of trade, foreign currency reserves fell precipitately and practically disappeared by the end of 1971.[33]

Developments in the state sector of the economy added to the inflationary pressures of government wage policies. The purchase of some enterprises by the state was financed by money creation. In addition, inefficiency in nationalized industries combined with price controls on most state-produced products resulted in enormous losses for state-run enterprises in 1972 and 1973. To cover these losses, the government increased the money supply drastically. With widespread tax evasion and the unwillingness of Congress to increase taxes, the government also resorted to running the printing presses to finance major social programs in housing, urban sanitation, and irrigation.[34] The money supply increased 100 percent in 1971, 98 percent in 1972, and 291 percent in 1973.[35]

With those massive increases in the money supply, galloping inflation was inevitable. There was no more slack in the economy, real output could not be increased without investment, and investment in both the private and public sectors was falling sharply.[36] Prices rose dramatically: 163 percent in 1972 and over 500 percent in the year of the military coup. (See Table 5.1.)

## The Anti-Allende Activities of the U.S. Government

In the decade between 1963 and 1973, U.S. involvement in covert action in Chile was extensive and continuous. According to a 1975 staff report of a U.S. Senate committee on intelligence activities, "[The CIA] financed activities covering a broad spectrum, from simple propaganda manipulation of the press to large-scale support for Chilean political parties, from public opinion polls to direct attempts to foment a military coup."[37]

The staff report disclosed that

> The Central Intelligence Agency spent more than $2.6 million in support of the [1964] election of the Christian Democratic candidate, in part to prevent the accession to the presidency of Marxist Salvador Allende. More than half of the Christian Democratic [Frei] candidate's campaign was financed by the United States, although he was not informed of this assistance. In addition, the [CIA] Station furnished support to an array of pro-Christian Democratic student, women's, professional and peasant groups. Two other political parties were funded as well in an attempt to spread the vote.[38]

Pulitzer Prize winning journalist Seymour M. Hersh (he also won several awards for his reporting on the CIA and Chile), wrote in 1983 that the staff report grossly understated U.S. involvement. According to Hersh, U.S. expenditure to support Frei's candidacy in the 1964 campaign was "at least $20 million . . . about $8 per voter." Frei won with 56 percent of the vote.[39]

During the Frei years, the CIA continued to operate throughout Chile, primarily to repress leftist political activities. At least 20 covert actions were undertaken in Chile between 1964 and 1969. Expenditures for those activities amounted to almost $2 million, of which one-fourth was "for specific major political action efforts."[40]

On September 15, 1970, nine days before the Chilean Congress was to decide whether Allende or Alessandri would be chosen as president, President Nixon met with CIA Director Richard Helms. He informed Helms "that an Allende regime in Chile would not be acceptable to the United States and instructed the CIA to play a direct role in organizing a military coup d'état in Chile to prevent Allende's accession to the Presidency."[41] Helms' handwritten notes taken during that meeting included such remarks as "full-time job — best men we have"; "$10,000,000 available, more if necessary"; "make the economy scream."[42]

Despite U.S. efforts, Allende was chosen as president by the Chilean Congress. But covert U.S. activities continued during the Allende years aimed at his destruction, and the Nixon administration did pursue a concerted program of making the Chilean economy "scream."

Approximately $7 million was spent on covert action in Chile during 1970–73. "U.S. policy sought to maximize pressure on the Allende government to prevent its consolidation and limit its ability to implement policies contrary to U.S. and hemispheric interests." A fundamental goal was a "desire to frustrate Allende's experiment in the Western Hemisphere and thus limit its attractiveness as a model."[43]

During the years of Allende's presidency, the CIA funded a wide range of propaganda activities. It produced several magazines with national circulations, gave substantial financial support to *El Mercurio,* Chile's major daily newspaper, and developed material for opposition party newspapers, two weekly papers, and all radio stations controlled by opposition parties. Funds were also channeled to right-wing paramilitary groups and to private sector groups opposed to Allende. Antigovernment strikes "were actively supported by several of the private sector groups which received CIA funds." The 1975 staff report of the Senate concluded that all observers agree that the devastating truckers' strikes "could not have been maintained on the basis of union funds."[44]

In addition to its activities aimed at disrupting political and economic conditions within Chile, the United States also exerted tremendous pressure on the Chilean economy through the international channels of trade and aid. When the Unidad Popular came to power in 1970, it was faced with a situation in which debt service charges and profit remittances from direct foreign investment comprised about 30 percent of the total value of Chilean exports. Consequently, the United States, with its power to adversely affect the flow of aid and credit to Chile, had a powerful tool for damaging the Chilean economy. In addition, the structure of Chilean imports (39 percent of which came from the United States, including the bulk of crucial spare parts and machinery) gave the United States "powerful leverage to disrupt the Chilean economy."[45]

In 1971, the U.S. Export-Import Bank announced that Chile could expect no loans or guarantees. Chile had received $600 million in credits from the bank since 1945. Chile had also made use of the bank's insurance and guarantee programs, which are crucial for a poor foreign government in obtaining credits from private banks and suppliers' credits for its imports. The effect of the bank's announcement was immediate. While private U.S. banks had supplied an average of $220 million in short-term credits in previous years, in 1972 Chile was able to get only $35 million in such credit. Furthermore, nearly all suppliers' credits were suspended, the U.S. Agency for International Development (AID) cut off all U.S. aid to Chile from the moment of Allende's victory, and the United States successfully pressured multilateral banks to sharply reduce lending to Chile.[46]

The impact of the above U.S. policies is reflected in the sharp decline in loans and grants to Chile from 1970 through 1973, the Allende years. Equally significant is the fact that U.S. military aid to Chile was increased over what it was in the previous six years. Since 1951, Chile has been the highest per capita recipient of military aid in Latin America, and in absolute terms ranks second only to Brazil. As Phillip J. O'Brien has written, "U.S. military aid, particularly since the 1960's has been designed not only to strengthen the recipient armed forces but also to tie these armed forces to the United States. If the need arose, the United States clearly would prefer not to have to intervene directly itself, but to leave it to its client armed forces."[47]

## The Alienation of the Petty Bourgeoisie

Chile is a country with a very large class of small shopkeepers, owners of workshops, owner-drivers of trucks, small peasantry, and other members of what can be called the petty bourgeoisie. Allende tried in his electoral campaign and early policies to reassure them by promising action only against the foreign corporations, the few large Chilean monopolists, and the big landowners.[48] The support, or at least neutralization, of the petty bourgeoisie was essential for Allende to remain in power. However, for several reasons, this large class soon became alienated from the government and emerged as a crucial force in the overthrow of Allende.

The petty bourgeoisie suffered great frustration as producers and had a difficult time as consumers. Owing to a desperate shortage of foreign exchange, many items were subject to strict import licensing. Hence, it became extremely difficult for a small manufacturer, a shopkeeper, or an owner of two or three trucks to obtain required spare parts, material, or commodities from abroad. As consumers, they were faced with a situation in which many items at fixed prices were unobtainable. "Meat was exceedingly scarce, and it was almost impossible to find sugar, flour, butter, margarine, rice. . . . It soon became very difficult to buy detergents, cigarettes, razor blades, toilet paper and toothpaste." In August 1972, the shopkeepers staged a 24-hour strike, their first since the government took office. In middle-class areas, unrest and protests mounted and housewives marched banging empty pots.[49]

In March of 1973, despite difficult and deteriorating conditions in Chile, Allende's Unidad Popular coalition won about 43 percent of the vote in congressional elections.[50] Although the opposition parties held on to their majority in Congress, the vote represented a seven point increase over what Allende had received in the 1970 presidential election. Allende attempted a political rapprochement with the leaders of the Christian Democratic party shortly after the March elections. After some delicate negotiations, a dialogue began at the end of July.[51]

On July 25, 1973, during the attempt at political rapprochement, the National Truck Owners Confederation began an indefinite walkout against the policies of government, a strike that ultimately proved fatal to the Allende regime. With the Chilean economy overwhelmingly dependent on road transport, the strike produced economic chaos. Professional people — lawyers, pharmacists, engineers, teachers, airline pilots — followed the lead of the truckers and went on strike. Shopkeepers struck for 48 to 72 hours every week. Of those developments Alec Nove has written,

> With no means of enforcing any policy the government could only watch the continuing collapse of the economy. Aware of the increasing likelihood of a coup, the striking bourgeoisie refused any compromise. . . . Allende had now neither policy nor power to impose a policy. He could only stagger on, improvising solutions to crises as they arose, until in the end the more ruthless elements in the armed forces destroyed him, the UP parties, and the constitution on that tragic day of September 11, 1973.[52]

## THE CHILEAN MIRACLE: THE TRIUMPH AND TRAGEDY OF IDEOLOGY

The close relationship between Professor Friedman and the military junta that overthrew Allende goes back to 1955. In that year, an agreement was signed between the University of Chicago and the Catholic University of Chile giving the opportunity to a large number of Chilean economists to undertake postgraduate work at the University of Chicago. Between 1955 and 1963, this exchange was financed by the United States Agency for International Development, and thereafter by

Chilean business people and others.[53] The Chileans studied under Professors Friedman and Arnold Harberger, and a number of them became ardent adherents of the Chicago school of economics.[54]

On returning to Chile, even prior to Allende's presidency, "the Chicago Boys" (the name by which they were popularly known in Chile) obtained important footholds in the media and established right-wing think tanks. During the Allende period, several of the Chicago Boys played an important role in carrying out media campaigns and organizing and coordinating actions against the government and met periodically and informally to discuss the economic situation. Early in 1973, "at the request of . . . Navy officers and certain business interests, a group of Chicago Boys met to draw up an economic plan to be implemented after the fall of Allende." Ten leading economists, eight Chicago Boys, and two sympathizers drew up the plan. "By the time of the coup, a 280-odd page plan had been written, and was in the hands of the Junta. Not surprisingly, virtually the day after the coup many of the authors of the plan entered the key Economic Ministries as 'advisers'."[55]

The analytical and philosophical framework of the Chicago school, through the extraordinary influence of the Chicago Boys, provided the intellectual rationale for the specific social, political, and economic policies vigorously imposed on Chilean society by the military junta. Therefore, to understand the specific policies of the junta it is necessary to have a clear picture of the basic ideas of the Chicago school, particularly as they have been developed by Milton Friedman.

Monetarism is a basic component of Friedman's analytical and philosophical framework. The "Keynesian revolution" in economic thought was, fundamentally, an attack on "the central proposition of conservative orthodoxy — the assumed or inferred tendency of the economy to full employment." Keynesians tend to view unemployment as "the overriding social problem" in capitalist economies. The monetarists' counterrevolution, on the other hand, is an attempt to restore the conservative orthodoxy, and their primary concern is inflation.[56] For the monetarists, as Friedman has stated, "inflation is always and everywhere a monetary phenomenon, produced in the first instance by an unduly rapid growth in the quantity of money."[57]

Robert J. Gordon has succinctly summarized the planks of the monetarist platform.

Plank 1: Without the interference of demand shocks introduced by erratic government policy, private spending would be stable.

Plank 2: Even if private planned spending is not completely stable, flexible prices create a natural tendency for it to come back on course.

Plank 3: Even if private planned spending is not completely stable, and prices are not completely flexible, an activist monetary and fiscal policy (as called for by the Keynesians) is likely to do more harm than good.

Plank 4: Even if prices are not completely flexible so that the economy (may generate excessive unemployment) in the short run, there can be no dispute regarding the increased flexibility of prices, the longer the period of time allowed for adjustment.[58]

In essence, then, the monetarists view a capitalist economy as inherently reasonably stable in the absence of attempts to manage the economy by activist monetary and fiscal policies. For the monetarists, it is precisely those activist policies that have generated periodic bouts of inflation and unemployment. To reduce or prevent unemployment, expansionary monetary and fiscal policies are undertaken, inevitably leading to inflation. To counter the inflationary pressures, contractionary policies are taken and the result is increased unemployment. The monetarists' distrust of the political process leads them to believe that with an activist policy, "the economy will be allowed to expand too far and too rapidly, inflation will accelerate," and the monetary authorities will then "be forced to cause another recession and bout of unemployment to fight the renewed acceleration of inflation."[59]

Opposing activist countercyclical swings in the money supply, monetarists argue that the economy would be better off with a constant growth rate rule. The only policy required to guarantee long-run full employment and full-time price stability is "a legislated rule instructing the monetary authority to achieve a specified rate of growth in the stock of money." For this purpose, Friedman defines the stock of money as including all currency outside commercial banks plus all deposits in commercial banks. So defined, Friedman's legislative rule would require the monetary authorities to increase the monetary stock "month by month and indeed, so far as is possible, day by day," at an annual rate somewhere between 3 and 5 percent, a rate roughly equal to the noninflationary growth potential of the economy.[60]

It must be emphasized, as is implicit from the planks of the monetarist platform, that the monetarists' agenda involves much more than just a concern with inflation. Hidden behind their legitimate concern about inflation and its causes, the monetarists' attack on activist monetary and fiscal policy is a radical attempt to lay the base for what they believe will be a more successful and more pure model of capitalist development, with almost complete reliance on free-market forces. As will be manifest when we look at the policies of the Chilean junta, monetarism involves structural reforms to eliminate previous "distortions" in the price system, the privatization of state enterprises to achieve "correct" pricing, the rapid reduction or elimination of tariff barriers and exchange controls, the elimination of government subsidies for basic necessities, social services, and private enterprises, the reduction of direct taxation, and the weakening of the bargaining power of trade unions. The long-term goal of the monetarist program is to restore conditions for higher profit in the private sector and thereby, they believe, generate higher levels of investment and economic growth.[61]

The coming into power of the junta allowed the Chicago Boys to join the government and pursue the implementation of their particular view of economic and social policies. Historically in Chile, political parties, the press, unions, Congress, and other institutions and groups played a very important role in the design and outcome of economic policies. Under the junta, on the other hand, the economic team was able to implement its program with very little institutional, political, or social restrictions.[62] Let us now look at the economic developments in Chile since the 1973 military coup.

Those developments can be divided into three phases: the initial phase, September 1973–April 1975; the shock treatment, April 1975–December 1976; and consolidation, 1977–81.

## The Initial Phase: September 1973–April 1975

The primary objective of the initial phase was to restitute market mechanisms in an economy with widespread controls and severe imbalances. Two early decisions were to implement across-the-board tariff reductions (thereby opening up the Chilean economy to international competition) and to free domestic prices from regulation. In addition, collective bargaining was suppressed and labor union activities sharply curtailed, state enterprises were privatized as quickly as possible, the exchange rate was drastically devalued, an attempt was made to attract foreign investment through a new investment code, and relations were normalized with main international financial institutions such as the World Bank, the International Monetary Fund (IMF), and private foreign banks. Shortly after the coup, the IMF and the World Bank rushed in teams "to give their blessing to the general direction proposed by the Chicago plan."[63]

The abrupt deregulation of prices resulted in a rate of inflation of 128.5 percent in the last quarter of 1973. Prices then stabilized at around 45 percent per quarter in 1974, an average rate similar to that prevailing in the last year of the Allende regime. By early 1975 there were clear recessionary signs: industrial production in the first quarter of 1975 was 15 percent below that of the last quarter of 1974, real wages were 40 percent below the 1970 levels, and unemployment rose sharply from 7 percent in the last quarter of 1973 to 13.3 percent in the first quarter of 1975. Serious balance-of-payments problems developed in the last quarter of 1974 when, primarily as a result of a sharp decline in the price of Chile's major export, copper, there was a loss of $375 million in reserves.[64]

Faced with these grim conditions — the continuance of rapid inflation, falling production, sharply rising unemployment, and a crisis in the balance of payments — Chile was ripe for some new policies.

## Phase 2: The Shock Treatment, April 1975–December 1976

Professors Friedman and Harberger visited Chile in March 1975. In numerous public appearances and media interviews they emphasized that applying palliatives instead of taking drastic measures to amputate the diseased parts of the economy ran the danger that the final costs would be higher. Friedman asserted that "the immediate cause of inflation is always a consequence of a larger increase in the amount of money than production and this is clearly so in the Chilean case." His prescription for Chile was simple: "The first necessity therefore is to end inflation, and the only way Chile can do this is by drastically cutting the fiscal deficit, preferably by reducing government expenditure . . . in Chile . . . gradualism seems to me impossible."[65]

More specifically, Friedman's primary recommendations were a 20 to 25 percent cut in government spending, which he described as his "most important" proposal, and the removal of both constraints and subsidies previously applied to private enterprise. Conceding that unemployment would rise if his recommendations were followed, Friedman advised the Chileans to enact assistance programs. However, Friedman said that the disruption would be temporary, citing as support for his position the smooth 1946 demobilization in the United States and the "economic miracles" achieved in occupied Germany and Japan within months after economic controls were removed.[66]

With a change of cabinet in April 1975, the Chicago Boys assumed what was in effect dictatorial control over economic policy. In the two highest posts, business types were replaced by monetarist economists Jorge Cauas and Sergio de Castro. Cauas was appointed super-minister in charge of most of the key ministries and de Castro, a Chicago Ph.D. and Harberger associate of some 20 years, was appointed minister of economy. The monetarists were now in a commanding position to put in place Friedman's recommendations, and they didn't hesitate.[67]

To rally support for their anti-inflationary measures, the Chilean regime borrowed a phrase from Friedman: "shock treatment" (or, as it appeared in the Chilean press, *tratamiento de 'shock'*). As *Business Week* then observed, "an already severe anti-inflationary policy was turned into one of Draconian harshness." Friedman's "only concern" at the time was "that they push it long enough and hard enough."[68]

Push it they did. However, the new policies were not limited to a contractionary shock on demand; they also aimed at a substantial restructuring of the economy that would have a long-term influence on Chilean society. Total government expenditures fell by 27 percent in real terms in 1975, with the public-investment component being cut in half. Financial deregulation led to a dramatic rise in the real rate of interest from 23.4 percent in the second quarter of 1975 to 178.4 percent in the third quarter. There was an additional reduction in real wages by changing the method of calculating cost-of-living increases. The average tariff was reduced from 54.7 percent to 32.3 percent between the first quarter of 1975 and the end of 1976, and there was a drastic devaluation of the exchange rate.[69] The privatization process continued, with public enterprises being transferred to private hands at sharply reduced prices because of the recession.[70]

Although the contractionary policies did slow down considerably the rate of increase in the price level (from 68 percent in the second quarter of 1975 to 29 percent in the last quarter), and the balance of payments went from deficit to surplus, the goals were achieved at the cost of a huge recession.[71] Gross domestic product fell 12.9 percent in 1975, and the unemployment rate bolted upward from 9.2 percent to 14.5 percent in 1975 and 14.8 percent in 1976. (See Table 5.1.) The increase in the official unemployment rate is significantly understated, as it does not take into account a make-work program established in 1975, the Minimum

Employment Plan (PEM). The program was set up as a mechanism aimed at palliating to some extent the negative consequences of the shock treatment on employment. The workers under the plan were employed by the municipal authorities on road sweeping, tidying public gardens, and similar tasks at the abysmal salaries of up to $30 per month.[72] If the reported unemployment rate of 14.8 percent in 1976 is adjusted to take into account those unemployed workers given the make-work jobs, then the 1976 unemployment rate figure is a more-accurate 19.8 percent, about three times the rate that prevailed in the decade of the 1960s and more than five times the rate in the Allende years. (See Table 5.1.)

*Fortune* magazine, certainly no sympathizer of Marxist Allende, wrote of the devastating impact of the shock treatment,

> The Chicago Boys foresaw — indeed, they sought — the contraction, but its severity and duration took them by surprise. The national output fell by 15 per cent in 1975 and wages slid to one-third below what they had been in 1970. Unemployment went to 20 percent, and stuck within three points of that level for the next four years. A crash program put heads of large families on the public payroll. There were outbreaks of mange and other infectious diseases. Beggars appeared on city streets, and the Catholic Church organized soup kitchens. That painful reality was a sobering contrast to what had been promised. In 1975, Milton Friedman predicted that the unemployed would rapidly find work. "You'd be surprised," he told a Santiago audience, "how fast people would be absorbed by a growing private-sector economy." The Chicago-trained president of the Central Bank predicted that inflation would fall from 343% that year to 10% by 1976. Inflation did drop — to 199% in 1976 and to 84% in 1977. The private sector, caught between limp demand and high interest rates, came back very slowly. Only in 1978 did output regain its prerecession level. In hindsight, it's clear that the shock treatment succeeded in bringing down inflation only by putting the country through a ringer. . . . Whatever the causes, certainly a democracy would demand more compassion and quicker results. Perhaps only an autocrat like Pinochet could clobber inflation with such a heavy hand.[73]

Even General Pinochet, a brutal autocrat who could never be accused of excessive compassion, had to concede that the social cost of the shock treatment was greater than he expected.[74]

## Phase 3: Consolidation, 1977–81

During the period of consolidation, many economic policy decisions were taken that aimed at the rapid conversion of Chile to a fully free-market economy. Tariff rates were slashed to an average of 10 percent, automobiles being the only exception. The Chilean peso was devalued several times until 1979, when it was fixed at 30 pesos to the dollar in an attempt to stabilize Chile's rate of inflation at the international rate. The tax treatment for foreign investment was liberalized, restrictions on the remittances of profits abroad were eliminated, and the ceiling on external borrowing by the private sector was gradually lifted. These developments in the area of foreign trade made Chile one of the most open economies in the world. Privatization continued so that of the 507 public enterprises in 1973, only 15 remained in government hands by 1980. Public sector employment was cut back by 21 percent between 1974 and 1978.[75]

Labor unions were barred from engaging in collective bargaining after the 1973 coup. Not until June 1979 was it again legal for unions to bargain collectively, but unlike in the years prior to the coup, the government imposed severe constraints. If 10 percent of the workers in an enterprise decided to form a union, they could do so and negotiate separately with management. However, workers who chose not to join could also negotiate with the firm, subject to the same conditions as unions. Any association of several unions was not allowed to bargain collectively, nor were workers in service sectors or the public sector. The maximum period allowed for a strike was 60 days and, if there was no agreement after the 60 days, either conditions prior to negotiations were accepted or the workers were fired. Any union member could go back to work after 30 days without sanctions, and as few as 10 percent of the workers could censor labor negotiations at any time.

A primary goal of the labor reform was to ensure that collective bargaining would take place in a decentralized manner that would not disrupt production except at a very localized level, and even then only temporarily. Furthermore, by atomizing the labor movement, the legislation sought to prevent labor unions from regaining the political power they long had had in Chile. Free markets, decentralization and political immobilization, and control were achieved at one blow.[76]

Social security reforms had the effect of privatizing massive pension funds. Workers' contributions to social security were mandatory and were deposited in private institutions that administered the funds, investing the workers' contributions in the capital market. The individual worker's rate of return depended upon the success of the firm chosen by the worker in investing in highly profitable investment instruments. Although the law guaranteed a minimum rate of return, the minimum was variable and dependent on the average profitability in the financial sector.[77] Other reforms involved the development of private enterprise for the provision of educational, health, housing, and nutrition services in competitive markets. The government guaranteed the provision of free minimum services only for the very poor.[78]

With respect to the objectives of the labor, social security, and social service reforms, Foxley has commented quite accurately,

> The intended objectives of economic reforms were then to decentralize public institutions, leave as many of these activities as possible to the private sector, let market decision making operate, and, in a general way, guarantee freedom of choice to individuals concerning the provision and access to basic social services.[79]

## FRIEDMAN AND THE CHILEAN MIRACLE: AN ASSESSMENT

When in 1975, Milton Friedman was denounced at demonstrations and sharply criticized by fellow Nobel laureates for his relationship with the Chilean junta, he reacted with controlled anger. In a letter to the New York *Times,* he expressed "dismay at the double standard" of his critics, since they nor anyone else ever criticized him for his earlier trips to the Soviet Union and Yugoslavia. He also asserted that he had never been an economic adviser to the junta and that his only personal contact had been a six-day visit to Chile in March 1975.[80] Furthermore, on the atmosphere in Chile at the time of his visit, Friedman wrote in 1975,

> It is perhaps not irrelevant that at two universities, the Catholic University and the University of Chile, I gave talks on "The Fragility of Freedom", in which I explicitly characterized the existing regime as unfree, talked about the difficulty of maintaining a free society, the role of free markets and free enterprise in doing so, and the urgency of establishing those preconditions for freedom. There was no advance or *ex post* censorship, the audiences were large and enthusiastic, and I received no subsequent criticism. Could I have done that in the Soviet Union? Or more to the point, in the Communist regime Allende was seeking, or Castro's Cuba?[81]

While attacking his critics for their double standard, Friedman himself was blatantly guilty of a double standard and selective presentation of data. He emphasizes the fact that there was no advance or ex post censorship when he spoke at the University of Chile and at Catholic University, while at the same time conveniently neglecting to mention the sweeping suppression of academic freedom at those universities. That Friedman spoke before "large and enthusiastic audiences" and "received no subsequent criticism" may have been owing not so much to the message he conveyed but rather to the fact that there had been a massive purge of the faculty and the student body prior to his arrival. The potential critics of Friedman and the junta had been suppressed or eliminated from the university environment. Robert J. Alexander, an authority on Latin America and a vigorous critic of the Allende regime, describes the situation of the universities under the junta during Friedman's visit as follows:

> The blow dealt by the military regime was perhaps felt most by the universities. All the country's universities were put under *delegados-rectors,* military men, most of whom were retired from active service. . . . Purges of varying degree were conducted in the faculties of all universities . . . lists were published of expelled professors, without explanation or forewarning. . . . At the University of Chile . . . professors affiliated with the Unidad Popular parties were suspended (44 out of 360 in the Law School, for instance). . . . Those professors who retained their jobs, unless they were of the far Right points of view, labored under severe handicaps. They did not know what they could and could not say without losing their jobs, or worse. . . . The United Nations-financed Facultad Latino Americana de Ciencias Sociales with graduate level programs in political science and economics were forbidden to hold classes. . . . Some 22,000 students — more than one-eighth of the student body — were dropped from the rolls of the country's eight universities . . . 8,000 from the University of Chile.[82]

Given these conditions, it is little wonder that Friedman was able to report that he received little criticism.

In response to his critics, Friedman was not only defending his role in Chile but was at the same time attempting to distance himself from the widely publicized brutal and repressive activities of the junta. The evidence indicates that his relationship with the junta was closer and more significant than he suggests. Moreover, an analysis of his statements with respect to that role and his assessment of the efficacy of the junta's policies tell us a great deal about Friedman's basic ideology and analytical framework.

When Friedman denies being an economic adviser to the junta, presumably he means that he acted in no official capacity. However, that he gave quite specific advice to the Pinochet regime during his six-day visit in March 1975 and that his advice was followed cannot be denied. Friedman spent his week in Chile (he went at Harberger's urging) recommending the shock treatment imposed by the junta shortly after his visit. His message was carried on TV and, according to *Fortune* magazine, he even "trooped over to Pinochet's office to give the general a one-hour course in monetary theory." *Business Week* and *Fortune* reported that despite Friedman's criticism of the repressive nature of the Chilean regime, the junta found his visit and public appearances quite helpful. Evidently the junta was able to blithely ignore his comments about the virtues of freedom, while taking advantage of his prestige to gain support for their economic program. *Business Week* reported that Friedman's appearances "served to create support for the junta" and *Fortune* observed that "the Chicago Boys realized that the Friedman-Harberger road show was good public relations for the drastic steps they were about to take," the imposition of the Friedman shock treatment.[83]

In defense of his relationship with the junta, Friedman argued,

> In spite of my disagreement with the authoritarian political system of Chile, I do not consider it as evil for an economist to render technical advice to the Chilean government, any more than I would regard it as evil for a physician to give technical medical advice to help end a medical plague.[84]

This position, together with Friedman's denial that his advice lent support to the junta, is inconsistent with the analytical framework that permeates his own best seller, *Free to Choose*. In the book's preface he writes,

> *Free to Choose* treats the political system symmetrically with the economic system. Both are regarded as markets in which the outcome is determined by the interactions among persons pursuing their own self-interests (broadly interpreted) rather than by the social goals the participants find it advantageous to enunciate. This is implicit throughout the book.[85]

On the basis of this hypothesis, Friedman should have concluded that the leaders of the military junta must have been "pursuing their own self-interest" rather than the "social goals" they found it "advantageous to enunciate," and that therefore the "outcome" of their efforts would be the perpetuation of a repressive authoritarian regime. That is, had he employed the hypothesis set forth in his *Free to Choose,* he would have predicted with considerable accuracy the precise nature of future developments in Chile.

Instead Friedman took a different tack. He asserted in 1975 that the Allende regime offered Chile only bad choices: either Communist totalitarianism, or a military junta. . . . As between the two evils, there is at least one thing to be said for the military junta — there is more of a chance for a return to a democratic society . . . my brief visit there persuaded me of one thing. The likelihood that the junta will be or can be temporary and that it will be possible to restore democracy hinges critically on the success of the regime in improving the economic situation and eliminating inflation. . . . Only success will make possible liberalization. . . . Insofar as we were able to give good economic advice, I believe that we contribute to strengthening the forces for freedom, not the reverse.[86]

Free markets, for Friedman, will provide the "necessary condition" for political freedom.

About a decade after the 1973 coup, Friedman declared Chile an economic miracle, a nation that had supported, as a matter of principle, a fully free-market economy. And what has happened to political freedom in Chile? The regime remains as brutally repressive as ever and General Pinochet shows no sign of relinquishing his authoritarian control. In an August 23, 1984, interview with the New York *Times,* Pinochet compared himself to the "best Roman Emperors," claiming a gift for applying military tactics and secrecy to political decisions, and asserting, "I don't have confidence in orthodox democracy."[87] Rather than free markets being a necessary condition for political freedom, it seems that in the Chilean case at least the suppression of political freedom may be a necessary condition for imposing free markets.

In a *Newsweek* article of January 1982, Friedman wrote of Chile's free-market experiment as follows:

Chile is an economic miracle. Inflation has been cut from 700 percent a year in mid-1974 to less than 10 percent a year. After a difficult transition, the economy boomed growing an average of about 8 percent a year from 1976 to 1980. Real wages and employment rose rapidly and unemployment fell. Imports and exports surged after export subsidies were eliminated and tariffs were slashed 10 percent. Many state enterprises have been denationalized and motor transport and other areas deregulated. A voucher system has been put into effect in elementary and secondary education. Most remarkable of all, a social security reform has been adopted that permits individuals to choose between participating in the government system or providing for their own retirement privately. Chile is an even more amazing political miracle. . . . This political miracle is the product of an unusual set of circumstances. The chaos produced by the Allende regime that precipitated the military takeover in 1973 discredited central economic control. In an attempt to rectify the situation, the military drew on a comprehensive plan for a free-market economy that had been prepared by a group of young Chilean economists, most, though not all, of whom had studied at the University of Chicago. For the first two years, the so-called "Chicago boys" participated in implementing the plan but only in subordinate positions, and there was little progress in reducing inflation. Somewhat in desperation, the junta turned major responsibility over to the Chicago boys. Fortunately, several of them combined outstanding intellectual and executive ability with the courage of their convictions and a sense of dedication to implementing them — and the economic miracle was on its way. Chile is currently having serious difficulties — along with much of the rest of the world. And the opposition to the free-market policies that had been largely silenced by success is being given full voice — from both inside and outside the military. This temporary setback will likely be surmounted. But I predict that the free-market policy will not last unless the military government is replaced by a civilian government dedicated to political liberty.[88]

Let us now turn to analysis of the above description by Friedman of economic and political developments in Chile. We will find that while he has selected some facts that tend to support his position, he has left out a good deal of readily available evidence that undermines his cavalier assertion that Chile is an economic miracle.

## The Record on Inflation

Friedman is correct in pointing to the sharp decline in the annual rate of inflation from an annual rate of about 700 percent in mid-1974 to less than 10 percent a year in 1981. When examined more closely, however, these figures suggest something less than a miracle.

After the shock treatment (April 1975 to December 1976), the rate of inflation fell sharply, from 340.7 percent in 1975 to 63.5 in 1977, and then stabilized at between 30 and 39 percent form 1978 to 1980. Not until 1981 did the rate of inflation fall below 10 percent. (See Table 5.1.) What does this record reveal? Clearly, from one viewpoint there was a sharp drop in the rate of inflation. But if we compare the rate of inflation in the eight years of the Chicago Boys, from 1974 through 1981, with the pre-Allende decade, the anti-inflation component of the miracle is somewhat tarnished. In seven of the eight years under the Chicago Boys, the rate of inflation was significantly higher than the 25.1 percent average of annual inflation rates during the 10 years prior to Allende. Furthermore, as will be discussed below, none of this takes into account the extraordinarily high social costs of reducing inflation by application of the Chicago model and the return of double-digit inflation after 1981.

## The Record on Economic Growth

Gross domestic product (GDP) did increase at about 8 percent per year, as Friedman notes, but here again a closer look at the relevant data reveals that those growth rates are considerably less than miraculous. For the entire 1974–81 period, which includes the shock-induced depression year of 1975, the economy grew at an average rate of about 4 percent per year, somewhat less than the 4.5-percent growth rate in the 1960–70 pre-Allende decade. A more meaningful figure is the per capita GDP as it takes into account the increase in population. In per capita terms, the GDP increased only 1.5 percent per year between 1974 and 1980, considerably less than the 2.3 percent per year achieved in the 1960s.[89]

The record is much worse when the severe depression that began in the last quarter of 1981 is taken into account. The accumulated annual growth rate of Chile's GDP was 1.5 percent during the 1974–82 period. This compares poorly with the average Latin American growth of 4.3 percent and with Chile's performance during the 1960s, when it grew at an average of about 4.5 percent. (See Table 5.1.)

The disastrous performance of the Chilean economy, after nine years of junta rule and the application of the Chicago model, is glaringly revealed when comparisons are made with other Latin American countries. Between 1970 and 1980, Chile's per capita GDP grew only 8 percent, while in Latin America (19 countries) it increased by 40 percent. All of Latin America was adversely affected by depressed conditions between 1980 and 1982, but the decline in Chile, 12.9 percent in per capita GDP, was much more severe than for Latin America as a whole, which had a decline of only 4.3 percent. For the entire period from 1970 to 1982, Latin America's per capita GDP increased by a substantial 34 percent, whereas Chile's actually declined by 4 percent. Looked at another way, Latin America started out in 1970 with a per capita GDP 26 percent lower than Chile's, but by the end of the period in 1982, its per capita GDP was higher than Chile's by 4 percent. (See Table 5.2.)

Roberto Zahler, in summarizing the results of Chile's free-market policies, observed that

> in average per capita terms, there has been no growth during these years in the Chilean economy. These results differ markedly from the advocates' claim that the new economic policy would make the country grow at much higher rates than in the previous thirty years which experienced an annual average rate of 4.0 percent.[90]

**TABLE 5.2**
**Per Capita Gross Domestic Product**
**(dollars at 1970 prices)**

|  | 1975 | 1980 | 1982 |
|---|---|---|---|
| Chile | 967 | 1,045 | 927 |
| Latin America[a] | 720 | 1,008 | 965 |

[a]Includes 19 countries.

*Source:* U.N., Economic Commission for Latin America, *CEPAL Review,* Chile, April 1983, p. 12.

## The Record on Real Wages and Unemployment

Friedman's ability to selectively choose data that will support his position is more blatant with respect to his assertion that real wages and employment rose rapidly and that unemployment fell between 1976 and 1980. True, real wages rose sharply after 1976, but what Friedman does not mention is that in 1976, the third year of junta rule, real wages had fallen by 35 percent below their 1970 level. By selecting 1976 as the base year for his calculations, a year when real wages were severely depressed, he is able to show a sharp increase. Friedman must be well aware of this since it was his recommended shock treatment that had depressed wages.

However, even with the increase, when Friedman wrote his *Newsweek* article in January 1982, real wages were still less than they were in 1970. When the economy went into a deep recession in 1982 and 1983 and inflation accelerated, real wages again fell sharply, by 10.9 percent. As a result, after a decade of junta rule, the economic miracle had driven real wages more than 13 percent below the level attained in 1970. (See Table 5.1.)

Officially reported unemployment did fall between 1976 and 1980, as Friedman states, but here again he has demonstrated his ability to use data selectively to support his economic-miracle thesis. Again he uses 1976 as a base, a year when the official unemployment rate reached 14.8 percent as a result of the depression induced by Friedman's recommended shock treatment. Official unemployment did fall gradually, to 11.8 percent in 1980, but that rate was still double the average annual unemployment rate in the 1960–70 period. (See Table 5.1.) A reduction in unemployment from 14.8 percent to 11.8 percent — a rate double historic rates — over a period of five years can by no stretch of any economist's imagination be termed an economic miracle.

Furthermore, the official unemployment rate grossly understates the true level of unemployment. When the shock treatment created a dramatic rise in unemployment, the Chicago Boys put in place the Minimum Employment Plan as a palliative to provide government make-work jobs at subsistence wages for some of the unemployed. If the unemployed workers in the PEM program are added to those officially listed as unemployed, then the unemployment rate jumps to 19.8 and 17.2 percent for 1976 and 1980, respectively. Those rates are three times the average of annual unemployment rates that Chile experienced in the years 1960 through 1970. In 1981, the combined official and PEM rate fell to 13.8 percent, still almost two and one-half times the rate of the 1960s. But even that high unemployment rate was temporary, as 1982 and 1983 saw the rate rise to well over 20 percent, the highest in Chilean history. Thus, in eight of the nine years from 1975 through 1983, the true unemployment rate was three to four times the average of annual unemployment rates of 5.6 percent of the previous decade. (See Table 5.1.)

## The Record on Imports and Exports

Imports and exports surged after export subsidies were eliminated and tariffs were slashed to 10 percent, as Friedman notes. With this freeing of international trade, exports and imports as a proportion of gross national product increased from less than 15 percent in 1961–70 to more than 22 percent in 1974–81.[91]

However, what Friedman does not mention is that imports grew at a much faster rate than exports, contributing to a huge balance-of-payments current-account deficit that increased from 4 percent of the GDP in 1974 to 16.5 percent of the GDP in 1981.

This development, together with monetary and credit policies that stimulated borrowing abroad and brought significant capital inflows into the Chilean economy, generated an enormous foreign debt. The Chilean foreign debt rose from $4.9 billion in 1975 to about $15.6 billion in 1981.[92]

For Chile to obtain the necessary currency for the repayment of its massive foreign debt, it had to earn more foreign currency from the sale of its exports than it spent on the purchase of imports. In order to achieve that excess of exports over imports, the government in 1981–82 relied on a traditional automatic mechanism that, theoretically, is supposed to operate as follows: a deficit in the balance of payments generates a loss of bank reserves; the loss of reserves induces a contraction in the money supply and a rise in interest rates; the rise in interest rates reduces borrowing and spending and, because of the reduced demand, domestic prices will fall; with the decline in prices, those goods become attractive to foreigners, so exports will rise, while at the same time imports will fall as foreign goods are now relatively more expensive; the surplus of earnings from exports over expenditures on imports can then be used to pay off the foreign debt. However, as Latin American specialist Alejandro Foxley observed, the adjustment mechanism "proved to be very slow, and the magnitude of the recession required to bring prices down, was too high to be sustainable, even in an authoritarian framework."[93] As the depression deepened in 1982, pressure began to mount for Chile to abandon its free-market policies.

## The Record on Denationalization

As noted previously, of 507 public enterprises in 1973, only 15 remained in government hands by 1980. The denationalization process was carried out under conditions that were extremely advantageous for the new owners. Because of the state's urgency to sell and its doing so in a time of deep recession, the enterprises were sold at sharply undervalued prices. Given the depressed conditions in the economy, only the large conglomerates, with liquid resources and access to cheap foreign capital, were able to buy the auctioned enterprises. Foxley has estimated that those firms that bought the public assets, because of the low sales price, received an implicit subsidy of up to 40 to 50 percent of the purchase value.[94]

*Latin America Economic Report,* in describing the denationalization process in 1976, related that "the role of public companies has been surrounded in secrecy, and details, particularly the purchasers, are hard to come by." A year later, the *Report* was able to state that

> twenty or so picturesquely named conglomerates . . . are disputing the carcass of Chile's dismembered economy. . . . Each of these groups is a kind of economic clan, with family links. . . . Much of their attention has been concentrated on buying up the denationalized companies which the government has sold off, often at absurdly lower prices.[95]

Denationalization of the social security system has similarly contributed to increased concentration of wealth. Private firms owned by two major business conglomerates were the recipients of 75 percent of the Social Security contributions. It is estimated that by 1987, these two groups will have amassed about $2 billion in deposits, nearly 10 percent of Chile's gross domestic product.[96]

The denationalization process also generated a major financial scandal. In 1981, *Fortune* magazine reported on the exploits of Javier Vial, chairman of the $13-billion BHC group, one of Chile's largest conglomerates. His 40-odd holdings included one-quarter of Chile's largest bank; the biggest lumber and home-appliance companies; as well as mines, metal processing plants, and a fishing fleet. Vial amassed large chunks of his empire by borrowing abroad and buying the state-owned enterprises that were put up for sale. He estimated that the assets he acquired from the government in 1975 were, by 1981, worth eight times what he paid for them.[97]

Three years later, as a result of what the *Wall Street Journal* reported as "Chile's most spectacular financial scandal in a decade," Javier Vial was sitting in prison along with nine other prominent bankers, a government official, and former members of President Augusto Pinochet's free-market economic team. The *Journal* went on to state,

> The scandal has its roots in the free-wheeling 1970s when Chile's economy was guided by disciples of Nobel prize-winning economist Milton Friedman. Borrowing freely from Professor Friedman's principles, they sought to change Chile from a state-run system into a no-holds-barred, free-market economy.
>
> Powerful business groups built large conglomerates using funds supplied by banks they controlled. The banks raised most of their funds abroad.
>
> The situation only came to light when BHC and several other conglomerates were forced to declare bankruptcy last year after they couldn't generate enough earnings to pay rising international interest rates on their loans. Their collapse was the key event that plunged the entire Chilean economy into a severe recession.[98]

Clearly contrary to Friedman's claim, the denationalization of state enterprises has produced results for Chilean society somewhat short of the miraculous.

## Developments since January 1982

In his January 1982 *Newsweek* article, Friedman wrote, "Chile is currently having serious difficulties. . . . This temporary setback will likely be surmounted."[99] Contrary to Friedman's faith in the ability of his miraculous free-market model to stage a comeback, the "temporary" setback, as this chapter is being written, has degenerated into a deep depression, the worst in Chilean history.

From 1982 to 1984, the unemployment rate, when those in the government's make-work programs for the unemployed are included, varied between 25 and 32 percent. Gross private domestic product fell 15 percent between 1981 and 1983, while the rate of inflation accelerated from 9.5 percent in 1981 to 20.7 and 23.1 percent in 1982 and 1983, respectively. The rise in unemployment and the fall in GDP was even greater than that experienced during the terrible shock treatment of 1975. Real wages dropped sharply, falling to 14 percent below what they were in 1970. (See Table 5.1.)

By 1983, Chile's foreign debt had soared to $17.5 billion from $11.1 billion in 1980. According to U.S. embassy representatives in Chile,

> The resultant annual external debt service (interest plus amortization) ratios are 15–25 percent of GDP and 70–80 percent of exports of goods and non-factor services. Management of these massive external payments will require a solid and sustained rate of economic growth, a continuing expansion of exports and careful management of the current account, prudent control of new external indebtedness, continuing arrangements with the IMF, rescheduling amortization payments to foreign commercial banks, and more credits from multilateral and official sources. The success of these efforts for the rest of the decade will be crucially affected by the price of copper, by international interest rates, and significantly, by Chile's ability to continue to increase its non-traditional exports and to attract foreign investment.[100]

The prospects for Chile being able to manage its external debt are, euphemistically speaking, extraordinarily bleak.

Bankruptcies have skyrocketed, and banks and financial institutions exhibited a ratio of bad loans over capital well in excess of 50 percent.[101] The government was forced to intervene in a number of major banks. Roberto Zahler commented wryly on the financial collapse,

> In view of the widespread failures and eventual crash of the private financial system, a massive government intervention took place early in 1983, *de facto*

> nationalizing it. Given the degree of firms' indebtedness to the banking system, the implementation of the Chilean economic model has created a new, original, "free market" road to socialism.[102]

The devastating economic crises brought tens of thousands into the streets in protest against the regime's economic and political policies. General Pinochet cracked down, sending in army troops to curb the demonstrators. According to an August 1984 report of the Roman Catholic Church, since the protests began in May 1983, 113 protestors have been killed and several thousand have been detained for political activity and protests. Pinochet has neutralized the nation's militant unions by firing thousands of protesting strikers and by jailing union leaders.[103]

In an attempt to restore economic calm, Pinochet made a series of cabinet changes. The first to be dismissed, in April 1982, was Sergio de Castro, Chile's arch-monetarist, a former student of Harberger and Friedman. Commenting on developments in Chile, the conservative British journal *The Economist* observed, "Chile, under the stern eye of President Pinochet, has provided laboratory conditions for a prolonged experiment by Mr. Milton Friedman's disciples. . . . Chile is another economic disaster. The 'Chicago boys' have gone grey watching their achievements . . . slowly wasting away."[104]

The *Wall Street Journal* ran a story on another cabinet shuffle in April 1984, which "analysts viewed as a major switch toward an increased government role in reviving the country's beleaguered economy." The *Journal* reported that "economic experts said the cabinet shakeup signals the final blow to Chile's so-called Chicago boys, who embraced the monetarist model of controlling the economy through the money supply."[105] The new ministers, reported the U.S. embassy in Chile, replaced economic teams that "took a free market-oriented approach towards economic policy making." The embassy noted that the new team held ministerial positions in the 1960s, that "they are viewed as pragmatic individuals who favor free enterprise, but who are also willing to increase the role of the state in the economy . . . in an effort to reduce high unemployment."[106]

Friedman concluded his January 1982 *Newsweek* article on the Chilean miracle with the following statement:

> I have long argued that economic freedom is a necessary but not sufficient condition for political freedom. I have become persuaded that this generalization, while true, is misleading unless accompanied by the proposition that political freedom in turn is a necessary condition for the long-term maintenance of economic freedom.[107]

The above statement is a drastic change from the position he took in 1975, when he attacked those who criticized him for giving advice to the junta. Then he said,

> The likelihood that the junta will or can be temporary and that it will be possible to restore democracy hinges critically on the success of the regime in improving the economic situation and eliminating inflation. . . . Only success will make possible liberalization. . . . In so far as we were able to give good economic advice, I believe that we contribute to strengthening the forces for freedom, not the reverse.[108]

After nine years of the economic miracle, Chileans continue to live under a brutally repressive regime. Clearly, the forces for freedom were not strengthened.

Why does Friedman modify his position in 1982 and assert that political freedom is a necessary condition for economic freedom? The answer seems clear. When the economic miracle collapses, Friedman will then be able to attribute its downfall to the absence of political freedom, thereby protecting the sacred validity of his free-market economic model.

## SUMMARY AND CONCLUSIONS

On the basis of our study of developments in Chile over the past couple of decades, we can now answer the questions posed in the opening section of this chapter concerning the relationship between Milton Friedman, his Chicago model, and the military junta.

### The Relationship of the Junta's Policies with Friedman's Philosophy

That the Chilean junta rigorously followed the free-market monetarist policies of Friedman and his Chicago school cannot be denied. The denationalization of state enterprises, sharp reductions in government spending, attempts to control the growth of the money supply, the destruction of the power of labor unions, the privatization of the social security system, and the elimination of export subsidies and the slashing of tariffs made Chile a clear-cut test of the Chicago model. Friedman himself stated as recently as 1982, fully seven years after Chile marched down the Chicago road, that the junta "supported a fully free-market economy as a matter of principle" and "turned major reponsibility over to the Chicago boys." The latter, asserts Friedman, "combined outstanding intellectual and executive ability with the courage of their convictions and sense of dedication to implementing them — and the economic miracle was on its way."[109]

While the junta leadership put in place Friedman's free-market principles, they clearly rejected his political philosophy. Free speech and freedom of the press have been harshly suppressed. Political opposition has been outlawed. In addition to those banished to internal exile in isolated villages, "tens of thousands of other Chileans, with their families, are exiled abroad, and thousands of others have passed through the jails, where torture, according to human rights activists, is common."[110]

## A Miraculous Experiment?

Contrary to Friedman's claim that Chile's free-market experiment is an economic miracle, the overwhelming evidence indicates that the experiment has been an economic disaster. In eight of the nine years under the Chicago model, the unemployment rate was in the double-digit range, three to four times greater than the average of annual employment rates in the decade prior to the takeover by the junta, and in 1982 and 1983 soared to well over 20 percent. Throughout most of those nine years, real wages were significantly less than what they were in 1970, and in 1983 they fell below the 1970 level by 13 percent.

The record on economic growth is equally deplorable. In the decade of the 1970s, while Latin America's (19 countries) per capita gross domestic product increased by 40 percent, Chile's rose by a mere 8 percent. By 1982, Chile's per capita GDP, as a result of a severe depression, was actually 4 percent lower than it was in 1970.

With the freeing of international trade, Chile's foreign debt has soared to $17.5 billion, leaving the country with a massive balance-of-payments problem. The necessity to manage that debt imposes severe constraints on the ability of the government to pursue policies that would stimulate economic growth and reduce its extraordinarily high level of unemployment.

Denationalization has resulted in increased concentration of industry and wealth, and a spectacular financial scandal involving a number of large conglomerates as well as former members of the junta's free-market team.

While inflation was brought down sharply with the shock treatment in 1975, Chile paid a high price in terms of a substantial fall in output and greatly increased unemployment. Although the inflation rate fell, in seven of the eight years of Chicago rule, from 1974 through 1981, the rate was significantly higher than in the decade of the 1960s. Furthermore, in the midst of a severe depression in 1982–83, the inflation rate again climbed steeply, exceeding 20 percent. Thus, after nine years of Chicago rule, Chile found itself mired in the worst of all posible economic straits — stagflation.

## The Moral Issue

Was there any justification for the moral outcry of Friedman's critics when he visited Chile and gave advice to the junta? Friedman is justified in attacking his critics for their double standard, since they did not criticize him for his earlier trips to the Soviet Union and Yugoslavia. However, for several reasons, Friedman cannot get off the moral hook so easily.

First of all, while he might not have acted in any official capacity as an economic adviser, he did give advice to the junta during his visit to Chile; the junta did follow his advice and did benefit from the prestige his name lent to their program.

Second, on his return from his 1975 visit to Chile, he wrote that he was permitted to speak freely at universities and even criticize the regime as unfree with no censorship or subsequent criticism. He asked, rhetorically, if he could have done that in the Soviet Union or Castro's Cuba. However, given his high-level contacts in Chile, he must have been aware of the thousands of dissidents, both faculty and students, who had been purged from Chilean universities. Yet, evidently, Friedman saw no reason to mention those developments in his letters of protest directed at his critics or in his interviews with the press.

Third, after nine years of junta rule, Friedman effusively praised the Chicago Boys for their "outstanding intellectual and executive ability," their "courage," and their "sense of dedication." These are the same Chicago Boys who participated as key members of a regime that had imprisoned, exiled, tortured, and killed thousands of Chileans. Compare Friedman's praise of his Chilean Chicago Boys with the following vitriolic comments he heaps upon U.S. bureaucrats:

> The lure of getting someone else's money is strong. Many, including the bureaucrats administering the program will try to get it for themselves rather than have it go to someone else. The temptation to engage in corruption, to cheat, is strong and will not always be resisted or frustrated. People who resist the temptation to cheat will use legitimate means to direct the money to themselves. They will lobby for legislation favorable to themselves, for rules from which they can benefit. The bureaucrats administering the program will press for better pay and perquisites for themselves — an outcome that larger programs will facilitate.[111]

Friedman, in his characterization of bureaucrats, makes manifest his fundamental ideological preconceptions that are hidden in his writings for an audience of professional economists. For Friedman, Washington bureaucrats who administer social programs are often corrupt, inefficient, or dishonest. The Chicago Boys, key members of Pinochet's brutal regime, Friedman sees as courageous men with a sense of dedication.

Furthermore, while Friedman is quite laudatory in his praise of the economic miracle supposedly wrought by the Chilean regime, his criticism of its authoritarian nature is extraordinarily mild in the light of its brutal behavior. Finally, as we have shown, he presented highly selective evidence in portraying Chile as an economic miracle, constructing a picture of the Chilean economy that bore little resemblance to reality.

In sum, one is forced to conclude that the moral outcry against Friedman's relationship with the junta was definitely justified. For 13 years, the Chilean people have not been free to choose.

## NOTES

1. *Newsweek,* January 25, 1982, p. 59.

2. U.S., Congress, Senate, Select Committee to Study Governmental Operations with Respect to Intelligence Activities, *Covert Action in Chile,* 94th Cong., 1st sess., 1975, p. 3.

3. Arturo, Valenzuela, "Eight Years of Military Rule in Chile," *Current History* 81 (1982): 64.

4. U.S., Senate, *Covert Action in Chile,* p. 61.

5. Valenzuela, *Eight Years,* p. 65.

6. New York *Times,* October 24, 1976, sect. 4, p. 14.

7. New York *Times,* December 2, 1977, p. 16; idem. December 14, 1976, pp. 55, 59.

8. Robert J. Alexander, *The Tragedy of Chile,* (Westport, Conn.: Greenwood Press, 1978), pp. 101–3; Paul E. Sigmund, *The Overthrow of Allende and the Politics of Chile, 1964–1976* (Pittsburgh: University of Pittsburgh Press, 1977), p. 46.

9.   Alexander, *The Tragedy*, pp. 94–103.

10.   Ibid., p. 10.

11.   Sigmund, *The Overthrow*, pp. 54, 92, 105.

12.   Alexander, *The Tragedy*, p. 48.

13.   Sigmund, *The Overthrow*, pp. 74–76.

14.   Ibid., p. 95.

15.   Alexander, *The Tragedy*, pp. 123, 124.

16.   Ibid., p. 125.

17.   Sigmund, *The Overthrow*, p. 120.

18.   Ibid., pp. 119–30.

19.   Alec Nove, "The Political Economy of the Allende Regime," in *Allende's Chile*, ed. Phillip J. O'Brien (New York: Praeger, 1976), p. 54.

20.   Barbara Stallings, *Economic Development in Chile, 1958–1973* (Stanford, Calif.: Stanford University Press, 1978), p. 260.

21.   Richard E. Feinberg, *The Triumph of Allende* (New York: New American Library, 1976), p. 263.

22.   Roberto Zahler, "Recent Southern Cone Liberalization Reforms and Stabilization Policies," *Journal of Interamerican Studies and World Affairs* 25 (1983): 539.

23.   Laurence Whitehead, "Inflation and Stabilization in Chile, 1970–77," in *Inflation and Stabilization in Latin America*, ed. Rosemary Throp and Laurence Whitehead (New York: Holmes and Meier, 1979), p. 69.

24.   Alexander, *The Tragedy*, pp. 147, 148; Sigmund, *The Overthrow*, p. 133.

25.   Alexander, *The Tragedy*, pp. 150–53.

26.   Ibid., p. 161.

27.   Sigmund, *The Overthrow*, p. 133.

28.   Nove, *The Political Economy*, pp. 56, 57.

29.   Stallings, *Economic Development*, p. 248.

30.   Nove, *The Political Economy*, pp. 58, 59.

31.   William Ascher, *Scheming for the Poor* (Cambridge: Harvard University Press, 1984), pp. 241, 242.

32.   Nove, *The Political Economy*, p. 59.

33.   Ibid., pp. 60–62.

34.   Sigmund, *The Overthrow*, p. 137; Ascher, *Scheming*, p. 241.

35.   Whitehead, *Inflation*, p. 66.

36.   Stallings, *Economic Development*, p. 248.

37.   U.S., Senate, *Covert Action in Chile*, p. 1.

38.   Ibid., p. 9.

39.   Seymour M. Hersh, *The Price of Power* (New York: Summit Books, 1983), p. 260.

40.   U.S., Senate, *Covert Action in Chile*, p. 17.

41.   Ibid., p. 23.

42.   Hersh, *The Price*, p. 274.

43.   U.S., Senate, *Covert Action in Chile*, p. 27.

44.   Ibid., pp. 29–31.

45.   Phillip J. O'Brien, "Was the United States Responsible for the Chilean

Coup," in *Allende's Chile*, ed. Phillip J. O'Brien (New York: Praeger, 1976), p. 224.

46.   Ibid., p. 232.

47.   Ibid., p. 235.

48.   Ascher, *Scheming*, p. 236; Nove, *The Political Economy*, p. 52.

49.   Nove, *The Political Economy*, p. 64.

50.   Sigmund, *The Overthrow*, p. 199.

51.   Ibid., pp. 218, 219.

51.   Nove, *The Political Economy*, p. 74.

53.   Phillip J. O'Brien, "The New Leviathan: The Chicago School and the Chilean Regime, 1973–1980," *IDS Sussex Bulletin* 13 (1981): 38.

54.   *Business Week*, January 2, 1976, p. 70.

55.   O'Brien, "The New Leviathan," pp. 40, 41; *Business Week* of January 12, 1976, reported the following on page 70: "Nothing, in fact, implicates the Chicago luminaries themselves. But the U.S. Senate Select Committee on Intelligence Activities disclosed last month that 'CIA collaborators' had helped plan economic measures that Chile's junta enacted immediately after seizing power. Committee witnesses maintain that some of Harberger's and Friedman's former students, widely known in Chile as 'The Chicago Boys,' received CIA funds for such research efforts as a 300 page economic blueprint that was given to leaders of the coup."

56.   Harry G. Johnson, "The Keynesian Revolution and the Monetarist Counter-Revolution," *American Economic Review* 61 (May 1971): 7–11.

57.   Milton Friedman, *Dollars and Deficits* (Englewood Cliffs, N.J.: Prentice-Hall, 1968), p. 18.

58.   Robert J. Gordon, *Macroeconomics* (Boston: Little, Brown, 1981), p. 365.

59.   Ibid., p. 369.

60.   Milton Friedman, *Capitalism and Freedom* (Chicago: University of Chicago Press, 1962), p. 54.

61.   Stephany Griffith-Jones, "Editorial," *IDS Sussex Bulletin* 13 (1981): 3.

62.   Zahler, *Recent Southern Cone Liberalization Reforms*, pp. 512–13.

63.   O'Brien, "The New Leviathan," pp. 41–42.

64.   Alejandro Foxley, *Latin American Experiments in Neoconservative Economics* (Berkeley: University of California Press, 1983), pp. 53–55.

65.   O'Brien, "The New Leviathan," p. 42.

66.   *Business Week*, January 12, 1976, p. 71.

67.   Ibid.

68.   Ibid., pp. 71–72.

69.   Foxley, *Latin American Experiments*, pp. 55–57.

70.   O'Brien, "The New Leviathan," p. 42.

71.   Foxley, *Latin American Experiments*, Table 8, pp. 50–51, 56.

72.   Alexander, *The Tragedy*, p. 405; Zahler, *Recent Southern Cone Liberalization Reforms*, p. 540.

73.   *Fortune*, November 2, 1981, p. 140.

74.   *Wall Street Journal*, November 1975, p. 1.

75.   Foxley, *Latin American Experiments*, pp. 61–65.

76.   Ibid., pp. 104–5.

77.   Ibid., pp. 105–6.

78.   Ibid., p. 108.

79.  Ibid., p. 104.
80.  New York *Times*, May 22, 1977, sect. 4, 18:1.
81.  *Wall Street Journal*, October 27, 1975, p. 8.
82.  Alexander, *The Tragedy*, pp. 387–88.
83.  *Fortune*, November 2, 1981, p. 138;  *Business Week*, January 12, 1976, p. 71.
84.  *Newsweek*, June 14, 1976, p. 5.
85.  Milton Friedman and Rose Friedman, *Free to Choose* (New York: Avon, 1981), p. x.
86.  *Wall Street Journal*, October 27, 1975, p. 8. Friedman's distinction between a totalitarian regime and the military junta is strikingly similar to the distinction later made by Jeane Kirkpatrick, United States Permanent Representative to the United Nations, between traditional dictators like the Shah and General Samoza, who supposedly offer a hope of gradual democratization, and totalitarian (Communist) dictatorships, who offer no such hope. President Reagan welcomed the distinction and "made the doctrine his own." See Seymour Maxwell Finger, "The Reagan Kirkpatrick Policies and the United Nations," *Foreign Affairs* 62 (1983/84): 438.
87.  New York *Times*, August 23, 1984, p. 1.
88.  *Newsweek*, January 25, 1982, p. 59.
89.  Foxley, *Latin American Experiments*, p. 45.
90.  Zahler, *Recent Southern Cone Liberalization Reforms*, p. 537.
91.  Foxley, *Latin American Experiments*, p. 525.
92.  Zahler, *Recent Southern Cone Liberalization Reforms*, pp. 532–33.
93.  Foxley, *Latin American Experiments*, p. 90.
94.  Ibid., p. 66.
95.  Alexander, *The Tragedy*, pp. 413–14.
96.  Zahler, *Recent Southern Cone Liberalization Reforms*, p. 544.
97.  *Fortune*, November 2, 1981, p. 142.
98.  *Wall Street Journal*, March 6, 1984, p. 38.
99.  *Newsweek*, January 25, 1982, p. 59.
100.  U.S., Department of Commerce, International Trade Administration, *Foreign Economic Trends and Their Implications for the United States, Chile* (Washington, D.C.: Government Printing Office, 1984), pp. 1, 17.
101.  Foxley, *Latin American Experiments*, p. 89.
102.  Zahler, *Recent Southern Cone Liberalization Reforms*, p. 549.
103.  New York *Times*, August 26, 1984, p. 12.
104.  *Economist*, April 30, 1983, p. 24.
105.  *Wall Street Journal*, April 3, 1984, p. 36.
106.  U.S., Department of Commerce, *Foreign Economic Trends*, p. 4.
107.  *Newsweek*, January 25, 1982, p. 59.
108.  *Wall Street Journal*, October 27, 1975, p. 8.
109.  *Newsweek*, January 25, 1982, p. 59.
110.  New York *Times*, December 10, 1982, p. 2; March 23, 1982, p. 27; June 16, 1983, p. A3; September 6, 1983, p. 2; *New York Review of Books*, February 3, 1983, p. 41; Providence Sunday *Journal*, August 21, 1983, p. 13.
111.  Friedman and Friedman, *Free to Choose*, p. 108.

# 6

# THE EVILS OF BIG GOVERNMENT: FRIEDMAN'S ATTACK ON THE WELFARE STATE

Big government is not the solution to our social problems, it is the primary cause of those problems. Not only does it threaten our economic and political freedom,[1] big government has slowed economic growth and depressed productivity,[2] stimulated a rise in criminality and violence,[3] weakened the family,[4] generated racial unrest,[5] lowered the quality of our schools,[6] and increased poverty.[7] So runs the litany of evils that, according to Milton Friedman, are the manifest products of big government.

In their preface to *Free to Choose,* the Friedmans write,

> Our principles offer no hard and fast line how far it is appropriate to use government to accomplish jointly what it is difficult or impossible for us to accomplish separately through strictly voluntary exchange. In any particular case of proposed intervention, we must make up a balance sheet, listing separately the advantages and disadvantages. Our principles tell us what items to put on the one side and what items on the other and they give us some basis for attaching importance to the different items.[8]

The above quotation suggests that what will follow in *Free to Choose* is a discussion of the advantages and disadvantages of government programs and a careful assessment of their costs and benefits. Instead, what we find there, as well as in Friedman's numerous popular essays, is a highly dogmatic polemic against all social programs. Government efforts to achieve greater equality in the distribution of income; social security for the aged; and programs aimed at protecting consumers, the environment, and workers on the job are uniformly attacked. Friedman's balance sheet on those social programs consists of substantial social costs with virtually no social benefits. His ideological posture is accurately reflected in a 1982 *Newsweek* article in which he asserted,

> There is a sure fire way to predict the consequences of a government social program adopted to achieve worthy ends. Find out what the well-meaning, public-interested persons who advocated its adoption expected it to accomplish. Then reverse those expectations. You will have an accurate picture of actual results. . . . I challenge my readers to name a government social program that has achieved the results promised by its well-meaning and public-interested proponents [who] have generally been the dupes of others who had very clear self-interested motives.[9]

Let us now turn to an examination of the evils Friedman attributes to big government.

## PRODUCTIVITY AND ECONOMIC GROWTH

A persistent theme that runs through Friedman's popular writings is his assertion that big government and excessive government spending have an adverse effect on productivity and economic growth. The following quotations from his various writings are indicative of his position:

> Deficits are bad primarily because they foster excessive government spending — the chief culprit, in my opinion, in producing both inflation and slow economic growth. By reducing private incentives to work, save, and engage in productive ventures, and by crowding out private investment, high government spending inhibits economic growth.[10]
>
> Irresponsible fiscal policy — excessive spending, burdensome and inequitable taxes, and massive deficits — does account for the sharp slowdown in economic growth in the past decade.[11]

A similar note was struck in President Reagan's first *Economic Report:*

> For several decades, an ever-larger role for the Federal Government and, more recently, inflation have sapped the economic vitality of the Nation. . . . The combination of these two factors . . . have played a major part in a fundamental deterioration in the performance of our economy. In the 1960's productivity in the American economy grew at an annual rate of 2.9 percent; in the 1970's productivity growth slowed by nearly one-half, to 1.5 percent.

Real gross national product per capita grew at an annual rate of 2.8 percent in the 1960's compared to 2.1 percent in the 1970's.[12]

Is big government the "chief culprit" in generating low productivity and slow economic growth as Friedman and Reagan contend? Although that connection is frequently made in his numerous popular writings, the evidence Friedman presents in support of his claim is striking by its total absence. To attribute the slowdown in economic growth in recent years to the expanded role of government is simplistic in the extreme, a product of Friedman's ideological bias. The process of economic growth is extraordinarily complex, and the relative significance of the many variables that affect the rate of growth has been the subject of intensive debate among economists. Investment in the education and training of the labor force, technological innovation, the development of a society's infrastructure, the availability of natural resources, investment in land and equipment, the willingness and ability of society to abstain from current consumption, expenditures on research and development, and efficiency in the use of capital and labor all are factors that may affect a society's rate of economic growth. Some government policies and taxation and expenditure programs may have a negative effect on economic growth, while other policies and programs may be a stimulus to growth. However, government activity in a capitalistic society, even when substantial, is only one element among many in the growth process. To assess Friedman's assertion that the expansion in the size of government has had a negative effect on growth, let us now turn to an examination of developments in a number of industrialized countries over the past couple of decades.

Government expenditures at all levels (federal, state, and local) did grow substantially as a percentage of gross national product (GNP) between 1929 and 1980, from 10 percent to 33.1 percent (see Table 6.1). Growth over the past couple of decades was owing primarily to the increase in spending on transfer programs that necessitate taxing some people for the benefit of others. Expenditures on transfer programs grew from about 5 percent of GNP in 1960 to 11 percent of GNP in 1980, with almost all of the increase a product of Social Security and other social programs that serve primarily middle-income groups and enjoy widespread political support.[13]

Despite the overall growth in government expenditures and the specific increase in transfer programs, the United States is far from being a welfare state by the standards of the rest of the industrialized world. In

**TABLE 6.1**
**Total Government Expenditures and Gross National Product,
1929–80**

(in billions of U.S. dollars)

|  | *Government Expenditures* | *GNP* | *Government Expenditures as Percent of GNP* |
|---|---|---|---|
| 1929 | 10.3 | 103.4 | 10.0 |
| 1940 | 18.4 | 100.0 | 18.4 |
| 1950 | 61.0 | 286.0 | 21.3 |
| 1960 | 136.4 | 506.5 | 26.9 |
| 1965 | 187.8 | 691.1 | 27.2 |
| 1970 | 313.4 | 992.7 | 31.6 |
| 1975 | 534.3 | 1,549.2 | 34.5 |
| 1980 | 869.0 | 2,626.1 | 33.1 |

*Source: Economic Report of the President, February 1982* (Washington, D.C.: Government Printing Office), pp. 242, 320.

1980, government expenditures as a percent of gross domestic product (GDP) was substantially lower in the United States than in all other major industrialized countries, except for Japan (see Table 6.2). Furthermore, between 1960 and 1980 the ratio of government expenditures to GDP rose much more rapidly in all the other industrialized nations. Over those two decades, the ratio in the United States increased about 19 percent, while in the other industrialized countries, the increases varied from 33 percent in France to a high of 111 percent in Sweden (see below).

*Percent Increase in Government Expenditures as a Percent of Gross
Domestic Product, 1960–80 (from data in Table 6.2)*

| | | | |
|---|---|---|---|
| Sweden | 111.3 | France | 33.5 |
| Netherlands | 85.5 | Italy | 51.5 |
| Belgium | 70.6 | United Kingdom | 36.8 |
| Norway | 65.2 | Canada | 40.8 |
| Austria | 51.1 | United States | 19.4 |
| Germany | 46.6 | Japan | 58.0 |

Outright government ownership of industry is also much more extensive in those countries than it is in the United States. In Western

Europe, of the major industries shown in Figure 6.1, telecommunications, electricity, railroads, and airlines are almost completely government owned, and government ownership is substantial in the gas, coal, steel, shipbuilding, auto, and oil industries. By contrast, government ownership of productive facilities in the United States is significant only in the electricity and railroad industries, but even in those industries public ownership is relatively small when compared with the almost 100-percent government ownership in other countries. The relatively greater role of government ownership in other countries is also reflected in employment statistics. While 3 percent of total employment in

## FIGURE 6.1
## The Government's Share of the Economy

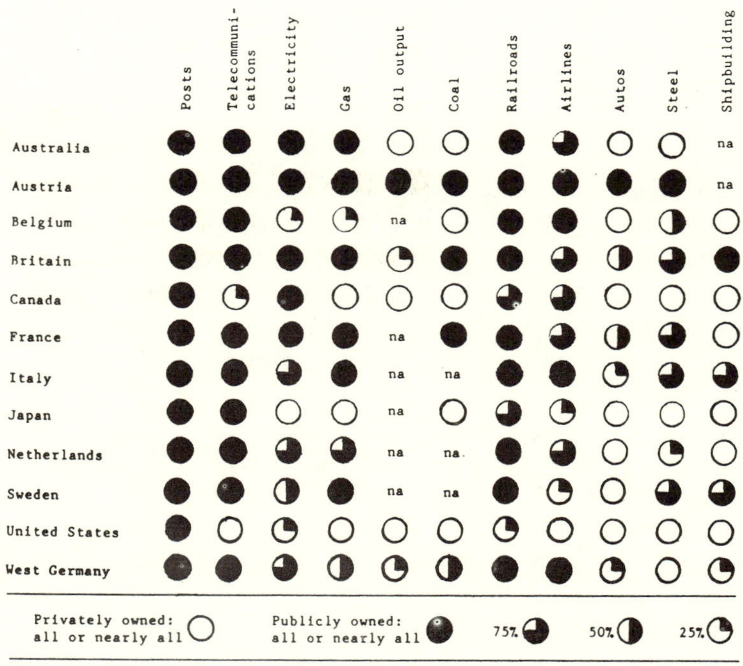

| | Posts | Telecommunications | Electricity | Gas | Oil output | Coal | Railroads | Airlines | Autos | Steel | Shipbuilding |
|---|---|---|---|---|---|---|---|---|---|---|---|
| Australia | ● | ● | ● | ● | ○ | ○ | ● | ◕ | ○ | ○ | na |
| Austria | ● | ◑ | ● | ● | ● | ● | ● | ◕ | ● | ● | na |
| Belgium | ● | ● | ◔ | ◔ | na | ○ | ● | ● | ○ | ◐ | ○ |
| Britain | ● | ● | ● | ● | ◔ | ● | ● | ◕ | ◐ | ◕ | ● |
| Canada | ● | ◕ | ● | ○ | ○ | ○ | ◕ | ◕ | ○ | ○ | ○ |
| France | ● | ● | ● | ● | na | ● | ● | ◕ | ◐ | ◕ | ○ |
| Italy | ● | ● | ◕ | ● | na | na | ● | ● | ◕ | ◕ | ◕ |
| Japan | ● | ● | ○ | ○ | na | ○ | ◕ | ◕ | ○ | ○ | ○ |
| Netherlands | ● | ● | ◕ | ◕ | na | na. | ● | ◕ | ○ | ◕ | ○ |
| Sweden | ● | ◑ | ◐ | ● | na | na | ● | ◕ | ○ | ◕ | ◕ |
| United States | ● | ○ | ◕ | ○ | ○ | ○ | ◕ | ○ | ○ | ○ | ○ |
| West Germany | ● | ● | ◕ | ◐ | ◔ | ◐ | ● | ● | ◕ | ○ | ◕ |

Privately owned: all or nearly all ○   Publicly owned: all or nearly all ●   75% ◕   50% ◐   25% ◔

na - Not applicable or negligible production.

*Source:* Adapted from a chart in *The Economist,* London, December 30, 1978, p. 39. Reprinted with permission.

the United States is in publicly operated market enterprises, in the other industrialized nations the percentage is two to four times greater, ranging from 6 to 13 percent.[14]

As the preceding discussion indicates, government in the United States is substantially less interventionist than it is in all other industrialized countries, except for Japan. Hence, if there were any validity to Friedman's assertion that government intervention in the economy is the chief culprit in causing slow economic growth, we would expect to find the United States with relatively high growth rates when compared with the other industrialized countries over the past several decades.

However, the data on growth rates are strikingly inconsistent with Friedman's claim. In the period between 1950 and 1973, all ten of the countries with higher government expenditures as a percentage of GDP and more extensive nationalization had higher growth rates in per capita GDP than did the United States. For the years from 1973 to 1979, seven of those ten countries had higher growth rates than the United States, and when the entire period from 1950 to 1979 is considered, only the United Kingdom had lower growth rates than did the United States (see Table 6.2).

Furthermore, the historical record in the United States indicates that growth was more rapid in the period of greater government intervention than it was when the government played a much smaller role in the economy (see Table 6.3). For almost three-fourths of the period between 1920 and 1960, starting with the New Deal in 1933, the government played a relatively large role in the economy. In those decades, the rates of growth as measured by product per capita, product per workers, and product per worker-hour were higher than they were in the years from 1840 to 1920, when the government's role in the economy, except for tariff protection, was negligible. Similarly, growth rates between 1950 and 1981 were higher than in the pre-1920 government-free years. Again, the data are inconsistent with Friedman's claim that government intervention retards economic growth. Thus both U.S. domestic experience and comparisons with foreign experience indicate there is no necessary conflict between social expenditures or government intervention and economic growth.

Let us take a closer look at two countries that Friedman has often cited to support his contention that laissez-faire conditions foster economic growth whereas government intervention retards growth: the United Kingdom and West Germany.

**TABLE 6.2**
**Government Expenditures as Percent of Gross Domestic Product and Growth Rates in Per Capita Gross Domestic Product**

| | Government Expenditures as Percent of Gross Domestic Product | | Growth Rates in Per Capita Gross Domestic Product | |
|---|---|---|---|---|
| | 1960 | 1980 | 1950–73 | 1973–79 |
| Sweden | 31.1 | 65.7 | 3.1 | 1.5 |
| Netherlands | 33.7 | 62.5 | 3.5 | 1.7 |
| Belgium | 30.3 | 51.7 | 3.6 | 2.1 |
| Norway | 29.9 | 49.4 | 3.1 | 3.9 |
| Austria | 32.1 | 48.5 | 5.0 | 3.1 |
| West Germany | 32.0 | 46.9 | 5.0 | 2.6 |
| France | 34.6 | 46.2 | 4.1 | 2.6 |
| Italy | 30.1 | 45.6 | 4.8 | 2.0 |
| United Kingdom | 32.6 | 44.6 | 2.5 | 1.3 |
| Canada | 28.9 | 40.7 | 3.0 | 2.1 |
| United States | 27.8 | 33.2 | 2.2 | 1.9 |
| Japan | 20.7 | 32.7 | 8.4 | 3.0 |

*Note:* GDP at constant prices.

*Source:* For government expenditures as percent of gross domestic product, *Economic Outlook* 31 (1982): 149. For growth rates in gross domestic product, Angus Maddison, "Capitalist Economic Performance since 1820," in *Technical Change, Employment and Investment,* edited by L. Jorberg and N. Rosenberg, Department of Economic History, University of Lund, Lund, 1982, p. 155.

Friedman views the post-World War II United Kingdom as an economic disaster and West Germany during the same period as an economic miracle. With respect to the British record, Friedman comments that

> since the end of World War II, British domestic economic policy has been dominated by the search for greater equality of outcome. . . . State-provided medical, housing, and other welfare services were greatly expanded. . . . Who can doubt the effect that the drive for equality has had on efficiency and productivity? Surely, that is the main reason why economic growth in Britain has fallen behind its continental neighbors, the United States, Japan and other nations over the past few decades.[15]

In sharp contrast to his assessment of the British experience, Friedman observes that West Germany, "a defeated and devastated country," became one of the strongest economies on the continent of

**TABLE 6.3**

**Rates of Growth in Product Per Capita, Product Per Worker, and Product Per Worker-Hour**

(in percents)

| | Product Per Capita | Product Per Worker | Product Per Worker-Hour |
|---|---|---|---|
| 1890–1913 | —* | — | 1.8 |
| 1913–48 | — | — | 2.2 |
| 1948–79 | — | — | 2.5 |
| 1840–80 | 1.26 | 1.04 | — |
| 1880–1920 | 1.61 | 1.26 | — |
| 1920–60 | 1.81 | 1.84 | — |
| 1950–69 | — | 2.30 | — |
| 1950–70 | 2.00 | — | — |
| 1970–80 | 2.10 | — | — |

*Data not available

*Source:* For product per worker-hour, Solomon Fabricant, "The Productivity Issue: An Overview," in *Productivity Prospects and Growth,* edited by Jerome M. Rosow (New York, Van Nostrand, 1981), p. 6. For product per capita and product per worker from 1840 to 1960, Simon Kuznets, "Notes on the Pattern of U.S. Economic Growth," in *The Reinterpretation of American Economic History,* edited by Robert W. Fogel and Stanley L. Engerman (New York, Harper and Row, 1971), p. 18. For 1950–69 product per worker, *Historical Statistics of the United States* (Washington, D.C.: U.S. Government Printing Office, 1974), Table F 10-16. For product per capita 1950–70 and 1970–80, *World Development Report, 1984* (New York, World Bank, Oxford University Press, 1984), p. 82.

Europe. What made it possible for West Germany to make such rapid progress? "It was the miracle of the free market," asserts Friedman.[16]

That the economic performance of the West German economy was substantially better than that of Great Britain over the past three decades cannot be denied. In 1958, per capita gross national product in Britain was $1,254, 24 percent greater than West Germany's $1,015. Over the next couple of decades their relative position was dramatically reversed. By 1981, as a result of its relatively rapid growth rate (fully double that of Britain's), West Germany's per capita GDP of $13,450 was 48 percent higher than Britain's $9,110.[17] However, those differential growth rates cannot be explained, as Friedman asserts without presenting any evidence, by the U.K.'s "drive for equality" and West Germany's adoption of free-market policies.

Contrary to Friedman's sharp distinction between the policies followed by the U.K. and West Germany, government played a massive role in the economy of both countries. In the two decades between 1962 and 1982, government expenditures as a percentage of gross domestic product varied between 34.2 and 47.4 percent in the United Kingdom while in free-market West Germany the corresponding figures were 35.6 and 49.4 percent (see Table 6.4). In 17 of the 21 years in that period, the total outlays of the government as a percentage of GDP were actually higher in West Germany. A similar pattern was also true of taxation. With respect to Social Security contributions by employers and employees, the amounts collected by the West German government as a share of GDP was about twice that collected in the United Kingdom.

Writing in 1965, Andrew Shonfield commented,

> The conventional image of the German Government would hardly lead one to anticipate the fact that it regularly takes in taxation in a higher proportion of the nation's output than the government of any advanced Western country. . . . It is especially interesting to compare the German with the British case, because of the remarkable persistence of a legend that Germany's much more rapid economic growth is correlated with the greater freedom of

## TABLE 6.4
## Government Expenditures, Tax Revenues, and Social Security Contributions as a Percentage of Gross Domestic Product: United Kingdom and West Germany

|  | Government Expenditures | | Tax Revenues | | Social Security Contributions | |
|---|---|---|---|---|---|---|
|  | U.K. | W.G. | U.K. | W.G. | U.K. | W.G. |
| 1950 | — * | — | 32.5 | 30.3 | — | — |
| 1955 | — | — | 29.0 | 32.2 | — | — |
| 1960 | — | — | 27.6 | 33.9 | — | — |
| 1962 | 34.2 | 35.6 | — | — | — | — |
| 1965 | 36.4 | 36.7 | 30.6 | 31.6 | 4.5 | 8.3 |
| 1970 | 39.2 | 38.6 | 37.3 | 32.9 | 5.0[a] | 10.5[a] |
| 1975 | 46.6 | 48.9 | 35.7 | 36.0 | 6.0 | 12.0 |
| 1980 | 45.4 | 48.3 | 36.0 | 37.8 | 6.1 | 12.8 |
| 1982 | 47.4 | 49.4 | 39.6 | 37.3 | 6.6 | 13.3 |

*Data not available.
[a]Figures are for 1972.

*Source:* For government expenditures as a percent of GDP, *Economic Outlook,* July 1984, Paris, p. 159. For tax revenue and social security contributions as a percent of GDP (1965–82) *Statistiques DeRecettes Publiques, 1965–1983,* OECD, Paris, 1984, p. 85 and Tables 16 through 19. For tax revenues 1950–60, *Statistics of National Accounts,* OECD, 1964.

her citizens from the attentions of the tax collector. It was true right at the beginning of the 1950's when the Labour Government was still in power in Britain, that the level of British taxation was higher than the German [32.5% of GNP in the U.K. and 30.3% in Germany]. But by 1960 the position had been dramatically reversed. . . . The increase in the absolute amount taken by the Germans in taxation over these years was even bigger than the figures suggest, because the rate of increase in the German national product between 1950 and 1960 was three times as great as the British. Indeed, the striking thing about the German case is that rising prosperity, which produced windfalls for the exchequer in the form of extra revenue . . . was not seized upon as a reason for cutting down the share of income claimed by the state from the nation. That is precisely what happened in Britain. . . . In the second half of the 1950's, the Germans embarked on a major expansion of their social security system. . . . In Britain the objective of tax reduction took priority over schemes for the extension of social welfare. But the high level of German taxation was not solely for the support of ambitious social welfare schemes. The money was needed for a variety of subsidies to support one or another of the activities favored by the state and also to help in the finance of the nation's capital investment at large. . . . Indeed, anyone judging the relative importance devoted to the role of the state in national economic policy by the obvious fiscal criteria — level of taxation, public saving, collective social expenditure — would be bound to conclude that the German policy makers belonged naturally with the Scandinavian group, while the British were allied with the Americans . . . and the other traditional antagonists of public initiative.[18]

Clearly, there is no basis for Friedman's simplistic assertions that "the miracle of the free market" was the source of Germany's rapid progress over the past three decades, while Britain lagged because of government intervention in the "drive for equality." In both countries, the state played a central role. In addition, the role of the state, as measured by government expenditures and taxation as a percent of GNP, was actually somewhat greater in Friedman's free-market Germany than it was in the welfare society of the United Kingdom.

Furthermore, the lag in economic growth in the U.K. behind other countries is not a recent phenomenon that developed over the past few decades. As British economist Samuel Brittan has written, "There is the long-standing gap between the growth rate of the United Kingdom and that of other industrial market economics" that "goes back over a hundred years."[19] One estimate by Angus Maddison indicates that the average level of output per head in 16 industrial countries rose more than sixfold between 1870 and 1976, but less than fourfold in the United Kingdom. Most significant for the present discussion, the data indicate that the

## TABLE 6.5
## Long-Term Growth Rates: Real Gross Domestic Product Per Head of Population: United Kingdom
### (in 1970 U.S. dollars)

|  | Average of 16 Advanced Countries | United Kingdom |
|---|---|---|
| Growth percent per annum |  |  |
| 1870–1976 | 1.8 | 1.3 |
| 1870–1913 | 1.5 | 1.0 |
| 1913–50 | 1.1 | 1.0 |
| 1950–70 | 3.8 | 2.3 |
| 1970–76 | 2.4 | 2.0 |
| GDP per head (in U.S. 1970 dollars) |  |  |
| 1870 | 666 | 956 |
| 1976 | 4,258 | 3,583 |
| Ratio of U.K. to average GDP per head |  |  |
| 1870 | — | 1.44 |
| 1976 | — | .84 |

*Note:* Arithmetical average of United States, Canada, Australia, Japan, United Kingdom, Germany, France, Italy, Switzerland, Netherlands, Belgium, Sweden, Denmark, Norway, Austria, Finland.

The only country with a slower growth rate than the United Kingdom over the century was Australia, where GDP per head in 1976 was 1.19 times that of the United Kingdom. U.S. growth over the century, 1870–1976, was 1.9 percent per annum, the Japanese 2.5 percent, the German 2.0 percent, and the French 1.9 percent.

*Source:* Samuel Brittan, "How British Is the British Sickness?" *Journal of Law and Economics* 21 (1978): 146.

British economy's growth lagged behind the average growth in the other 16 countries throughout the hundred-year period, not as Friedman states, just over the past few decades (see Table 6.5). The lag in the British growth rate is "historically deep-seated," not a recent development, beginning long before that nation took on significant aspects of a welfare state.[20]

## THE GROWTH OF GOVERNMENT AND THE INCREASE IN CRIME

As the following quotations make manifest, Friedman sees the increased role that the government has played in the economy as a major factor contributing to increased crime and violence:

> In the past few decades, there has been a decline in the moral climate. We
> see it in the rise in crime statistics, in the lack of respect for property, in
> the kind of rioting that broke out in New York, in the problems of
> maintaining discipline in the elementary schools. Why? I submit to you that
> a major factor has been a change in the philosophy that has been dominant, a
> change from belief in individual responsibility to belief in social
> responsibility.[21]
>
> The tendency to turn to the government for solutions promotes violence
> in at least three ways: (1) it exacerbates discontent; (2) it directs discontent at
> persons, not circumstances; and (3) it concentrates great power in the hands of
> identifiable individuals.[22]
>
> When the law interferes with people's pursuit of their own values, they
> will try to find a way around. They will evade the law, they will break
> the law, or they will leave the country. Few of us believe in a moral code
> that justifies forcing people to give up much of what they produce to
> finance payments to persons they do not know for purposes they do not
> approve of. When the law contradicts what most people regard as moral and
> proper, they will break the law. When people start to break one set of laws,
> the lack of respect for the law inevitably spreads to all laws, even those that
> everyone regards as moral and proper — laws against violence, theft, and
> vandalism. Hard as it may be to believe, the growth of crude criminality in
> the U.K. in recent decades may well be one consequence of the drive for
> equality. We in the United States have not gone as far as the U.K. in
> promoting equality of outcome, yet many of the same consequences are
> already evident — from a failure of egalitarians to achieve their objectives and
> a reshuffling of wealth that by no standards can be regarded as equitable to a
> rise in criminality.[23]

Here again, Friedman sees reliance on government as the source of
evil, particularly in the turn toward government in the drive for equality.
Here again, Friedman presents little evidence to support his position other
than the simplistic observation that violence and crime have increased in
the United Kingdom and the United States in recent decades.

Friedman is correct in stating that there has been a rise in crime
statistics in both the United States and the U.K in the past few decades.
Among students of criminology, arguments about the reasons for the
increase abound. For Friedman, the economist, the explanation is simple:
his ideological blinders direct him toward the growth in the welfare state
as a major factor underlying the growth in criminality and violence. For
criminologists, the answers are many and complex and there is little
consensus.

1. Changes in crime rates may reflect a changing age structure of the population. In 1979, although those between the ages of 15 and 20 made up only 15 percent of the population, one-third of those arrested were from that age group. There was a steady decline in the numbers arrested as age increased. The postwar baby boom in England and in the United States generated in the 1960s and early 1970s a temporary increase in the proportion of the population between 15 and 20 years of age, the ages most prone to commit offenses. Hence, part of the increase in crime since 1960 may be explained by the change in the age composition of the population.[24] Lending support to that hypothesis is the fact that since 1980, along with a decline in the offense-prone age group as a proportion of the population, there has been a decline in crime rates, both violent and against property.[15]

2. A significant part of the increase in crime rates may be explained by the way in which the data have been collected. The national figures on crime are compiled from data voluntarily submitted to the Federal Bureau of Investigation (FBI) by law-enforcement agencies of the states or by various local agencies. In 1960 there were about 2,500 reporting agencies. By 1977 the number of agencies participating in the FBI program had increased to over 10,000.[16] With the substantial increase in the reporting base there was, predictably, an increase in reported crime rates. As a result, there is some debate among criminologists as to whether the increase in crime is real or just apparent.[27]

3. Criminologists have recently become interested in "opportunity theory" as an explanation of the post-World War II rise in crime. The tremendous proliferation of durable consumer goods and their decreased weight, the shift from activities at home toward activities outside the home, and increased vacations away from home that leave the home unguarded all provide greater opportunity for crimes against property. The shift in activity patterns away from the home also moves people into positions of vulnerability on the streets and in bars, increasing the opportunity for violent crimes.[28]

4. Other variables that criminologists have analyzed as contributing to higher crime rates are increases in unemployment, lower labor-force participation rates, inequality in the distribution of income, and changes in the legal definition of crime.[29]

As Friedman has noted, the United States has not gone as far as the United Kingdom in promoting equality of outcome. Therefore, if the welfare state, with its emphasis on social responsibility rather than individual responsibility, is a major factor contributing to a rise in crime statistics as Friedman contends, we would expect to find higher crime rates in the U.K. than in the United States. By all significant measures of crime, however, we find just the opposite: per 100,000 of population, the homicide rate is ten times higher, the grand larceny rate more than 70 percent higher, and the juvenile crime rate 26 percent higher in the United States than in the U.K. (see Table 6.6).

The governments of all the countries listed in Table 6.6 are substantially more interventionist than is the government of the United States. The total population of those countries is almost exactly the same as the population of the United States, yet the number of homicides in the United States is eight and one-half times greater (20,432 as compared with 2,392).[30] Looked at another way, the homicide rate in the United States is from three to eighteen times greater than in those European

**TABLE 6.6**
**Crime Rates**

### (per 100,000 of population)

|  | *Homicides* | *Grand Larceny* | *Juvenile Crime* |
|---|---|---|---|
| Austria | 1.4 | 1,214 | 23.6 |
| Denmark | .5 | 1,724 | 30.3 |
| Finland | 3.0 | 131 | 25.8 |
| France | 1.0 | 388 | 10.6 |
| West Germany | 1.2 | 1,611 | 27.5 |
| Netherlands | .8 | 864 | 24.8 |
| Norway | .7 | 815 | 56.5 |
| Sweden | 1.2 | 1,427 | — * |
| England and Wales | .9 | 1,001 | 24.8 |
| United States | 9.2 | 1,744 | 31.3 |

*Note:* Grand larceny comprises robbery and burglary.
*Data not available.

*Source:* The data on homicides are for 1979 and are from *Statistical Abstract of the United States, 1981,* U.S. Department of Commerce (U.S. Government Printing Office, Washington, D.C.), 1981, p. 178. The other data are from George Thomas Kurian, *The Book of World Rankings* (Facts on File, New York), 1979, pp. 340–341 and 345. The data are based on the resources of INTERPOL which is currently the only international organization collecting international crime statistics.

countries. The grand larceny rate is higher in the United States than in all the countries, and the juvenile crime rate is higher than in all but one. Clearly, contrary to Friedman's contention, there seems to be little relationship between an interventionist government and the crime rate.

In a recently published book, *Tyranny of the Status Quo,* Friedman devotes an entire chapter to crime and again asserts that the growth of government is an important factor contributing to the increase in crime. The "change in the climate of opinion, since the time of the New Deal . . . shifted emphasis from individual responsibility to societal responsibility" and, says Friedman,

> encouraged the view that people are creatures of their environment and should not be held responsible for their behavior. . . . If people who are poor hold the view that poverty is not their own fault but the fault of society at large then it is perfectly understandable that their reaction is "since society is responsible for my poverty, I have the right to act against society and take what I need or want."[31]

On the same pages that the above quotes appear, he makes some comparisons between crime in India and crime in the United States, forgetting what he had written about India five years earlier in *Free to Choose.* In that volume, as discussed in Chapter 4, he attributed India's difficulties in economic development to its socialist programs. In *Tyranny of the Status Quo,* in an attempt to demonstrate that poverty is not a cause of crime, he points out that poverty is more prevalent, more degrading, and more intolerable in India than in the United States, "yet, there is less chance of being mugged or robbed on the streets of Bombay or Calcutta at night than on the streets of New York or Chicago."[32]

Here again Friedman uses evidence selectively in order to attack government. Big government he sees inhibiting economic development in India and a major factor generating increased crime in the United States. Desiring to explain away poverty as a cause of crime in the United States, he cites India's relative safety. But how could India be relatively safe if, as Friedman has argued, the government plays such a substantial role there and big government is a major factor in generating crime? The obvious inconsistency does not seem to bother Friedman. By this intellectual legerdemain, Friedman achieves two of his goals: he is able to blame big government both for low economic growth and increased crime while at the same time assigning to the poor responsibility for their poverty.

# THE GENERATION OF RACIAL UNREST
# AND THE PROGRESS OF BLACKS

Although Friedman does recognize the existence of widespread prejudice against blacks in U.S. society, he attributes limitations on their progress and the generation of racial unrest to liberals and misguided government programs. Only with reliance on the market — on "competitive private enterprise" — he argues, can there be a permanent solution to the problems of blacks in the United States.

In reaction to the widespread racial rioting that rocked the United States in the summer of 1967, Friedman in December of that year wrote,

> Liberals ... encouraged Negroes to look primarily to government for relief. ... Many of the problems the Negro faces in America today were produced or aggravated by governmental measures proposed, supported, and executed by liberals. ... The drive for further legislative measures, and particularly the techniques adopted [welfare, minimum wage legislation, public housing, slum schools provided by the government] have awakened the sleeping giant of racial prejudice among the whites in the North. The encouragement of unrealistic and extravagant expectations has produced frustration, outrage and a sense of betrayal among the Negroes in the North. Unwittingly, the liberals have set race against race.[33]

To blame liberals and the drive for legislation, as Friedman does, for having "awakened the sleeping giant of racial prejudice" and setting "race against race" is a gross distortion of the history of race relations in the United States. The giant of racial prejudice never slept. On the contrary, violence in race relations — race riots, lynching of blacks, bombings of their homes and churches, black outrage and frustration — has been endemic in U.S. society since the end of slavery, long before the emergence of any significant liberal influence.

Race riots resulting in the destruction of life and property exploded in Memphis and New Orleans in 1866; New York City in 1900; Springfield, Ohio in 1904; Atlanta in 1906; Springfield, Illinois in 1908; East St. Louis, Philadelphia, and Houston in 1917; Chicago, Washington, and 23 other cities and towns in 1919; Tulsa in 1921; and in Detroit and Harlem in 1943.[34] Throughout those years, "lynching, beating and bombing by whites ... supplemented legal systems of restraint designed to maintain white supremacy."[35] Between 1882 and 1946, 3,245 blacks were known to be the victims of lynch mobs, 178 as recently as the period betwen 1927 and 1946.[36]

In the same 1967 article referred to above, Friedman asserts that "Negroes have made great progress in the past century, thanks to their own efforts and to the opportunities offered them by a market system."[37] In *Capitalism and Freedom,* he argued that

> Negroes [and other minorities] have the most at stake in the preservation and strengthening of competitive capitalism. . . . Instead of recognizing that the existence of the market has protected them from the attitude of their fellow countrymen, they mistakenly attribute the residual discrimination to the market. . . . I believe strongly that the color of a man's skin or the religion of his parents is, by itself no reason to treat him differently. . . . I deplore what seems to me the prejudice and narrowness of outlook of those whose tastes differ in this respect from mine and I think the less of them for it. But in a society based on free discussion, the appropriate recourse is for me to seek to persuade them that their tastes are bad and that they should change their views and their behavior, not to use coercive power [of the state] to enforce my tastes and my attitude on others.[38]

In still another article, Friedman wrote that, "the tendency to turn to the government for solutions promotes violence" as "it exacerbates discontent" and "directs discontent at persons." Every extension "of the area over which explicit agreement is sought through political channels strains further the fragile threads that hold a free society together" and "may well disrupt the society — as our present attempt to solve the racial issue by political means is clearly doing." How should we deal with the racial problem? Friedman's answer: "We must husband the great reservoir of tolerance in our people, their willingness to abide by majority rule — not waste it trying to do by legal compulsion what we can do as well or better by voluntary means."[39]

Is the "great reservoir of tolerance" husbanded and violence lessened by avoiding legal compulsion and relying instead upon the market forces of competitive capitalism as Friedman suggests? The answer is clearly in the negative. The racial riots, the lynchings, the beating of blacks and bombing of their homes and churches occurred, for the most part, during the heyday of competitive capitalism in the United States, the period from the end of the Civil War to the 1920s. During those years, there was no significant drive for protective legislation for blacks except for the decade after the Civil War, no great liberal influence, and the market did little to protect blacks from the attitude of their fellow countrymen.

What validity is there in Friedman's contention that "Negroes have made great progress in the past century?" Again, contrary to Friedman's assertion, the evidence indicates blacks made relatively little economic progress in the 65 years following the Civil War. Of the economic condition of blacks in the beginning of World War II, Gunnar Myrdal, in his classic study *An American Dilemma,* wrote,

> The economic situations of the Negroes in America is pathological. Except for a small minority enjoying upper or middle class status, the masses of American Negroes, in the rural South and in the segregated slum quarters in Southern and Northern cities, are destitute. They own little property, even their household goods are mostly inadequate and dilapidated. Their incomes are not only low but irregular. They thus live from day to day and have scant security for the future. Their entire culture and their individual interests and strivings are narrow.[40]

Myrdal's bleak assessment is consistent with the pre-World War II data on black income. In 1939, the median wage and salary incomes of nonwhite males and females were only 41 percent and 36 percent, respectively, of those of white males and females, far short of the "great progress" suggested by Friedman. Not until the severe labor shortages of the World War II and postwar years opened up opportunities for nonwhites did income differentials begin to narrow significantly, at least for nonwhite males (see Table 6.7). As Professor Richard B. Freeman,

**TABLE 6.7**
**Median Wage and Salary and Total Money Income of Persons, Nonwhite as a Percent of White**

|  | *Median Wage and Salary Income* | | *Total Money Income of Persons* | |
|---|---|---|---|---|
|  | *Male* | *Female* | *Male* | *Female* |
| 1939 | 41 | 36 | —* | — |
| 1948 | 60 | 43 | 54 | 43 |
| 1950 | 61 | 37 | 54 | 45 |
| 1955 | 59 | 43 | 53 | 52 |
| 1960 | 60 | 50 | 53 | 62 |
| 1964 | 59 | 58 | 57 | 71 |
| 1968 | 66 | 72 | 61 | 81 |
| 1976 | 73 | 97 | 63 | 95 |
| 1980 | — | — | 63 | 96 |

*Data not available.

*Source:* U.S., Department of Commerce, Bureau of the Census, *Current Population Reports,* Consumer Income Series P-60 (Washington, D.C.: Government Printing Office).

an authority on blacks in the labor market has stated, "For over half a century [1890 through 1960] black men made little or no economic progress relative to whites, except during World War II."[41]

Instead of relying on the market forces of competitive capitalism and free discussion to persuade those who discriminate that their "tastes" are bad, as Friedman counseled, blacks along with white liberal allies in the mid-1950s turned toward massive nonviolent action, the courts, and federal legislation to break down discriminatory barriers. The next two decades, the 1960s and 1970s, saw a substantial growth in government intervention aimed at securing equality for blacks.

The civil rights movement caught fire with the Montgomery, Alabama bus boycott of 1955–56, which "captured the imagination of the nation and the Negro community in particular." The boycott resulted in a court-ordered desegregation of buses in Montgomery and similar movements spread to other southern cities. Increasing impatience among blacks led to a "rising tempo of nonviolent direct action in the late 1950's, culminating in the student sit-ins of 1960 and the inauguration of what is popularly known as the 'Civil Rights Revolution.'"[42]

This revolution led to two major federal initiatives in the 1960s designed to reduce market discrimination against minorities and redistribute income in their favor: Title VII of the Civil Rights Act of 1964, later amended (1972), and Executive Order No. 11246. As summarized by Professor Freeman,

> Title VII made discrimination by employers (Section 703a), employment agencies (703b), and unions (703c) illegal in a wide variety of areas of employment, including hiring, firing, compensation, and the terms, conditions, and privileges of employment, and union membership. . . . The second major action in the sixties was Executive Order No. 11246 (1965), which requires that federal contractors, who employ about one-third of the United States work force, "not discriminate" in employment and take "affirmative action" to recruit, employ, and promote qualified minority workers. The Executive Order established a potentially powerful sanction on miscreants by giving contracting agencies and the Office of Federal Contract Compliance (OFCC) the power to "cancel, terminate, suspend, or cause to be cancelled, terminated or suspended" contracts which fail to comply with non-discrimination provisions. . . . The Executive Order required substantial, formal equal employment administrative procedures which, if carried out, would revolutionize traditional personnel policy.[43]

Contrary to Friedman's assertion that government intervention had an adverse impact on blacks, Professor Freeman's studies concluded that these governmental efforts to penalize discriminators and shift the demand for labor in favor of discriminated-against groups appear to have greatly altered the market for blacks. Courts place significant penalties on discriminators, in some cases ordering recalcitrant employers to hire given numbers or proportions of minorities. State, local, and federal government agencies sought black candidates for jobs. Company personnel policies changed, with many instituting energetic affirmative action programs.[44]

Summarizing his findings, Professor Freeman wrote,

Specific groups of black workers — women, young men, young male college graduates — experienced relatively large economic gains. By the 1970's, black women had earnings as high as, or higher than, comparable white women in the country as a whole; young black male college graduates earned as much as their white counterparts; and the black-white income ratio for young men in general was 0.85, considerably above ratios in years past. As a result of increased incomes for highly educated and skilled black workers, the historic pattern of declining black-white income ratios with ascending skills no longer prevails.[45]

Most important for our discussion, Professor Freeman found that

much of the improvement in the black economic position that took place in the late sixties appears to be the result of governmental and related antidiscriminatory activity associated with the 1964 Civil Rights Act. Previous time trends, more education for blacks, and the general boom of the period cannot account for the sharp increase in relative incomes and occupational position of blacks after 1964. . . . All told, the evidence presented in this study tells a remarkable story of social and economic change in the sixties. Discriminatory differences that had persisted for decades began collapsing with surprising speed.[46]

The data presented in Tables 6.7 and 6.8 show the relative economic improvement in the position of blacks during the 1960s and 1970s discussed by Professor Freeman. The data in Table 6.8, taken from one of Professor Freeman's studies, show the striking change in the path of black-white earnings and relative occupational position that occurred around 1964 (when the Civil Rights Act was enacted) from a very slight upward trend before 1964 to a marked upward trend afterward.

The census surveys used by Freeman and many others who have studied black labor markets consist of one-time interviews with a different cross-section of families each year. Using wage-rate data from the University of Michigan's *Panel Study of Income Dynamics,* Professor Greg J. Duncan also studied black-white differentials. These

## TABLE 6.8
## Ratios of Nonwhite to White Economic Position and Annual Changes in Ratios, 1949–64 and 1964–76

|  | Year | | | Annual Change | |
|---|---|---|---|---|---|
|  | *1949–50* | *1964* | *1976* | *Before 1964* | *After 1964* |
| Males |  |  |  |  |  |
| Median income, |  |  |  |  |  |
|     professionals | .57 | .69 | .84 | 1.1 | 2.1 |
| Relative number of |  |  |  |  |  |
|     professionals | .39 | .45 | .65 | 0.4 | 1.8 |
|     managers | .22 | .22 | .41 | 0.0 | 1.7 |
| Females |  |  |  |  |  |
| Relative number of |  |  |  |  |  |
|     professionals | .47 | .60 | .83 | 0.9 | 2.1 |
|     clericals | .15 | .33 | .69 | 1.3 | 3.3 |

*Source:* Richard B. Freeman, *Labor Economics,* 2d ed. (Englewood Cliffs, N.J.: Prentice-Hall, 1979), p. 100.

data were collected by interviewing families in 1968 and performing follow-up interviews with the same families (and their offshoots) each year thereafter. His recently published study concluded that "the upward trend in the relative earnings of black men, observed by many in data from the Census Bureau, shows up in the Panel Study data as well" (see Table 6.9). The rising ratio, Duncan found, was "due more to the favorable position of black men just entering the labor force than to any improvement in the position of black men already in the labor market." He also observed that "government policies may have led to a favorable position for black labor market entrants," but that the evidence supporting this conclusion is indirect.[47]

President Reagan's view on the close relationship between the increase in crime and the growth in government as well as on the adverse effect on blacks of the legislative programs developed by liberals are strikingly similar to the views set forth by Friedman. In an address before a national meeting of Chiefs of Police, President Reagan asserted,

> The truth is that today's criminals, for the most part, are not desperate people seeking bread for their families. . . . They do really believe . . . that the

**TABLE 6.9**
**Black-to-White Wage Ratios**
(in percent)

| | All Workers (age 25–54) | Young Workers Only (age 25–34) |
|---|---|---|
| 1967–70 average | .65 | .72 |
| 1971–74 average | .70 | .78 |
| 1975–78 average | .76 | .80 |

*Source:* Greg J. Duncan, *Years of Poverty Years of Plenty* (Ann Arbor: The University of Michigan, Survey Research Center, 1984), p. 145.

world owes them a living. . . . It has occurred to me that the root cause of our other major domestic problem — the growth of government and the decay of the economy — can be traced to many of the same sources of the crime problem. . . . Many of the social thinkers of the 1950's and 1960's who discussed crime only in the context of disadvantaged childhoods and poverty-stricken neighborhoods were the same people who thought that massive government spending could wipe away our social ills.[48]

Compare these comments with those of Friedman's cited on pages 89 to 92 of this chapter.

On blacks, in an address delivered to the National Black Republican Council, President Reagan had this to say:

Our economic hardship is not some kind of mysterious malaise, suffered by people who have suddenly lost their vitality. . . . The record is there for all to see. . . . With the coming of the Great Society, government began eating away at the underpinnings of the private enterprise system. The big taxers and spenders in the Congress had started a binge that would slowly change the nature of our society, and even worse, it threatened the character of our people. . . . Perhaps the saddest part of the whole story is that much of this Federal spending was done in the name of helping those it hurt the most — the disadvantaged. . . . Government programs intended for the poor created a new kind of bondage for millions of American citizens by making them dependent on welfare and other benefits.[49]

And in a speech before the National Urban League, the President said,

To a number of black people, the U.S. economy has been something of an underground railroad: it has spirited them away from poverty to middle class prosperity and beyond. But too many blacks remain behind. . . . I believe many in Washington over the years have been more dedicated to making needy people Government dependent rather than independent . . . yet in spite of the money and the hopes the Government has never lived up to the dreams of poor people.[50]

Again, compare the similarity of these comments with those of Friedman's cited on pages 92 and 94.

## NOTES

1. *Newsweek*, November 10, 1980, p. 94.

2. Milton Friedman and Rose Friedman, *Free to Choose* (New York: Avon, 1981), pp. xx, 145–46; *Newsweek*, March 5, 1979, p. 87; February 23, 1981, p. 70; August 23, 1982, p. 59.

3. *Newsweek*, June 24, 1968, p. 90; November 10, 1980, p. 94; Milton Friedman, *Bright Promises, Dismal Performance*, ed. William R. Allen (New York: Harcourt, Brace, Jovanovich, 1982), pp. 86–87; Friedman and Friedman, *Free to Choose*, p. 136.

4. *Newsweek*, November 19, 1979, pp. 69–70; Friedman, *Bright Promises*, p. 43.

5. *Newsweek*, December 11, 1967, p. 89.

6. Friedman and Friedman, *Free to Choose*, pp. 140–43.

7. *Newsweek*, October 18, 1968, p. 104; Friedman, *Bright Promises*, pp. 42–45.

8. Friedman and Friedman, *Free to Choose*, p. ix.

9. *Newsweek*, October 25, 1982, p. 111.

10. *Newsweek*, February 23, 1981, p. 70.

11. *Newsweek*, August 23, 1982, p. 59.

12. *Economic Report of the President, February 1982* (Washington, D.C.: Government Printing Office, 1982), pp. 3, 4.

13. John L. Palmer and Isabel V. Sawhill, *The Reagan Record* (Cambridge, Mass.: Ballinger, 1984), pp. 75, 183.

14. Charles E. Lindblom, *Politics and Markets* (New York: Basic Books, 1977), p. 113.

15. Friedman and Friedman, *Free to Choose*, pp. 135–36.

16. Ibid., p. 47.

17. U.N., *Statistical Yearbook* (New York: United Nations, 1970), p. 605; *World Bank Atlas* (Washington, D.C.: International Bank for Reconstruction and Development, 1982), p. 22.

18. Andrew Shonfield, *Modern Capitalism* (New York: Oxford University Press, 1965), pp. 265–66.

19.   Samuel Brittan, "How British Is the British Sickness," *Journal of Law and Economics* (197): 245.

20.   Ibid., p. 247.

21.   Friedman, *Bright Promises*, pp. 86–87.

22.   *Newsweek*, June 24, 1968, p. 90.

23.   Friedman and Friedman, *Free to Choose*, p. 136.

24.   Paul Brantingham and Patricia Brantingham, *Patterns in Crime* (New York: Macmillan, 1984), pp. 140–43.

25.   U.S., Department of Commerce, Bureau of the Census, *Statistical Abstract of the United States, 1984*   104th ed. (Washington, D.C.: Government Printing Office, 1984), p. 176.

26.   Daryl A. Hellman, *The Economics of Crime* (New York: St. Martin's Press, 1980), p. 8.

27.   Brantingham and Brantingham, *Patterns*, p. 160.

28.   Ibid., pp. 155–58.

29.   Ibid., pp. 246–48, 202.

30.   U.S., Department of Commerce, *Statistical Abstract, 1984*, p. 181.

31.   Milton Friedman and Rose Friedman, *Tyranny of the Status Quo* (New York: Harcourt, Brace, Jovanovich, 1984), pp. 134–35.

32.   Ibid.

33.   *Newsweek*, December 11, 1967, p. 89.

34.   J. Paul Mitchell, ed., *Race Riots in Black and White* (Englewood Cliffs, N.J.: Prentice-Hall, 1970), p. ix; William M. Tuttle, Jr., *Race Riots* (New York: Atheneum, 1972), pp. 11–14; August Meier and Elliot Rudwick, *From Plantation to Ghetto* (New York: Hill and Wang, 1970), p. 177.

35.   Mitchell, *Race Riots*, p. 2.

36.   Ibid., pp. 31–32.

37.   *Newsweek*, December 11, 1967, p. 89.

38.   Milton Friedman, *Capitalism and Freedom* (Chicago: University of Chicago Press), pp. 21, 111.

39.   *Newsweek*, June 24, 1968, p. 90.

40.   Gunnar Myrdal, *An American Dilemma* (New York: McGraw-Hill, 1964) 1: 205.

41.   Richard B. Freeman, *Labor Economics*, 2d ed. (Englewood Cliffs, N.J.: Prentice-Hall, 1979), p. 98.

42.   Meier, *From Plantation to Ghetto*, p. 257.

43.   Freeman, *Labor Economics*, pp. 120–24.

44.   Ibid., p. 89.

45.   Richard Freeman, "Changes in the Labor Market for Black Americans, 1948–1972," in *Brookings Papers on Economic Activity*, no. 1 (Washington, D.C.: The Brookings Institution, 1973), p. 118.

46.   Ibid., p. 119.

47.   Greg J. Duncan, *Panel Study of Income Dynamics* (Ann Arbor: Survey Research Center, University of Michigan, 1981), pp. 144–47.

48.   New York *Times*, September 29, 1981, p. A18.

49.   Ibid., September 16, 1982, p. A23.

50.   Ibid., June 30, 1981, p. D21.

# 7

# FREEDOM, EQUALITY, POWER, AND THE GROWTH OF GOVERNMENT

The concept of *freedom* is central to Friedman's political economy. It appears in the title of his two major popular books, *Capitalism and Freedom* and *Free to Choose,* and in many of the approximately 300 columns he wrote for *Newsweek* between 1966 and 1982. Despite the key role he assigns to freedom in his popular writings, Friedman makes no serious attempt at analysis of the concept. What, precisely, is the nature of freedom? What are its components? What is necessary for its existence? What are the forces that threaten or severely limit freedom? How can freedom be protected or enhanced?

In order to gain insight into the nature and significance of Friedman's answers to these questions, it is first necessary to set forth his model of freedom. This will include the abstract principles he enunciates concerning the meaning of freedom, the conditions he sees necessary for its existence, and the forces he believes threaten its survival. We will then take a critical look at his model. This will involve (1) comparing his views with those of John Stuart Mill, the great nineteenth century proponent of freedom; (2) a discussion of the relationship of freedom to equality and power; (3) questions concerning how the decentralization of government power affects freedom; (4) an analysis of Friedman's argument that the rise and growth of the welfare state is primarily because of the influence of intellectuals, bureaucrats, and special interests; and (5) an examination of Friedman's view that the welfare state threatens freedom.

## FRIEDMAN'S MODEL OF FREEDOM

Friedman sees an "intimate connection between economics and politics" and argues that "only certain combinations of political and economic arrangements are possible, and that in particular, a society which is socialist cannot be democratic."[1] He stresses that there are only two ways of organizing the economic activities of millions: "one is central direction involving the use of coercion — the technique of the army and of the modern totalitarian state. The other is voluntary cooperation of individuals — the technique of the marketplace." Exchange in the marketplace, *"provided the transaction is bi-laterally voluntary and informed,"* can bring about "co-ordination without coercion. A working model of a society organized through voluntary exchange is a *free private enterprise exchange economy* — what we have been calling competitive capitalism."[2] Such a society will provide its members with "economic freedom" and the freedom to own property. Its members will thus have the "freedom to choose": how much to spend and on what items; how much to save and in what form; how much to give away and to whom; how to use their resources; and which occupation to enter.[3]

In a simple society of independent households ("a collection of Robinson Crusoes"), where each household controls resources enabling it to produce goods and services either directly for itself or for exchange, Friedman observes that no exchange will take place unless both parties benefit from it. The incentive for engaging in exchange is the increased product made possible by division of labor and specialization. Both parties gain and cooperation is achieved without coercion. Then, without so much as a pause for reflection, Friedman asserts there is a fundamental similarity between exchange in that simple society and exchange in a complex modern economy: "As in that simple model, so in the complex enterprise and money-exchange economy, cooperation is strictly individual and voluntary provided . . . that enterprises are private . . . and that individuals are free to enter or not to enter any particular exchange."[4]

For Friedman, "freedom in economic arrangements is itself a component of freedom broadly understood, so economic freedom is an end in itself." Even more, he finds that economic freedom is also an "indispensable means toward the achievement of political freedom."[5] On the relationship between economic freedom and political freedom, he reasons as follows:

> The great advantage of the market . . . is that it permits wide diversity. It is in political terms, a system of proportional representation. Each man can vote, as it were, for the color of the tie he wants and get it; he does not have to see what color the majority wants and then, if he is in the minority, submit. It is this feature of the market that we refer to when we say that the market provides economic freedom. Political freedom means the absence of coercion of a man by his fellow men. The fundamental threat to freedom is power to coerce, be it in the hands of a monarch, a dictator, an oligarchy, or a momentary majority. The preservation of freedom requires the elimination of such concentration of power to the fullest possible extent and the dispersal and distribution of whatever power cannot be eliminated — a system of checks and balances. By removing the organization of economic activity from the control of political authority, the market eliminates this source of coercive power. It enables economic strength to be a check to political power rather than a reinforcement.[6]

Friedman sees the principal threat to freedom as the growth in the power and influence of the federal government. He contends that although the Soviet Union is perceived by Americans as the immediate danger, "it is not the real threat to our national security. The real threat is the welfare state."[7] As has already been discussed, he argues that to avoid the threat that the government poses to freedom, its scope must be limited and its power dispersed to the lower levels of government outside Washington (see Chapter 2 of this volume).

Friedman notes that there has been a profound change in belief concerning the role of government, from "the view that government's role is to serve as an umpire to prevent individuals from coercing one another" to the belief that "government's role is to serve as a parent charged with the duty of coercing some to aid others."[8] The goal of the former view was to provide equality of opportunity, the goal of the latter to provide equality of outcome, a goal that Friedman sees as giving rise to the welfare state, the "real threat" to freedom.

In discussing the relationship between equality and freedom, Friedman draws a sharp distinction between equality of opportunity and equality of outcome. Equality of opportunity for him means that

> no arbitrary obstacles should prevent people from achieving those positions for which their talents fit them and which their values lead them to seek. Not birth, nationality, color, religion, sex, nor any other irrelevant characteristic should determine the opportunities that are open to a person — only his abilities. Equality of opportunity . . . is an essential component of liberty.[9]

By equality of outcome, Friedman means the goal of "fair shares for all." Government measures to achieve that goal, according to Friedman, are in clear conflict with liberty and in fact reduce liberty. With respect to the use of the fairness criterion, Friedman states,

> "Fairness" is not an objectively determined concept. . . . "Fairness" like "needs," is in the eye of the beholder. If all are to have "fair shares," someone or some group of people must decide what shares are fair — and they must be able to impose their decisions on others, taking from those who have more than their "fair" share and giving to those who have less. . . . If what people get is determined by "fairness" and not by what they produce, where are the "prizes" to come from? What incentive is there to work and produce? . . . What assures that people will accept the roles assigned to them and perform those roles in accordance with their abilities? Clearly, only force or the threat of force will do.[10]

## FRIEDMAN AND JOHN STUART MILL ON CAPITALISM AND FREEDOM

Friedman's first foray into national politics was as an adviser to Senator Goldwater in the 1964 presidential election. On reading Friedman's discussion of freedom, one is reminded of that memorable passage in Senator Goldwater's speech on accepting the nomination for president by the Republican party in 1964. In a blistering attack on moderate opponents within the party, Goldwater proclaimed, "Extremism in the defense of liberty is no vice! And . . . moderation in the pursuit of justice is no virtue."[11] In examining Friedman's analysis of freedom, one is forced to conclude that for him extremism in the defense of capitalism is no vice, and moderation in the defense of the laissez-faire market no virtue. As Nobel Laureate Kenneth Arrow remarked in a book review of Friedman's *Free to Choose,* "The concept of freedom, though it appears in the title of the book, is not analyzed. . . . As the title suggests, the Friedmans advocate an emotional libertarianism."[12]

Friedman's emotional libertarianism leads him to the extremist position of drawing a sharp dichotomy concerning the ways of organizing economic activity: central direction involving the use of coercion (the technique of the modern totalitarian state) or voluntary cooperation (the technique of the marketplace). The former he finds inconsistent with economic freedom and destructive of political freedom; the latter he sees as the source of economic freedom, which, he asserts, is an end in itself and a necessary condition for the achievement of political freedom. Within the framework of that simplistic dichotomy, using emotion-laden terms like *coercion* and *freedom* (Who would favor coercion or oppose freedom?), he then mounts an attack against any activity by the government that goes beyond the limited role he assigns to it in his laissez-faire framework. The proper role for the government, he holds, includes national defense, protection of individuals in the society from coercion by their fellow citizens, the establishment of general rules to facilitate voluntary exchange, and a few activities where strictly voluntary exchange is either exceedingly costly or impossible (see Chapter 2 of this volume for a discussion of these limitations). Government action beyond those severe limitations he finds coercive and an infringement on freedom.

Friedman quotes with approval the following passage from John Stuart Mill's classic essay *On Liberty*:

> The sole end for which mankind are warranted, individually or collectively, in interfering with the liberty or action of any of their number is self protection. . . . The only purpose for which power can be rightfully exercised over any member of a civilized community, against his will, is to prevent harm to others. His own good, either physical or moral, is not sufficient warrant. . . . The only part of the conduct of any one for which he is amenable to society, is that which merely concerns himself, his independence is, of right, absolute. Over himself, over his body and mind, the individual is sovereign.[13]

The passage from Mill's essay *On Liberty* was selected by Friedman because it expresses views on aspects of freedom similar to his own. But he makes no mention of Mill's major work in economics, one of the most influential texts of any time, *Principles of Political Economy,* in which Mill expounds views on socialism, capitalism, and freedom diametrically opposed to those of Friedman.[14]

Of Mill's views on socialism in his *Principles,* Joseph Schumpeter had this to say:

> Emotionally, socialism always appealed to him. He had little taste for the society he lived in and plenty of sympathy with the laboring masses. . . . There is no reason to doubt his statement in the preface to the third edition (1852) which was to the effect that he never intended to condemn socialism "regarded as an ultimate result of human progress" and that his objections merely rested on "the unprepared state of mankind." . . . He came to believe that capitalism was near to having done its work so that purely economic objections (to socialism) were losing part of their force. . . . He refused to

entertain the idea of transition by revolution. . . . Such views *define* Evolutionary Socialism.[15]

Mill was even more explicit in his classic *Autobiography,* in which he wrote,

> Our ideal of ultimate improvement went far beyond Democracy, and would class us decidedly under the general designation of Socialists. . . . The social problem of the future we considered to be, how to unite the greatest individual liberty of action, with common ownership in the raw material of the globe, and an equal participation of all in the benefits of combined labor. . . . The deep-rooted selfishness which forms the general character of existing society, is *so* deeply-rooted only because the whole course of existing institutions tends to foster it.[16]

Thus, in sharp contrast to the views held by Friedman, Mill — whose *On Liberty* is perhaps the most cogently argued and most frequently quoted defense of freedom — saw no necessary conflict between freedom and the organization of society along socialist lines.

On the workers' freedom to choose during the laissez-faire period in England, the period Friedman glorifies as a "golden age," [17] Mill had this to say: "The generality of labourers in this and most other countries have as little choice of occupation or freedom of locomotion, are practically as dependent on fixed rules and on the will of others, as they could be on any system short of actual slavery."[18]

Friedman looks at competition in free enterprise capitalism and sees the impersonal forces of the market generating voluntary cooperation without coercion. Mill's perception of the operation of the market yields a drastically different picture:

> I cannot . . . regard the stationary state of capital and wealth with the unaffected aversion so generally manifested toward it by political economists of the old school. I am inclined to believe that it would be, on the whole, a very considerable improvement on our present condition. I confess I am not charmed with the ideal of life held out by those who think that the normal state of human beings is that of struggling to get on; that the trampling, crushing, elbowing, and treading on each other's heels, which form the existing type of social life, are the most desirable lot of human kind, or anything but the disagreeable symptoms of one of the phases of industrial progress.[19]

The foregoing is in sharp contrast to the picture of nineteenth century British laissez-faire capitalism drawn by Friedman.

## FREEDOM, EQUALITY, AND POWER

From Friedman's perspective, the two major components of freedom are economic freedom and political freedom. Economic freedom he defines as the freedom to choose which goods and services to buy, how much to save, how much to give away and to whom, and which occupation to enter. Only under a system of competitive capitalism can there be economic freedom; only under competitive capitalism are people free to choose. Economic freedom he sees as an indispensable means toward political freedom. Political freedom for him "means the absence of coercion of man by his fellow man." The market, by removing the organization of economic activity from the control of political authority, "enables economic strength to be a check to political power." (See Chapter 2 of this volume.)

Friedman sees the relationship between power and freedom in the political sphere, but fails to see the obviously intimate connection between power and what he refers to as economic freedom. An individual may be free to choose but the freedom is meaningless unless he has the power to choose. Friedman may have learned much from his "great and revered teacher Frank Knight," but he must have missed Knight's lectures on the relationship between freedom and power in a system of voluntary exchange. On that relationship, Knight wrote,

> The fatal defect in the utilitarian doctrine of maximum freedom as a goal of social policy is its confusion of freedom and power. Its advocates overlook the fact that freedom to perform an act is meaningless unless the subject is in possession of the requisite means of action, and that the practical question is one of power rather than of formal freedom. As its actual test of equality of freedom, the utilitarians set up voluntary exchange. That is, no individual is to be asked to make a sacrifice at the behest of another unless he receives in return what he himself considers a full equivalent. Plausible this argument undoubtedly is, but there is a gaping hole in the logic. An "equivalent" to the choosing individual himself is simply the maximum that the other party will pay, a standard of force with no flavor of fairness. An ostensible provision for "fair" equivalence comes in only through the workings of the competitive market, establishing a general scale of prices. Thus the *most* that exchange relations can do is to assure that each individual shall keep, quantitatively unimpaired, the stock of values originally possessed, as measured by free exchange among persons whose original stocks were whatever they happened to be. The principle merely settles the ethical problem by decreeing fixity for all eternity of the *existing* distribution of means of enjoyment as measured by a process the results of which depend on the starting point. By a twofold *petitio-principii* it sanctifies the *status quo*. Its ethic is in the first place the

right to keep what one has. But it does not stop there. . . . It also sets up
the right to use what one has to get more, without limit![20]

On the power of labor in the exchange relationship, Knight observes
that

the inalienability of control over one's own person . . . results in placing in
an especially weak position anyone who owns productive capacity only as
embodied in his own person in the form of labour power. . . . The man
without "property" in the usual meaning of the term, is dependent upon a
practically continuous opportunity to market his services.[21]

On the relationship between economic power and accumulation and
inheritance, Knight comments that

freedom of accumulation not only carries with it the possibility of cumulative
increase in the inequality of *economic* power, and creates a strong tendency in
that direction; in addition economic power confers power in other forms,
including political power. . . . Freedom is a sound ethical ideal,
but *"effective" freedom depends on the possession of power as well as mere
absence of interference, at the hands of other individuals or of "society."*
Liberal societies have as a matter of course, if gropingly, recognized these
problems in practice and have tried to meet them through such measures as
progressive income and inheritance taxation. [Emphasis added][22]

Liberal societies and Friedman's teacher, Frank Knight, have
recognized those problems, but not Milton Friedman. In long chapters
devoted to the distribution of income in *Free to Choose* and *Capitalism
and Freedom,* there is not so much as a mention of the "commonplace
idea that poverty is in many ways a restriction of personal freedom."[23]
The poor, because of their lack of economic power, are not so free to
choose what to spend and on what items, how much to save and in what
form, how much to give and to whom, and which occupations to enter.
Neither are the poor so free to choose in the political arena. This
Friedman himself inadvertently admits when, in the context of a
discussion on poverty and welfare programs, he observes with respect to
the poor that

their disadvantage in the political market is likely to be greater than in the
economic. Once well-meaning reformers who may have helped to get a
welfare measure enacted have gone on to their next reform, the poor are left to
fend for themselves and they will almost always be overpowered by the
groups that have already demonstrated a greater capacity to take advantage of
available opportunities.[24]

In a chapter entitled "Who Protects the Worker," Friedman concludes that in a competitive free market a worker is protected from coercion by the employer because of the existence of other employers for whom he can work, and an employer is protected from exploitation by his employees by the existence of other workers whom he can hire. Workers are free to choose which occupation to enter, an "essential part of economic freedom."[25] Coordination through voluntary cooperation benefits both parties to an economic transaction *"provided the transaction is bi-laterally voluntary and informed."*[26] As in a simple society where "each household uses the resources it controls," so "in the complex enterprise and money-exchange economy, cooperation is strictly individual and voluntary," provided that enterprises are private and individuals are free to enter or not to enter any particular exchange.

Friedman, in support of his various positions, frequently cites passages from *The Wealth of Nations* by his favorite economist, Adam Smith. In Friedman's *Free to Choose,* the index attributes 24-page citations to Smith. The only reference by Friedman to Smith in the chapter "Who Protects the Worker" is in a passage in which Friedman argues that the influence of labor unions on wages has been overestimated. Friedman there states, "'The higgling and bargaining of the market' — as Adam Smith termed it — whereby the wages of most workers in the United States are determined is far less visible, draws less attention, and its importance as a result greatly underestimated."[27] In writing about the workers' freedom to choose, while citing Smith on the higgling and bargaining of the market, Friedman conveniently forgets the following famous passage in *The Wealth of Nations* on the relative position of masters and workmen:

> A landlord, a farmer, a master manufacturer, or merchant, though they did not employ a single workman, could generally live a year or two upon the stocks which they have acquired. Many workmen could not subsist a week, few could subsist a month, and scarce any a year without employment. In the long-run, the workman may be as necessary to his master as his master is to him, but the necessity is not so immediate. We rarely hear, it has been said, of the combination of masters, though frequently of workmen. But whoever imagines, upon this account, that masters rarely combine, is as ignorant of the world as of the subject. Masters are always and everywhere in a sort of tacit, but constant and uniform combination, not to raise the wages of labor above their actual rate. To violate this combination is everywhere a most unpopular action, and a sort of reproach to a master among his neighbors and equals.... Masters too sometimes enter into particular combinations to sink the wages of labour even below this rate.[28]

In another famous passage in *The Wealth of Nations* not mentioned by Friedman, Smith wrote of the effects of specialization,

> the employment of the far greater part of those who live by labour, that is, of the great body of the people, comes to be confined to a very few simple operations, frequently to one or two. . . . The man whose whole life is spent in performing a few simple operations . . . has no occasion to exert his understanding, or to exercise his invention in finding out expedients for removing difficulties which never occur. He naturally loses, therefore, the habit of such exertion, and generally becomes as stupid and as ignorant as it is possible for a human creature to become. The torper of his mind renders him, not only incapable of relishing or bearing a part in any rational conversation, but of conceiving any generous, noble, or tender sentiment, and consequently of forming any just judgment concerning many of the ordinary duties of private life. . . . In every improved and civilized society this is the state into which the labouring poor, that is, the greater body of the people, must necessarily fall, unless government takes some pains to prevent it.[29]

For Smith, the ordinary worker in a complex enterprise and money-exchange economy, because of weak bargaining position and the adverse effects of specialization, was not so free to choose.

The fundamental similarities Friedman sees between his simple society and the complex enterprise and money-exchange economy can only be explained by the tunnel vision produced by his ideological blinders. In the simple society, where each household uses the resources it controls, the household has the option to refuse to engage in exchange and, as Friedman himself notes, use its resources "directly by producing goods for its own immediate use."[30] Contrary to Friedman's claim, no such simple option exists for labor in the complex enterprise and money-exchange economy. With the separation of capital and labor in a capitalistic economy and with labor having few resources of its own even in a wealthy society, labor is not so free to choose. For the transaction between the owner of capital and labor to be truly voluntary and free of coercion, labor must be free to enter into any exchange or into none at all. Laborers without assets are not free to opt out of the market. Thus, for labor, where there is little or no choice there is coercion.

This becomes patently clear when there is termination of an exchange relationship by an employer. Suppose a worker, for any reason, is fired or laid off by an employer. As Charles E. Lindblom has observed, on termination people must move, leave their homes, change their occupations — any of a number of possible major changes, none of their own choosing. In addition, the mere threat of termination can be as constraining, as coercive, as menacing as an authoritative governmental command. A person whose style of life and family livelihood have for years been built around a particular job, occupation or location finds a command backed by a threat to fire him indistinguishable in many consequences for his liberty from a command backed by the police and the courts. . . . *Income — earning property is a bulwark only for those who have it!* Those who do not are vulnerable to coercion when jobs are scarce and insecure to the degree that jobs may become scarce. Unemployment compensation and other welfare programs are — by such a line of analysis — necessary to freedom in markets.[31]

Millions of workers have little to offer in the market other than their labor. Their personal resources are meager or nonexistent. Even in a wealthy country like the United States, 40 percent of the families had less than $1,000 in liquid assets and 64 percent less than $5,000 (see Table 7.1). Financial assets and income-earning property protect the freedom to choose of those who have such assets and property. For those workers who do not, when jobs are scarce or insecure in a modern economy, the impersonal forces of the market (of which Friedman is so enamored) rather than enhancing the worker's freedom, make him vulnerable to coercion. For the worker with meager assets, it is the welfare state,

**TABLE 7.1**

**Percentage Distribution of Families by Holdings of Total Financial Assets and Liquid Assets, 1983**

| Dollars | Total Financial Assets | Liquid Assets |
|---|---|---|
| None | 12 | 12 |
| 1–999 | 27 | 28 |
| 1,000–1,999 | 9 | 10 |
| 2,000–4,999 | 13 | 14 |
| 5,000–9,999 | 10 | 10 |
| 10,000–24,999 | 12 | 13 |
| 25,000 and more | 17 | 13 |

*Note:* Financial assets include liquid assets plus stocks, other bonds, nontaxable holding (municipal bonds and shares in certain mutual funds), and trusts. Liquid assets include checking accounts, savings accounts, money market accounts, certificates of deposit, IRA and Keogh accounts, and savings bonds.

*Source:* Robert B. Avery, Gregory E. Elliehausen, and Glenn B. Conner, "Survey of Consumer Finances," *Federal Reserve Bulletin* 70 (1984): 680.

Friedman's bête noire, with its unemployment compensation and other welfare programs, that reduces vulnerability to coercion in the market and, hence, enhances the freedom to choose. Given the history of periodic recessions and depressions that have plagued all capitalistic countries since the industrial revolution, the provision of unemployment compensation in protecting the worker's freedom to choose is one of the significant achievements of the welfare state.

## DECENTRALIZATION OF GOVERNMENT POWER AND FREEDOM

In answer to the question How can we benefit from the promise of government while avoiding its threat to freedom? Friedman replies with two broad principles: (1) the scope of government must be limited, and (2) government power must be dispersed. By the dispersion of government power, Friedman means that "if government is to exercise power, better in the county than in the state, better in the state than in Washington." The rationale he presents for this position is that if one does not like what the local community or state does, one can move to another. The mere possibility, he asserts, will act as a check. But there are few alternatives if an individual objects to what Washington imposes. For Friedman, "The preservation of freedom is the protective reason for limiting and decentralizing government power."[32]

That decentralizing government power preserves freedom is yet another of Friedman's simplistic assertions. Not only is it belied by U.S. history, it is even inconsistent with some of his own writings.

Rather than protecting freedom, state governments have often been a powerful force in restricting freedom. It is incredible that Friedman could so easily forget the role of state governments in the defense of slavery. It took a Civil War and the national government — Friedman's much-despised Washington — to end the institution of slavery despite fierce resistance on the part of state governments.

In the decades following the Civil War, all southern state governments passed Jim Crow laws harshly restricting the freedom of blacks. Blacks were not free to choose where to eat, which school to attend, in which recreations to participate, and even in which cemeteries to be buried. Political freedom for blacks was also sharply restricted by a combination of poll taxes, literacy tests, and residency requirements aimed at driving them away from the voting booth. In effect, "The Constitutional amendments guaranteeing equality before the law and at the ballot box had been practically nullified by the turn of the century — all in the name of State's rights."[33]

It took Supreme Court rulings and legislation by Congress — the central government in Washington — and the protests of a massive national civil rights movement in the 1950s and 1960s to finally break down the legal barriers to black freedom erected by decentralized state and local governments. Thus, for our 26 million black citizens, the freedom to choose has been increased greatly by the national government in the face of stiff resistance by state governments.

An area of considerable concern to Friedman is that of occupational licensure, the restriction of the right to practice or engage in an occupation to those individuals licensed by the state. He has written extensively on the subject and devoted a full chapter to it in his popular work *Capitalism and Freedom*.[34] Friedman argues that the licensure requirement, invariably justified by the need to protect the consumer, is in reality primarily a device for restricting entrance into a profession or occupation in order to protect or enhance the incomes of those already licensed — an analysis with which many if not most economists would agree. He sees occupational licensure as a severe restriction on the economic freedom of those barred from pursuing a particular career and on the freedom of consumers to choose who will provide them with services. Friedman is particularly forceful in attacking organized medicine for its use of the licensure mechanism to engage in restrictive practices in the provision of medical services.

That occupational licensure is widespread cannot be denied. It has been estimated that some 800 different occupations are licensed in the United States, from phrenologists to physicians.[35] A short list of licensed occupations is presented in Table 7.2.

The striking aspect of Table 7.2, for our present purposes, is what it tells us about Friedman's argument that decentralization of government power is a necessary condition for protecting freedom. All the 64 occupations listed are being regulated by state governments. Furthermore, of the some 800 occupations being regulated in the United States, almost all are regulated by states or municipalities, very few by Washington. In addition, the only significant attempts to curb the adverse effects of licensure have not come from the states or municipalities but from the Federal Trade Commission (FTC), an agency of the national government.[36] Friedman himself quotes a chairman of the FTC on the ridiculous extent to which states have engaged in occupational licensing.[37]

# TABLE 7.2
## Number of States that Regulate Certain Occupations

| | | | |
|---|---|---|---|
| Abstractor | 12 | Acupuncturist | 12 |
| Aerial duster | 8 | Ambulance attendant | 32 |
| Auctioneer | 24 | Audiologist | 30 |
| Boiler inspector | 26 | Chauffeur | 34 |
| Collection agent | 22 | General contractor | 20 |
| Specialty contractor | 5 | Well driller | 31 |
| Driving instructor | 40 | Electrician | 15 |
| Elevator inspector | 12 | Funeral director | 29 |
| Employment agency | 39 | Engineer | 49 |
| Forester | 12 | Geologist | 9 |
| Guide | 24 | Hearing aid dealer | 41 |
| Landscape architect | 35 | Librarian | 23 |
| Marriage counselor | 6 | Masseur | 15 |
| Medical lab technician | 8 | Medical lab director | 15 |
| Midwife | 28 | Milk sampler | 30 |
| Mine foreman | 19 | Projectionist | 6 |
| Naturopath | 11 | Nursing home administrator | 49 |
| Occupational therapist | 10 | Occupational therapy assistant | 6 |
| Optician | 19 | Outfitter | 4 |
| Pest control applicator | 23 | Pesticide applicator | 18 |
| Pharmacist's assistant | 17 | Physical therapy assistant | 21 |
| Physician's assistant | 25 | Plumber | 30 |
| Polygraph examiners | 21 | Private detective | 35 |
| Private patrol agent | 17 | Psychologist | 48 |
| TV technician | 4 | Radiologic technician | 10 |
| Sanitarian | 33 | School bus driver | 12 |
| Securities agent | 49 | Harbor pilot | 25 |
| Shorthand reporter | 13 | Social worker | 20 |
| Soil tester | 7 | Surveyor | 49 |
| Tree surgeon | 11 | Veterinarian | 16 |
| Watchmaker | 10 | Watchman/guard | 9 |
| Weather modifier | 21 | Weighmaster | 21 |

*Source:* Jeffrey M. Berry, "The States Occupational Licensing Debate," *State Government News* (1982): 10–14.

Friedman states that "few things have a greater effect on our lives than the occupation we may follow." How should we deal with the problem of occupational licensure? "Widening freedom to choose in this area," he asserts, *requires limiting the power of the states*" (emphasis added). So important is the issue to him that he proposes the following constitutional amendment: "No state shall make or impose any law which shall abridge the right of any citizen of the United States to follow any occupation or profession of his choice."[38]

In recommending the use of a national action to control the power of the state, Friedman has, in essence, denied the validity of his own basic principle that the dispersion of government power to the states and local levels is fundamental for the protection of freedom.

In the case of occupation licensure, as with the rights of blacks, it has been the national government — Washington — that has promoted freedom, whereas the state and local governments have restricted freedom. The evidence in these two important areas of social concern is manifestly inconsistent with Friedman's dispersion thesis concerning the relationship between government power and freedom. History provides the massive evidence with respect to freedom of blacks. Ironically, in the case of occupational licensure, much of the evidence for refutation of his thesis is provided by Friedman himself.


## INTELLECTUALS, BUREAUCRATS, AND SPECIAL INTERESTS

Given the obvious benefits that Friedman maintains flow from limited government and the dispersion of power to state and local levels, how can the pronounced increase in the role of the national government be explained? To explain that development, Friedman constructs a scenario consisting of intellectuals who led the movement, bureaucrats who fed on it, and special interests who took advantage of it to serve themselves. And it was all made possible by the widely accepted "myth" that the Great Depression of the 1930s was a failure of free-market capitalism.

"In the 1920's and 1930's," he states, "intellectuals in the United States were overwhelmingly persuaded that capitalism was a defective system" but they had little effect on government policy until the Great Depression of the early 1930s. The "myth" that the depression was a failure of the free market led the public to join the intellectuals in a changed view of the relative responsibilities of individuals and government. . . . The view that government's role is to serve as an umpire to prevent individuals from coercing one another was replaced by the view that government's role is to serve as a parent charged with the duty of coercing some to aid others. These views have dominated developments in the United States during the past half-century.[39]

Again we find Friedman engaging in a cavalier treatment of both history and economics. He states correctly that in the 1930s the Great Depression "was widely interpreted as a failure of free market capitalism." He labels that interpretation a "myth" and instead blames incompetent monetary policy, stating,

> *We now know*, as few knew then, that the depression was not produced by a failure of private enterprise, but rather by a failure of government in an area in which the government had from the first been assigned responsibility — "to coin money, regulate the value thereof, and of foreign coin," in the words of Section 8, Article 1, of the U.S. Constitution.[40] [Emphasis added]

When Friedman asserts, "We now know the cause of the Great Depression," he must be referring to the kingly *we,* since there is considerable disagreement among economists concerning both the causes and severity of cycles of prosperity and depression. In the recently published twelfth edition of *Economics* by Nobel Laureate Paul Samuelson (now jointly authored with William D. Nordhaus), the authors state, "Most theories today stress the importance . . . of consumption goods and investment. And when we compile a list of cycle theories, we could easily find dozens." The text lists seven of "the better known theories" and the names of 16 prominent economists associated with the different theories. Friedman is only one of the 16.[41]

Another Nobel laureate in economics, Kenneth Arrow, commented as follows on Friedman's claim that the Great Depression was caused by a failure in monetary policy, not by a failure in free-market capitalism:

> The reader should be warned that the sole emphasis on incompetent monetary policy as the cause of the Great Depression is disputed by serious scholars, who point to other factors. It must be noted that the really bad turns in monetary policy did not come until the end of 1930, by which time the recession was already very severe. When one adds that the Great Depression, while the worst in capitalist history, had some very serious precursors, notably in 1893 and 1873, and fluctuations of smaller amplitude were

continuous, the conclusion is hard to avoid that instability of a considerable magnitude is endemic in the free enterprise system even with a stable monetary policy.[42]

Friedman's incredible assertion that "we now know" that it was a failure of monetary policy that caused the Great Depression, when he surely knows that a large majority of economists disagrees with him, can only be explained by his profound ideological bias against almost any kind of government role in the economy.

That a "myth" created by intellectuals concerning the failure of the free market led the public to join intellectuals in a changed view of the relative responsibilities of individuals and government and that the combination of those factors generated the welfare state is itself a myth — a Friedman myth.

For the American people, the failure of free-market capitalism in the Great Depression was no myth, it was stark reality. By 1933, the gross national product had fallen to half its 1929 peak. Unemployment reached a high of about 25 percent in 1933 and averaged about 18.2 percent for the entire decade. Millions of families saw their savings wiped out as over 8,000 banks went under between 1930 and 1933. Many thousands lost their homes; in 1933 alone 25,000 mortgages were foreclosed. *Fortune* reported in February 1933 that some 200,000 young men and boys rode the rails from city to city across the country for want of something better to do. As poverty and hunger spread in the depths of the depression, organized looting of food became a nationwide phenomenon. Rebellious incidents flared up in normally conservative farm communities and in urban centers. As fear spread throughout the land, there was even talk of revolution by prominent businessmen, leaders of labor and farm organizations, and in the halls of Congress. Bankers, businessmen, and labor leaders clamored for action by Washington as the system collapsed.[43]

It was in response to the grim reality of these conditions — to the failure of the free-market system — not in response to any myths or plans generated by intellectuals, that President Roosevelt and Congress were led to take actions that ultimately laid the basis for the welfare state.

The intellectuals whose views, according to Friedman, produced the New Deal legislation of the 1930s comprised President Roosevelt's Brain Trust. As already indicated, Friedman greatly exaggerates their influence. That this is true is manifest from an examination of the origins of the two most important laws passed in the 1930s, the National Labor Relations Act (NLRA) and the Social Security Act.

The NLRA gave the National Labor Relations Board the power to prohibit "unfair labor practices" by employers who sought to block unionization, to order and conduct elections to determine whether workers wanted to bargain collectively, and if so to allow them to choose whom they wanted to represent them. Rather than reflecting Roosevelt's views or those of his Brain Trust, the president actually opposed the NLRA, successfully blocking its passage in 1934. The bill was reintroduced in the Senate in 1935 by Senator Wagner and, although Roosevelt still wanted no part of it, it was passed by an overwhelming margin of 63 to 12. As historian Robert S. McElvaine states, "Seeing that the legislation would pass anyway, President Roosevelt decided to gain whatever credit he could for a popular law that he had never supported. He suddenly announced that the Wagner bill was on his 'must' list of legislation."[44]

In a speech titled "Economic Myths and Public Opinion," Friedman had this to say about the origins of the Social Security Act:

> Maybe Social Security is a good thing. I'm not for the moment talking about that. I happen to think it is not. I think it's a terrible program, but maybe I'm wrong. *I'm here concerned with the myth. Did Social Security reflect a grass roots demand for services? The answer is no. It was sold under false pretenses.*[45] [Emphasis Added]

With respect to those who have written in support of Social Security, Friedman comments,

> Apparently they have regarded themselves as an elite group within society that knows what is good for other people better than those people do for themselves, an elite that has a duty and a responsibility to persuade the voters to pass laws that will be good for them, even if they have to fool the voters in order to get them to do so.[46]

Again we find Friedman claiming that an elite group of intellectuals generated a major social program by creating a myth that there was a grass-roots demand for services. That there was no grass-roots demand for the Social Security Act is yet another Friedman myth belied by history. During the Great Depression the security of millions of people vanished with the collapse of banks, insurance companies, and private pension plans.[47] Old people were particularly hard hit by unemployment, as many were dependent on others for support. In response to these conditions, a tremendous grass-roots movement burst forth in support of Dr. Francis E. Townsend's Townsend Plan. By late 1934, he had rallied hundreds of thousands of aged behind the plan, which called for a monthly pension of $200 for all citizens over 60 years of age. People were to receive the pension provided they would forego gainful employment and agree to spend every pension dollar within 30 days. The response to the plan was nothing short of phenomenal as Townsend Clubs sprouted throughout the country. With an estimated 7,000 clubs, their leaders claimed 3.5 million members. Other estimates placed the membership at closer to the 2 million signatures in support of their plan, a number of petition signers not matched by any cause in U.S. history. When asked in December 1935 whether they favored government pensions for the needy aged, a massive 89 percent of a cross-section of Americans answered in the affirmative.[48] Contrary to Friedman's claim, there was nothing mythical about the enormous grass-roots support for government-financed pension programs for the aged.

Friedman's attack on intellectuals is benign when compared with his vitriolic treatment of the government bureaucracy. He accuses bureaucrats of incompetence, massive waste, needlessly expanding programs, elitism, and the crudest self-interest. And most serious, he believes that as a class they have been a major factor in encouraging the growth of government and the erosion of our freedom. For Friedman, government employees are not civil servants, they are "bureaucrats," with all the invidious connotations the word carries for ideologues opposed to government programs. A few quotations from his numerous references to bureaucrats will give the reader some insight into the kind of crude populist appeal that permeates much of Friedman's writing for the general public.

From Friedman's perspective, money allocated for programs for the poor is

siphoned off by . . . a massive bureaucracy at attractive pay scales.

Special interests that benefit from specific programs press for their expansion — foremost among them the massive bureaucracy spawned by the programs.

The more bureaucratic an organization, the greater the extent to which useless work tends to displace useful work.

Bureaucrats spend someone else's money. Little wonder the amounts spent explode.

They inevitably become persuaded that they are indispensable, that they know more about what should be done than uninformed voters or self-interested businessmen.[49]

An examination of the index to Friedman's *Free to Choose* yields quick insight into his profound ideological bias. In a volume purportedly dealing with the freedom to choose in the modern U.S. economy, there are 55 page citations under bureaucracy, all dealing with social or regulatory activities of the government, but not a single reference to the immense civilian bureaucracy in the Defense Department. He attacks the "huge empire" of the Department of Health, Education and Welfare (HEW). (HEW was divided in 1979 into two agencies, the Department of Health and Human Services and the Department of Education.) Friedman states that more than one out of every hundred employees in the United States worked for HEW. That is, they worked for HEW or in programs for which HEW had responsibility but were administered by state and local units. As a result, he says, "All of us are affected by its activities."[50] It is odd, to say the least, that in *Free to Choose* there is not a single reference to any constraint on our freedom to choose as a result of the ubiquitous military-industrial-union-university complex inextricably tied to the mammoth Defense Department bureaucracy.[51] Indeed, HEW's 147,000 employees (4.8 percent of total civilian employment by the federal government) is less than one-seventh of the 1.1 million civilians employed by the Department of Defense (see Table 7.3). The latter employs about 36 percent of the civilians working for the federal government, and if those on the payrolls of the Veterans Administration and the National Aeronautics and Space Administration are counted as part of the military establishment, the figure increases to about 45 percent. Even that figure is somewhat understated, since it does not include those engaged in military projects in the Central Intelligence Agency (CIA) and in the Energy Department.

Friedman's discussion of the Energy Department is particularly interesting because it indicates how he uses data in his popular writings in order to make an ideological point. He states that price controls on oil and other forms of energy by the U.S. government strengthened the Organization of Petroleum Exporting Countries (OPEC) cartel, created shortages,

**TABLE 7.3**
**Civilian Employment of the Federal Government by Branch and Agency, August 1985**

| | |
|---|---|
| Total, all agencies | 3,065,770 |
| Legislative branch | 39,996 |
| Judicial branch | 18,285 |
| Executive branch | 3,007,489 |
| Executive departments | 1,824,296 |
| State | 25,479 |
| Treasury | 132,125 |
| Defense | 1,107,098 |
| Justice | 64,374 |
| Interior | 80,459 |
| Agriculture | 121,870 |
| Commerce | 35,448 |
| Labor | 18,503 |
| Health and Human Services | 142,476 |
| Education | 4,921 |
| Energy | 16,897 |
| Housing and Urban Development | 12,270 |
| Transportation | 62,376 |
| Independent agencies | 1,181,687 |
| U.S. Postal Service | 756,392 |
| Veteran's Administration | 248,664 |

*Source:* U.S., Office of Personnel Management, *Federal Civilian Workforce Statistics, Monthly Release* (Washington, D.C., 1985), pp. 10–13.

and required the introduction of major command elements in the United States in order to allocate the scarce supply (by a Department of Energy spending in 1979 about $10 billion and employing 20,000 people). . . . Removing price controls . . . would show how useless, indeed harmful, are the activities of the 20,000 employees of the Department of Energy. It might even occur to someone how much better off we were before we had a Department of Energy.[52]

The clear impression created by these statements is that the Energy Department's activities consisted primarily of regulating prices and allocating scarce supplies — an impression that is extraordinarily far from being at all accurate. Of the 20,000 employees of the department, about 3,600 were engaged in atomic energy defense activities and in nuclear-fission research in coordination with the National Aeronautics and Space Administration and the Department of Defense. An additional approximately 8,000 were employed by the Western Area Power, Bonneville Power, and the Southeastern Power Administrations, which administer government power projects created years before the establishment of the Energy Department in 1977. Still another 4,000 were involved in the overall administration of the department. In sum, only about 4,000 of the 20,000 were involved in the regulatory administration function of the department, somewhat less than the 20,000 suggested by Friedman.[53]

In addition to the Department of Health, Education and Welfare, specific agencies singled out for criticism by Friedman for their bureaucratic intervention in the economy are the Occupational Safety and Health Administration, the Consumer Product Safety Commission, the Environmental Protection Agency, the National Endowment for the Humanities, the National Science Foundation, the Food and Drug Administration, the National Transportation Safety Board, the Interstate Commerce Commission, the Department of Housing and Urban Development, and the Department of Energy.[54] The 51,357 workers in those agencies are only 1.7 percent of the total civilian employment by the federal government. If we add to that number every employee of the Departments of Agriculture, Health and Human Services, and Education, the figure for all those agencies attacked by Friedman for their bureaucratic interventionism amounts to about 10 percent of federal civilian employees. This is still much less than one-third of those employed by the military establishment (see Tables 7.3 and 7.4), with respect to which Friedman has nary a comment in *Free to Choose.*

Defense expenditures are discussed in *Tyranny of the Status Quo,* a recently published book he wrote with his wife, Rose Friedman. In that volume, for the first time Friedman comments on the waste and inefficiency in the military establishment and the role of special interests in securing military expenditures. He discusses congressmen protecting unnecessary military bases located in their districts, private firms advertising for specific expenditures on military projects that will enhance their profits, and branches of the military services lobbying for their own interests. Undoubtedly, Friedman's belated reference to the problem is a result of the recent, in his words, "steady stream of scandals about the procurement of military supplies."[55] However, although this material appears in a chapter entitled, "Defense," the main thrust and thesis of the chapter is an attack on the welfare state.[56]

## TABLE 7.4
## Employment in Selected Departments and Agencies, 1984

| | |
|---|---|
| Occupational Safety and Health Administration | 2,355 |
| Consumer Product Safety Commission | 595 |
| Environmental Protection Agency | 10,464 |
| National Endowment for the Humanities | 247 |
| National Science Foundation | 1,194 |
| Food and Drug Administration | 7,191 |
| National Transportation and Safety Board | 333 |
| Interstate Commerce Commission | 1,190 |
| Department of Energy | 16,897 * |
| Department of Housing and Urban Development | 12,270 * |

*Figures are for 1985.

*Source:* U.S., Congress, *Budget of the United States Government, Appendix, Fiscal Year 1985* (Washington, D.C.: Government Printing Office, 1985).

In an uncharacteristic display of humility in that chapter, he states, "We are not ourselves defense experts. We do not know the right amount of money to spend in order to assure the safety of our country."[57] Only four pages later, after a discussion of the decline in defense spending since the 1950s, he unceremoniously drops his mantle of humility concerning his expertise in military matters and states without qualification, "The growth of the welfare state has increasingly absorbed the taxable capacity of the nation and is inexorably driving the United States into [a] state of impotence in international affairs."[58]

In that same volume, Friedman again vents his spleen on the federal bureaucracy. In a section entitled, "Tyranny of Bureaucracy," he reasons as follows:

The key characteristics of bureaucrats are these: first they spend other people's money; second they have a bottom line, a proof of success, that is very distant and difficult to define. Under these circumstances, a major incentive for every bureaucrat is to become more powerful — and this is true whether the bureaucrat is dominated by broad and unselfish interests or by narrow and selfish interests. In either case being more powerful will enable the bureaucrat to pursue those interests more effectively. In most cases, the way for a bureaucrat to become more powerful is to have more people under his or her control — to expand the scope of whatever piece of the gigantic governmental structure is that bureaucrat's domain.[59]

Since congressmen, the president, and the members of his cabinet cannot be familiar with all the activities of the government, whether it is legislation or administration, Friedman concludes that

> inevitably the conduct of the government is delegated to bureaucrats. The number of bureaucrats has grown immensely in the course of years. From 1932 to 1982, the population of the United States didn't quite double, but the total number of employees of the federal government multiplied almost fivefold.[60]

Friedman selects the 1932–82 years to support his argument that bureaucrats have the incentive to expand the number of people under their control and, therefore, are an important element in explaining the growth of government. However, if we break down the 1932–82 period chosen by Friedman, we get a dramatically different picture that is manifestly inconsistent with his thesis.

If Friedman's analysis were correct, employment by the federal government should grow relative to the growth in population or, at a minimum, keep pace with it. Instead what we find over the past three decades is that while the population and employment in the private sector rose by 53 and 58 percent, respectively, federal employment grew by only 42 percent (see Table 7.4). That is, there was a relative decline in federal employment.

Even more significant for a test of Friedman's thesis are the developments after 1965. He refers to the "explosion in welfare activities" after President Lyndon Johnson declared a War on Poverty in 1964.[61] If Friedman's thesis were valid, we should have witnessed a corresponding explosion in the federal bureaucracy. The explosion never occurred. Since 1965, while the population increased 20 percent, federal employment grew only 15 percent. Furthermore, the percentage increase in private sector employment of 38 percent over the same period was more than twice the employment increase in the federal sector (see Table 7.5).

Bureaucrats may have a desire to increase their power and influence, as Friedman suggests, by increasing the number of people under their control. If so, contrary to his assertion, those bureaucrats at the federal level have in recent decades met with little success in expanding their empires.

**TABLE 7.5**

**U.S. Population and Employment by the Private Sector and by the Federal Government, 1950–82**

   **(population in millions, employment in thousands)**

| | | | | Percent Change | |
|---|---|---|---|---|---|
| | *1950* | *1965* | *1982* | *1950–82* | *1965–82* |
| Population | 152.3 | 194.3 | 232.3 | 53 | 20 |
| Employment | | | | | |
|    Private sector | 49,096 | 56,299 | 77,772 | 58 | 38 |
|    Federal government | 1,928 | 2,378 | 2,739 | 42 | 15 |

*Source:* U.S. Bureau of the Census, *Statistical Abstract of the United States: 1985* (105th edition), Washington, D.C., 1985, p. 6 for population data and p. 631 for farm employment, U.S. Department of Labor, *Monthly Labor Review*, April 1985, Washington, D.C., p. 73, for private sector employment other than farm.

## SPECIAL INTERESTS

On the role of special interests in generating big government, Friedman writes,

> We rail against "special interests" except when the "special interest" is our own. Each of us knows that what is good for him is good for the country — so our "special interest" is different. The end result is a maze of restraints and restrictions that makes almost all of us worse off than we would be if they were all eliminated. We lose more from measures that serve other "special interests" than we gain from measures that serve our "special interests."[62]

In his popular books and in his almost 300 articles in *Newsweek,* Friedman attacks numerous special interests: workers and businessmen, who call for tariff protection in the textile, shoe, cattle, sugar, auto, and steel industries; teachers and school administrators, who want to maintain control over public elementary and high school education; presidents of state universities, who want government subsidies; the millions in occupations protected by licensing; the merchant marine with its government subsidies and protection from competition in U.S. coastal waters; the postal workers and their government monopoly of the mail service; the railroad and trucking industries, which seek government protection from competition; the aged, who get Social Security; labor unions protected by labor legislation; scientists, artists, and actors, who get government grants; businessmen and workers, who with the aid of their congressmen, lobby for military contracts; and, above all, the federal bureaucracy.

When we total all of those interests it adds up to just about the entire U.S. population. Friedman himself recognizes this as he states, "There is hardly any of us who is not engaged in 'interested sophistry' in one area or another."[63] He decries that behavior, but in doing so he ends up in an anomalous position: while justifying the free market on the grounds that it maximizes political liberty, he denounces almost everything people do with that liberty.

Friedman's belief that big government and restraints on the free market were a product of the ideological influence of socialist intellectuals and the activities of bureaucrats and special interests is contradicted by history. The fundamental causes of the restraints imposed on the free market were the weaknesses and failures of the market itself; and government grew as the institutional mechanism for the imposition of those restraints. Karl Polanyi develops this thesis in his discussion of the movement away from laissez-faire in the last quarter of the nineteenth century by various countries of a widely dissimilar political and ideological configuration.

> Victorian England and the Prussia of Bismarck were poles apart, and both were very much unlike the France of the Third Republic or the empire of the Hapsburgs. Yet each of them passed through a period of free trade and laissez-faire, followed by a period of antiliberal legislation in regard to public health, factory conditions, municipal trading, social insurance, shipping subsidies, public utilities, trade associations and so on. . . . Under the most varied slogans, with different motivations a multitude of parties and social strata put into effect almost exactly the same measures in a series of countries in respect to a large number of complicated subjects. . . . *Intellectual fashions played no role whatever in this process. . . . It is incorrect to say that the change to social and national protectionism was due to any other cause than the manifestation of the weaknesses and perils inherent in the self-regulatory market system.*[64] [Emphasis added]

More recently, Professor Edward Herman commented along similar lines,

> The growth of government has closely followed perceived failings of the private market system, especially in terms of market instability, income insecurity, and the proliferation of negative externalities. Some of these deficiencies of the market can be attributed to its very success, which have generated more threatening externalities and created demands for things the market is not well suited to provide. It may also be true that the growth of

the government further weakens the market. This does not alter the fact that powerful underlying forces — not power hungry bureaucrats or frustrated intellectuals — are determining the main drift.[65]

## THE WELFARE STATE AS A THREAT TO FREEDOM

As discussed previously, Friedman stresses that there are only two ways of organizing the activities of millions. "One is central direction involving the use of coercion — the technique of the army and of the modern totalitarian state. The other is voluntary cooperation — the technique of the marketplace" (see p. 103, this volume). Friedman's construction of the paradigm and his use of obviously emotive words like *coercion, voluntary,* and *totalitarian* are a distortion of reality and an attempt to force the reader into his simplistic ideological corner. It distorts reality by selecting two extreme points on a continuum and comparing them as if they were the only two possibilities. In presenting his readers with only two choices, the "coercion" of the totalitarian state or the "voluntary cooperation" of the marketplace, Friedman knows full well which will appeal to his audience. He has, in effect, loaded the dice. In doing so, he can then discuss the modern welfare state, argue that it uses coercion in many of its activities, and thereby damn it in a not-too-subtle process of guilt by association with the technique of the totalitarian state.

Clearly, however, there is so vast a difference in the technique of coercion in the welfare state from that employed in the totalitarian state that it amounts to a difference in kind. The welfare state relies on the citizens' participation in and commitment to democratic processes, while the totalitarian state commonly resorts to authoritarian suppression of its citizenry.

Friedman often invokes the views of prominent historical figures to support his position that the welfare state involves coercion and threatens freedom. In an epigraph to *Free to Choose,* he establishes the theme of the book with a quotation from a dissenting opinion by Supreme Court Justice Louis Brandeis in the case of *Olmstead v. United States.*

Experience should teach us to be most on guard to protect liberty when the government's purposes are beneficial. Men born to freedom are naturally alert to repel invasion of their liberty by evil-minded rulers. The greater dangers to liberty lurk in insidious encroachment by men of zeal, well-meaning but without understanding.[66]

Since Friedman uses that statement as an introduction to all that follows in *Free to Choose,* the impression is created that Justice Brandeis was attacking the intellectuals and bureaucrats who supported the move toward the welfare state. Nothing could be further from the truth. The Olmstead case concerned the question of the legality of wiretapping by government officials.[67] The Brandeis statement quoted by Friedman was in fact a trenchant criticism of zealous government officials who had engaged in wiretapping. In no sense can the quotation be interpreted as a warning by Justice Brandeis of a threat to liberty by proponents of the welfare state. On the contrary, his views on social experimentation by government were diametrically opposed to those held by Friedman. In a case involving state licensing of private enterprise, Brandeis wrote,

> There must be power in the States and the Nation to remold, through experimentation, our economic practices and institutions to meet changing social and economic needs. I cannot believe that the framers of the Fourteenth Amendment, or the States which ratified it, intended to deprive us of the power to correct the evils of technological unemployment and excess productive capacity which have attended progress in the useful arts. . . . To stay experimentation in things social and economic is a grave responsibility. Denial of the right to experiment may be fraught with serious consequences for the nation.[68]

Justice Brandeis was a staunch defender of individual liberty, but unlike Friedman, he saw no inconsistency with that position and his belief that the government must play an active role in the economy. Brandeis "consistently displayed a social consciousness and a willingness to experiment with new approaches to pressing economic problems."[69] In addition, again unlike Friedman, Brandeis did not believe that the worker's freedom and decent working conditions were protected by unconstrained competition in the labor market. In a path-breaking brief submitted to the Supreme Court, Brandeis presented statistical, historical, sociological, and economic data to support social legislation by the state of Oregon that stated that no female shall be employed in any factory or laundry more than ten hours during any one day.[70] The Court upheld the Oregon law.

Justice Brandeis's views on the freedom of workers in the marketplace were markedly different than the views held by Friedman. Before a U.S. commission on industrial relations, Brandeis testified,

> My observation leads me to believe that while there are many contributing causes to unrest, that there is one cause which is fundamental. That is the

necessary conflict — the contrast between our political liberty and our industrial absolutism. We are as free politically as it is possible for us to be. . . . On the other hand, in dealing with industrial problems, the position of the ordinary workers is exactly the reverse. The individual employee has no effective voice or vote. And the main objection, as I see it, to the very large corporation is, that it makes possible — and in many cases makes inevitable — the exercise of industrial absolutism. . . . The result, in the cases of these large corporations, may be to develop a benevolent absolutism, but it is an absolutism all the same. There develops within the State a state so powerful that the ordinary social and industrial forces existing are insufficient to cope with it.[71]

For Justice Brandeis, the worker in a world of large corporate enterprise is not so free to choose. In effect, he rejected Friedman's contention that freedom of exchange protects the employee from coercion by the employer because of other employers for whom he can work.

In an article in which Friedman attempts to show that the hardship of unemployment is not nearly so great as is popularly believed, he glaringly contradicts two of his main theses, (1) that the worker is free to choose and (2) that no government social programs have achieved the results promised by its proponents. In that article, he states,

The growth of government transfer payments in the form of unemployment insurance, food stamps, welfare, social security, and so on, has reduced drastically the suffering associated with involuntary unemployment. A worker who has been laid off and expects to be recalled after a reasonable interval, as most laid-off workers are, may enjoy nearly as high an income when unemployed as when employed. . . . At the very least, he need not be so desperate to find another job as his counterpart was in the 1930's. He can afford to be choosy and to wait until he is either recalled or a more attractive job turns up.[72]

By admitting the existence of involuntary unemployment, Friedman is in essence, denying that freedom of exchange in the market protects the worker's freedom to choose. Unemployment is not the worker's choice. Furthermore, in stating that unemployment insurance and other government transfer programs have reduced the suffering associated with involuntary unemployment, he has inadvertently admitted that the social programs have at least achieved one of the major goals of its proponents. In addition, since those social programs have made it possible for the worker to be "choosy" in seeking employment, to that extent the welfare state has increased his freedom.

In discussing the impact on liberty of the drive for equality in the welfare state, Friedman exercises his freedom to choose in the way he selects and characterizes countries and makes comparisons among them. In discussing what he sees as a conflict between freedom and equality of outcome, he states that every attempt to make egalitarianism an overriding principle in organizing society invariably ends in a state of terror. As clear and convincing evidence, he cites the USSR, the People's Republic of China, and Cambodia.[73] Friedman seems to forget that all three of those societies were under authoritarian rulers prior to the drive for egalitarianism after the Communist takeovers. He also ignores the fact that terror was a basic instrument of the czars and Chiang Kai-shek in capitalist Russia and capitalist China before they were overthrown by the Communists.[74] Neither does he allude to the reign of terrror instituted in Chile when his own Chicago Boys were operating a free-market economy.

Most egregious of all is his failure to mention those welfare states where the drive for egalitarianism has been particularly strong for at least half a century with no terror and no loss of freedom: Sweden, the United Kingdom, and the Netherlands. As Nobel Laureate Paul Samuelson observed with respect to freedom in welfare states and in free-market economies,

> Why should there be a perverse empirical relation between the degree to which public opinion is, in fact, tolerant and the degree to which it relies on free markets? In our history, the days of most rugged individualism — the Guilded Age and the 1920's — seem to have been the ages least tolerant of dissenting opinion. . . . For years libertarians have been challenged to explain what appears to most observers to be the greater political freedoms and tolerances that prevail in Scandinavia than in America. In Norway, a professor may be a Communist, a Communist may sit by right on the board of the Central Bank or as an alternate board member. The BBC and the Scandinavian airwaves seem, if anything, more catholic in their welcome to speakers of divergent views than was true in McCarthy America or is true now. In 1939, I was told that none of this would last; active government economic policy had to result in loss of civil liberties and personal freedom. One still waits.[75]

## NOTES

1.  Milton Friedman, *Capitalism and Freedom* (Chicago: University of Chicago Press, 1962), p. 8.
2.  Ibid., p. 13.

3.   Milton Friedman and Rose Friedman, *Free to Choose* (New York: Avon, 1981), pp. 56–58.

4.   Friedman, *Capitalism,* p. 14.

5.   Ibid., p. 8.

6.   Ibid., pp. 15–16.

7.   Milton Friedman and Rose Friedman, *Tyranny of the Status Quo* (New York: Harcourt, Brace, Jovanovich, 1984), p. 73.

8.   Friedman and Friedman, *Free to Choose,* p. xix.

9.   Ibid., pp. 119–26.

10.   Ibid.

11.   William Manchester, *The Glory and the Dream* (Boston: Little, Brown, 1973), p. 1257.

12.   Kenneth Arrow, "Book Review," *New Republic,* 86 (March 22, 1980), p. 26.

13.   Friedman and Friedman, *Free to Choose,* p. xvi.

14.   John Stuart Mill, *Principles of Political Economy* (New York: Augustus Kelley, 1969), pp. 209–17. Published in 1848, as late as 1919 this essay was still being used at Oxford; see Robert Lekachman, *A History of Economic Ideas* (New York: McGraw-Hill, 1959), p. 177.

15.   Joseph Schumpeter, *History of Economic Analysis* (New York: Oxford University Press, 1954), p. 532.

16.   John Stuart Mill, *Autobiography* (New York: Columbia University Press, 1944), pp. 162–63.

17.   Friedman and Friedman, *Free to Choose,* p. xvii.

18.   Mill, *Political Economy,* p. 210.

19.   Ibid., p. 748.

20.   Frank H. Knight, *Freedom and Reform* (Port Washington: Kennikat Press, 1947), pp. 4–5.

21.   Ibid., p. 65.

22.   Ibid., pp. 4, 5, 65, 67, 382, 384.

23.   Arrow, "Book Review," p. 26.

24.   Friedman and Friedman, *Free to Choose,* p. 109.

25.   Ibid., pp. 57, 236; Friedman, *Capitalism,* pp. 14–15.

26.   Friedman, *Capitalism,* p. 13.

27.   Friedman and Friedman, *Free to Choose,* p. 219.

28.   Adam Smith, *The Wealth of Nations* (New York: Random House, 1937), pp. 67, 68.

29.   Ibid., pp. 734–35.

30.   Friedman, *Capitalism,* p. 13.

31.   Charles E. Lindblom, *Politics and Markets* (New York: Basic Books, 1977), pp. 48–50.

32.   Friedman, *Capitalism,* pp. 2–3.

33.   John M. Blum et al., *The National Experience* (New York: Harcourt, Brace, and World, 1963), pp. 380–81.

34.   Friedman, *Capitalism,* Chapter 9; Milton Friedman and Simon Kuznets, *Income from Independent Professional Practice* (New York: National Bureau of Economic Research, 1945), pp. 8–21.

35.   Kenneth J. Meier, *Regulation* (New York: St. Martin's Press, 1985), p. 1975.

36.   Ibid., pp. 188–91.

37.   Friedman and Friedman, *Free to Choose*, p. 229.

38.   Ibid., p. 293.

39.   Ibid., pp. xviii, xix; Friedman, *Capitalism*, p. 196.

40.   Friedman and Friedman, *Free to Choose*, p. 63.

41.   Paul Samuelson and William D. Nordhaus, *Economics* (New York: McGraw-Hill, 1985), p. 195.

42.   Arrow, "Book Review," p. 27.

43.   Robert S. McElvaine, *The Great Depression* (New York: Times Books, 1984), Chaps. 2, 6; Sherman J. Maisel, *Macroeconomics* (New York: W. W. Norton, 1982), pp. 112, 113; Carl N. Degler, *Out of Our Past* (New York: Harper & Row, 1959), pp. 379–416.

44.   McElvaine, *The Great Depression*, pp. 258–59.

45.   Milton Friedman, *Bright Promises, Dismal Performance: An Economist's Protest*, ed. William R. Allen (New York: Harcourt, Brace, Jovanovich, 1983), p. 70.

46.   Friedman and Friedman, *Free to Choose*, p. 96.

47.   Bruno Stein, *Social Security and Pensions in Transition* (New York: Free Press, 1983), p. 19.

48.   Ibid., pp. 100–1; McElvaine, *The Great Depression*, pp. 241, 242.

49.   Friedman and Friedman, *Free to Choose*, pp. 88, 99, 105, 108, 284–85.

50.   Ibid., p. 87.

51.   Friedman finally found it necessary to discuss the Defense establishment in his 1984 publication *Tyranny of the Status Quo*. However, in a brief chapter, he says nary a word about the size of the Defense bureaucracy, but does attack the welfare state because it absorbs the "taxable capacity" of the nation, thereby driving the nation into a "state of impotence in international affairs." See Chapter 4 and pp. 73, 74.

52.   Friedman and Friedman, *Free to Choose*, pp. 9, 210.

53.   U.S., Congress, *Budget of the United States Government, Appendix, Fiscal Year 1981*, 96th Cong. 2d sess., pp. 395–425.

54.   Friedman and Friedman, *Free to Choose*, pp. 60, 100, 184–92, 193–200, 194, 202–3, 208–12, 232, 233, 280.

55.   Friedman and Friedman, *Tyranny*, p. 77.

56.   Ibid., pp. 69–80.

57.   Ibid., p. 70.

58.   Ibid., p. 74.

59.   Ibid., pp. 48, 49.

60.   Ibid., p. 47.

61.   Friedman and Friedman, *Free to Choose*, pp. 86–87.

62.   Ibid., p. 31.

63.   Ibid., pp. 30–31.

64.   Karl Polyani, *The Great Transformation* (New York: Rinehart, 1944), pp. 145–47.

65.   Edward Herman, *Corporate Control, Corporate Power* (Cambridge: Cambridge University Press, 1981), pp. 300–1.

66.   Friedman and Friedman, *Free to Choose,* epigraph.

67.   James Morton Smith and Paul L. Murphy, eds., *Liberty and Justice* (New York: Alfred A. Knopf, 1958), pp. 402–3.

68.   New State Ice Co. v. Liebmann, 285 U.S. 280 (1931), p. 311.

69.   Smith and Murphy, *Liberty and Justice,* p. 406.

70.   Ibid., p. 344.

71.   U.S., Department of Labor, Commission on Industrial Relations, *Final Report and Testimony,* vol. 8, Senate Document no. 415, 64th Cong., 1st sess., pp. 7659–60.

72.   Friedman, *Bright Promises,* p. 347.

73.   Friedman and Friedman, *Free to Choose,* p. 126.

74.   Nathaniel Peffer, *The Far East* (Ann Arbor: University of Michigan Press, 1958), pp. 314, 390–91; Warren Bartlett Walsh, *Russia and the Soviet Union* (Ann Arbor: University of Michigan Press, 1958), pp. 345–46.

75.   Paul Samuelson, "Personal Freedom and Economic Freedoms in the Mixed Economy," in *The Business Establishment,* ed. Earl Cheit (New York: Wiley, 1964), pp. 127–28.

# 8

# A "RAGBAG" OF SOCIAL PROGRAMS

"I challenge my readers to name a government social program that has achieved the results promised by its well-meaning and public-interested proponents."[1] This sweeping generalization by Friedman, in a *Newsweek* column in 1982, is a theme that is constantly reiterated in his popular essays and books. Aside from his persistent criticism of the Federal Reserve monetary authorities, no other subject receives so much of his attention as the social programs of the welfare state. In addition to denouncing Social Security, by far the major welfare-state effort in the United States, he damns what he refers to as that "ragbag of well over 100 federal programs that have been enacted to help the poor."[2]

This chapter will examine Friedman's views on Social Security and his assessment of that "ragbag" of other federal programs enacted to help the poor and will conclude with a brief discussion of Friedman's recommended alternative as a substitute for all the social programs.

## SOCIAL SECURITY

The discussion in this section will focus on the old age and survivors insurance (OASI) component of the Social Security program. Benefit payments to retired workers and their dependents and to survivors of deceased workers from OASI amounted to approximately $150 billion in 1983, by far the largest component of federal social welfare expenditures. In 1983 there were more than 32 million beneficiaries; 90 percent of the labor force is covered by the program. The average monthly benefit in

1983 was $441 for retired workers and $396 for widows and widowers.[3]

Financing for OASI is provided by a payroll tax on employers and employees. When tax collections exceed outlays for benefits, the surplus is credited to a trust fund and invested in federal government securities. The trust fund is no more than a contingency fund. In essence, the system is on a pay-as-you-go basis, with workers currently employed paying for the current benefits of the aged.

While the normal retirement age is 65, reduced benefits are available for those retiring at age 62 and increased benefits are paid to workers who choose to retire past age 65. The amount of the benefit also depends on the average lifetime earnings of the claimant and on the number of the claimant's dependents. An important feature of the benefit structure is that it is weighted to favor lower-wage earners.

To qualify for benefits, an individual must work for a minimum number of years in jobs covered by the system. The worker is credited with a quarter of coverage for every $250 earned in any year, up to a maximum of four quarters per year. To be eligible for benefits, a worker must accumulate a quarter of coverage in at least one-fourth of the years between 1950 (or from age 21, if later) and the year before age 62. Starting in 1991, 40 quarters of coverage will be needed. The system is financed by a tax on wages up to a limit called the *wage base*. In 1985, employers and employees each paid 7.05 percent of wages up to $39,600. Of the 7.05 percent, 5.70 percent was for old age, survivors, and disability insurance (OASDI), and 1.35 percent was for health insurance (Medicare).

Social Security may be a sacred cow that no politician can question, but not so for Milton Friedman. Some of his most acerbic criticisms are aimed at the Social Security program, particularly at its old-age-and-survivors-insurance component. In a number of his publications, going at least as far back as 1967, he has argued that since its inception in the 1930s, Social Security has been promoted through "misleading and deceptive advertising."[4] As evidence, he cites a government booklet published annually, *Your Social Security*, and accuses the unsigned authors of Orwellian doublethink. He comments that in that document (1) payroll taxes are labeled "contributions," hence giving the impression that the taxes are voluntary; (2) the trust funds are treated as if they played an important role, when they are in fact too low to finance future benefits; (3) an impression is fostered that a worker's benefits are financed by his or her contributions, when in fact the benefits paid to retired workers are actually financed by the taxes paid by persons at work; and (4) workers are said to be earning protection for themselves, when in fact they are paying taxes to finance payments to persons who are not working.[5]

Friedman asserts that Social Security has been a target of complaints from all sides:

> Persons receiving payments complain that the sums are inadequate to maintain the standard of life they have been led to expect. Persons paying Social Security taxes complain that they are a heavy burden. Employers complain that the wedge introduced by the taxes between the costs to the employer of adding a worker to his payroll and the net gain to the worker of taking a job creates unemployment. Taxpayers complain that the unfunded obligations of the Social Security system total many trillions of dollars, and that not even present high taxes will keep the system solvent for long.

Friedman concludes the litany with the observation, "And all complaints are justified."[6] Let us look at his criticisms.

## THE TRUST FUND

To understand Friedman's criticism of the characterization of the trust fund in the booklet *Your Social Security,* it is necessary to see how the fund arises and how it increases or decreases.

The Social Security payroll taxes are collected by the Internal Revenue Service and credited to the fund. Benefit payments and the program's administrative expenses are disbursed by the fund. In essence, when the taxes collected exceed the disbursements, the fund grows and when the disbursements are greater than the tax intake, the fund shrinks.

Friedman criticizes the booklet's statement that the contributions by the workers and employers are pooled into special trust funds. The impression given by that statement is that the workers' benefits are being financed by their own contributions. Friedman is absolutely correct when he asserts that in fact taxes collected from persons at work are used to pay benefits to retired persons or to their dependents and their survivors. The system is on a pay-as-you-go basis, with current taxes financing current benefits. The trust fund is actually only a small fraction of annual benefits. At the end of 1980, for example, the trust fund of $22.8 billion was only 18 percent of the $123.8 billion in benefits paid in 1981. In essence, the Social Security taxes of $122.6 billion in 1981 financed the benefits paid that year.[7]

Clearly, as Friedman argues, the fund is in no sense an insurance reserve. The fund does, however, have two functions. First of all, it acts as a buffer if there is a mismatch between revenues and disbursements. For example, there may be a sharp fall in revenue as a result of a large increase in unemployment, or there may be a substantial increase in outlays with inflation, since benefits are indexed to the cost of living. Unless those economic shocks are too great, the fund acts as a buffer for the system by meeting the mismatch between receipts and disbursements.

A second function of the fund is as a barometer. A steady fall in the fund, or a failure to meet some target size in the future is a signal that something must be done — either raising taxes and/or decreasing benefits.[8]

Unfortunately, the attention given to the trust fund in the popular press when the fund reached low levels in the late 1970s and early 1980s fostered groundless fears among the general public that Social Security was on the verge of bankruptcy. In essence, the maintenance of benefit payments does not depend upon the trust fund but upon the willingness of those working to finance the program through current taxation. The criticisms by Friedman and others did little to assuage those fears.

## THE LONG-RUN SOLVENCY PROBLEM

Friedman claims that taxpayers are justified in their complaint that the "unfunded obligations of the Social Security system total many trillions of dollars, and that not even the present high taxes will keep it solvent for long."[9] He states,

> The long-run financial problems of Social Security stem from one simple fact: the number of people receiving payments from the system has increased and will continue to increase faster than the number of workers on whose wages taxes can be levied to finance those payments. In 1950 seventeen persons were employed for every person receiving benefits: by 1970 only three: by early in the twenty-first century, if present trends continue, at most two will be.[10]

What Friedman has presented as a "simple fact" is really not so simple. The impression one is left with by his analysis is that workers will be carrying a heavier and heavier burden because the number of beneficiaries of Social Security will be growing more rapidly than the number of workers who must support them. In assessing the long-run problems of OASI, however, it is misleading to focus only on a prospective increase in the number of beneficiaries relative to the number of workers. Several other demographic variables must be considered in order to arrive at a balanced assessment of the burden likely to be borne by future generations of workers.

The real burden carried by the working-age population is not simply a function of the relative size of the elderly population. The aged are not the only ones dependent on those of working age for their food, clothing, and shelter. So too are the young. A more meaningful measure of the real burden for those of working age is the dependency ratio — the ratio between those 65 years of age and over plus the population under age 20 to the population aged 20 to 64.

On the assumption that the fertility rate will gradually move to 2.1 births per woman by the year 2005, Professor Bruno Stein finds that the dependency ratio declines from .829 in 1975 to .662 in 2010. The reciprocal of the dependency ratio tells us the average number of people in the 20-to-64-year age group who share the burden of supporting all dependents. In 1975, 1.2 individuals in the working-age group shared the burden of supporting a dependent. By 2010 the figure rises to 1.5.[11] That is, in 1975, six individuals in the working-age group shared the burden of carrying five dependents, and by 2010 the burden is reduced as five dependents will be shared by 7.5 individuals in the working-age group.

Several factors combined explain the declining dependency ratio between 1975 and 2010. During this period, the relatively small group born between 1920 and 1945 will be retiring, while the post-World War II baby boom will have added substantial numbers to the labor force. In addition, the baby-boom generation has had falling birth rates. Combining these elements — a larger working-age population and a growing number of aged, offset by a declining proportion of children in the population — the result is a declining dependency ratio.

Between 2010 and 2035, the dependency ratio will rise. This will occur because during those years, the large baby-boom generation of the post-World War II period reaches retirement, while its lower fertility will have reduced the working-age population as a share of the total population. Despite these developments, by 2035 the dependency ratio will be .828, virtually the same as the 1975 level.[12] That is, the burden on the working-age population in 2035 will be no greater than it was in 1975.

The fact that there is no greater burden for the working-age population does not mean there is no long-term difficulty in the financing of Social Security. There is a very real problem that must be faced, but it is clearly not that of a growing total burden for workers, as suggested by Friedman.

Professor Bruno Stein has succinctly commented on the real long-term problems of Social Security. On observing that the declining number of children that need to be supported offsets the growing number of aged people, resulting in long-run constancy of the dependency ratio, Professor Stein concluded as follows:

> It can be argued that if the nation was capable of supporting its dependents in 1975, it should be capable of doing so again at some future point if the burden on the working population is no greater. In real terms, this means that resources that are not needed for the young can be reallocated for use by the aged. The usual way of getting a reallocation is through the market mechanism. There, consumers use their income to bid for the goods and services they want, and sellers respond by shifting the quantity and array of goods that they offer. In this case, however, the market mechanism cannot make the reallocation. This is because much of the income of the aged depends on Social Security, which relies on the willingness of the population to be taxed. Thus, even though the resources may be available, their transfer from the young to the old becomes a political rather than an economic issue.[13]

With projected stable and low fertility rates, the young will be a smaller percentage of the total population. As a result, resources not needed for the young can be shifted to use for the aged. For the reasons noted by Professor Stein, the problem is political, not economic, and its solution depends on the willingness of the population to be taxed to support the aged. The increased taxes that will be required to finance Social Security need not necessarily entail a net increase in the burden for workers, however, as less taxes will be needed for expenditures on education and less private expenditures will be necessary for child care.

## COMPULSION, FEAR, LIES, AND THE PROMISE OF FUTURE BENEFITS

Following are some choice comments Friedman has made with respect to Social Security:

The Social Security program involves a transfer from the young to the old. To some extent such a transfer has occurred throughout history — the young supporting their parents, or other relatives in old age. *Moral responsibility is an individual matter, not a social matter.* Children helped their parents out of love or duty. *They now contribute to the support of someone else's parents out of compulsion and fear.*

Individuals who would not lie to their children, their friends or colleagues, have propagated a false view of Social Security. Their intelligence and exposure to contrary views make it hard to believe that they have done so unintentionally and innocently. Apparently they have regarded themselves as an elite group within society that knows what is good for other people better than those people do for themselves, *an elite that has a duty and responsibility to persuade the voters to pass laws that will be good for them, even if they have to fool the voters in order to get them to do so.*

Workers paying taxes today derive no assurance from trust funds that they will receive benefits when they retire. Any assurance derives solely from the willingness of future taxpayers to impose taxes on themselves to pay for benefits that present taxpayers are promising themselves. The one-sided "compact between the generations," foisted on generations that cannot give their consent, is a very different thing from a "trust fund."[14] [Emphasis added]

An examination of these comments on Social Security can provide some insight into Friedman's values and economic philosophy.

Friedman asserts that moral responsibility is an individual matter, not a social matter. One can gain some insight into the degree of Friedman's concern with moral responsibility by examining his treatment of poverty and the distribution of income. As Kenneth Arrow observed on his reading of *Free to Choose,*

One would have no idea from this book of the extent of income inequality. Hard-working individuals can vary in their incomes by a factor of one thousand. . . . [The Friedmans'] lack of interest in the distribution of income appears heartless when (in another context) they observe, "persons with lower incomes on the average have a shorter life span than persons with higher incomes."[15]

The context in which that statement by Friedman appears is in a discussion of the supposed adverse effect of Social Security on the poor. Friedman writes,

Children from poor families tend to start work — and start paying employment taxes — at a relatively early age; children from higher income families at a much later age. At the other end of the life cycle, persons with lower incomes on the average have a shorter life span than persons with higher incomes. The net result is that the poor tend to pay higher taxes for more years and receive benefits for fewer years than the rich — all in the name of helping the poor.[16]

Friedman employs these facts when he wants to use them to attack the Social Security program. Once having cited those facts, however, he expresses no concern or feelings of compassion or moral responsibility for the children of poor families who tend to start work at a relatively early age or for the poor who have a shorter life span.

Witness the different treatment Friedman gives to an individual who has been able to accumulate $100,000 in financial assets. In a *Newsweek* column Friedman quotes from a letter he received from a reader:

During the past 47 years, I have worked and managed to save about $100,000. I have it invested in U.S. Savings Bonds and bank certificates of deposit. . . . Could you give me any idea how I should proceed to protect what I have? . . . Perhaps the only safety one has is to cash his bonds and bury the money.[17]

In 1970, three years before this letter was received by Friedman, 60 percent of the families in the United States had total financial assets of less than $2,000, while only 1 percent had been able to amass as much as $100,000. For families in which the age of the family head was over 65, the category in which Friedman's reader belonged, the median total financial asset holdings was only about $11,000 in 1983 and was considerably less in 1973 when the letter was written.[18]

When Friedman discusses expenditures on poverty programs, he finds the amounts spent "clearly overkill."[19] When he looks at the census figures on those living below the poverty level, he sees a "gross overestimate."[20] When he notes that children of the poor start to work at a much younger age than children of those with higher incomes and that the poor have shorter life spans, rather than expressing any feeling of compassion or sense of moral responsibility for the poor, he uses the data to attack the Social Security program.

Now note the difference in his response to the reader in the top 1 percent of families with financial assets who is troubled about what to do with his $100,000 in savings.

The writer of this moving letter was concerned about the danger of "bankruptcy coming upon the U.S." That danger is illusory, but the threat to his life savings from inflation is real. . . . We badly need to develop institutional arrangements that will provide the small saver with an inflation-proof asset with assured real yield and that will reduce in other ways as well the ravages of inflation.[21]

Friedman devotes the entire column to various ways that the writer of the "moving letter" might invest his $100,000 to protect his savings. For the poor, he has no advice; for the reader with $100,000 in savings, Friedman's cup of compassion runneth over.

Let us now turn to an examination of Friedman's assertions (1) that individuals who regard themselves as an elite group have fooled the voters into supporting Social Security, (2) that under Social Security children contribute to the support of someone else's parents out of compulsion and fear, and (3) that any assurance that workers today will receive the benefits promised when they retire depends solely on the willingness of future taxpayers to impose taxes on themselves to pay for benefits the present taxpayers promised themselves.

Formerly, notes Friedman, children helped their parents out of love or duty. With the advent of Social Security, he claims children now contribute to the support of someone else's parents out of compulsion and fear. When asked in a debate "Why it should be consumer sovereignty . . . if an individual buys whatever he wants, but not be consumer sovereignty when a number of individuals band together and decide they want to have social security with some kind of benefits paid by the government and for which they want to contribute?" Friedman responded,

I believe there is a philosophical difference between consumer sovereignty in which 100 percent of the people decide to join a program and a situation in which 51 percent of the people impose taxes on the other 49 percent of the people. . . . If 51 percent of the people vote to shoot the other 49 percent of the people, is that appropriate consumer sovereignty?[22]

This last point made by Friedman, the analogy between 51 percent of the people voting to shoot the other 49 percent and a majority of the voters opting for Social Security, is worthy of a witty high school debater, not a Nobel Prize winner, and deserves no comment. What does merit comment is his objection, in the context of a discussion of Social Security, to 51 percent of the people imposing taxes on the other 49 percent, and that under Social Security children contribute to the support of someone else's parents out of compulsion and fear. What are the facts with respect to the public's support for Social Security?

In a poll conducted by Gallup in January 1983, those polled were told that it was estimated that the federal government would have a deficit as much as $200 billion in fiscal 1984, unless some steps were taken to reduce the deficit, and that there were only a few ways that the deficit could be reduced. They were then asked, "Please tell me whether you approve or disapprove of the following: Make cuts in 'entitlement' programs such as Social Security, and the like."[23] The results are shown in Table 8.1. In every age group, support for Social Security was overwhelming, from 81 to 85 percent. Although not shown in the table, Gallup found virtually similar support by region, by political affiliation, by religion, by city size, and whether or not those questioned were members of labor unions.

Most important of all, 84 percent of those under 30 years of age and 83 percent of those in the 18-to-24-year group supported Social Security, indicating that Friedman's charge that children paid taxes under Social Security out of compulsion and fear is completely baseless and a product of his ideological blinders. Clearly, if the young disapproved of Social Security, they were under no compulsion and fear to say so in a poll conducted by Gallup.

Furthermore, Friedman's objection to 51 percent of the people imposing taxes on the other 49 percent, in the context of a discussion of

**TABLE 8.1**
**Should Programs Such as Social Security Be Cut?**
**A Gallup Poll**

|  | *Approve* | *Disapprove* | *No Opinion* |
|---|---|---|---|
| National | 12% | 83% | 5% |
| Age |  |  |  |
| Total under 30 | 12 | 84 | 4 |
| 18–24 years | 12 | 83 | 5 |
| 25–29 years | 11 | 85 | 4 |
| 30–49 years | 12 | 85 | 3 |
| Total 50 and older | 12 | 82 | 6 |
| 50–65 years | 14 | 81 | 5 |
| 65 and older | 10 | 82 | 8 |

*Source: The Gallup Report,* Report no. 208, February 1983, p. 20.

Social Security, is a gross distortion of reality. What the Gallup poll indicates is that 83 percent of the people are willing to impose taxes on all the people, including themselves, in order to finance Social Security.

When Friedman states that the benefits promised to workers today depend solely on the willingness of future taxpayers to impose taxes on themselves and that workers paying taxes today derive no assurance from trust funds that they will receive benefits when they retire, he is raising the specter that Social Security may not deliver on its promises. He is correct in stating that the benefits promised to workers today depend upon the willingness of future taxpayers to impose taxes on themselves. However, given the overwhelming support for Social Security even among the young, given the fact that even conservative politicians find it necessary to support Social Security (as Friedman himself notes), given the century-long history of support for social insurance for the aged in Western Europe and for half a century in the United States, there seems little danger that there will be any serious erosion of promised benefits.[24] The specter raised by Friedman is little more than mythology.

Friedman's charge that an elite group has fooled voters into supporting Social Security by propagating falsehoods is particularly odd coming from an individual who professes to be such a strong proponent of democracy and freedom. Evidently he believes that the overwhelming majority of all the voters in the United States and in all the democratic countries of Western Europe have been fooled by elite groups for the more than half-century they have supported social insurance for the aged. Alternatively, is it possible that the charge he has leveled at the intellectual proponents of Social Security is in fact applicable to Friedman — that he regards himself as a member of "an elite group within society that knows what is good for other people better than those people do for themselves?"

## WHO PAYS, WHO BENEFITS?

The tax to finance Social Security is a flat rate on wages up to a maximum. Since wages earned above the maximum and income earned from property are not subject to the tax, the tax is regressive, bearing most heavily on those with low incomes. Benefits paid, however, are calculated in accordance with a formula that is progressive. That is, the benefit schedule is weighted in favor of those with lower earnings.

In the 1972 debate, referred to above, Friedman stated that "social security combines a highly regressive tax with largely indiscriminate benefits and, in overall effect, probably redistributes income from lower to higher income persons."[25] During the question period, Friedman was confronted with the following statement by Robert Myers, a Temple University professor and formerly chief actuary of the Social Security Administration: "I can't quite understand, and therefore, I'd like to see a real quantitative demonstration of, Dr. Friedman's thesis that social security transfers money from the poor to the middle class. I think it does just the opposite because of the heavily weighted benefit formula."[26]

In a sharp departure from his usually aggressive debating style, Friedman's response was extraordinarily weak. He admitted that "it's extremely difficult to get a really satisfactory analysis of the redistribution involved in social security," that maybe he (Friedman) was "wrong," that he hadn't looked at it as much as Professor Myers, that Myers' "judgment is probably better than mine." Friedman concluded, "Maybe I'm wrong, and I would like to see a really satisfactory analysis of it," but then stated that he still believed his "judgment" was correct.[27]

A year later, without there having been any "really satisfactory analysis" such as he had said he thought was necessary (when confronted by an expert), in a long interview for *Playboy* magazine (when not confronted by an expert), Friedman returned to his assertive self. With no qualification he stated flatly that the lower-class person "pays more taxes and gets less in benefits. This biases the whole program in favor of the well-to-do, who don't need the money, as opposed to the poor, who do."[28] When Friedman deals with the general public, his academic role of intellectual caution and humility slips away and the ideologue is revealed.

More recently, in *Free to Choose* he again claims that Social Security is biased against the poor in favor of the middle class. Again, he offers no quantitative analysis and presents his assessment of the distributive impact as if it were an undisputed fact.[29] No mention is made of the fact that students of Social Security have taken a position diametrically opposed to Friedman's with respect to the net effect of Social Security taxes and benefits on the distribution of income. Let us take a closer look at the impact of Social Security on the poor.

The Social Security payroll tax, as Friedman emphasizes, is highly regressive. This is so for most ranges of the income scale, because the tax does not apply to earnings above a maximum and because beyond that point, property income, which is not subject to the tax, becomes increasingly important as a source of income as income rises. However, contrary to Friedman's suggestion, the regressivity of the tax does not apply to the poor if one defines the poor as those living below the government-determined poverty level. Congressional action in the latter part of the 1970s significantly reduced the impact of Social Security taxes on the poor.

To lessen the burden of the Social Security tax on those with low incomes, Congress in 1975 introduced a refundable income tax credit of 10 percent of earnings up to $4,000. The credit was phased down to zero between $4,000 and $8,000 of income. Since 1979 the credit has been applied to the first $5,000 of earnings, phasing down to zero between $6,000 and $10,000 of income. The credit applied to persons with children and is refundable because cash payments are made to those persons not subject to the income tax.

In 1983 there were approximately 5.8 million families living below the poverty level of about $10,000, and they had a median income of $5,604. As a result of the income tax credit, almost all of those families had their Social Security taxes reduced substantially. Joseph Pechman estimates that "about 71 percent of the combined employer-employee payroll tax is eliminated for eligible workers earning less than $5,000."[30]

Henry J. Aaron of The Brookings Institution reviewed a number of studies of the impact of Social Security on the distribution of income, conducted his own study, and concluded that

> on balance, it is clear that such factors as differential mortality and age of entry [the factors cited by Friedman] offset, but do not eliminate, the progressivity of the social security benefit formula, that survivors and disability insurance reinforce it, and that social security has provided relatively larger lifetime wealth increments to cohorts with low earnings and, within those cohorts, to workers with low earnings.[31]

The Social Security program has dramatically reduced the number of aged living in poverty. To discuss that effect, it is first necessary to discuss how the government measures poverty. The poverty index is based solely on money income and does not include noncash benefits, such as food stamps, Medicaid, and public housing that may be received by low-income persons. Money income includes the sum of the amounts received from earnings, Social Security and public assistance payments, dividends, interest and rent, unemployment and workers' compensation, government and private employee pensions, and other periodic income. The index is based on a 1961-economy food plan constructed by the Department of Agriculture and reflects the different requirements of families based on their size and composition. The poverty thresholds are adjusted every year to reflect changes in the consumer price index. In

1983, for example, the poverty threshold for a four-person family was $10,178.[32]

Between 1959, the first year for which such data are available, and 1984, the percentage of those under 65 years of age below the poverty level fell by 30 percent, while the percentage of aged living in poverty declined by 65 percent (see Table 8.2). In 1984, the percentage of the under-age-65 group living in poverty increased by about 37 percent over what it was in 1969. During that same period, the percentage of aged living in poverty fell steadily, so that by 1984 it was more than 50 percent lower than it had been in 1969. The improvement in the relative position of the aged poor is equally dramatic for those persons below 125 percent of the poverty level; while the percentage of those under age 65 actually increased by 24 percent between 1969 and 1984, the percentage of aged plummeted by 40 percent.

Social Security is the largest single source of income for the aged. It is particularly important for the elderly poor, as it provides them with 76 percent of their income.[33] Between 1959 and 1984, while those over 65

## TABLE 8.2
### Percent of Persons below Poverty Level and below 125 Percent of Poverty Level, by Age, 1959–84

|  | Persons below Poverty Level | | Persons below 125 Percent of Poverty Level | |
|---|---|---|---|---|
|  | Below Age 65 | Age 65 & Over | Below Age 65 | Age 65 & Over |
| 1959 | 21.2 | 35.2 | — * | — |
| 1967 | 12.6 | 29.5 | — | — |
| 1969 | 10.7 | 25.3 | 15.5 | 35.2 |
| 1970 | 13.2 | 24.6 | 16.0 | 33.9 |
| 1973 | 10.5 | 16.3 | 14.6 | 26.8 |
| 1980 | 12.7 | 15.7 | 17.2 | 25.7 |
| 1981 | 13.8 | 15.3 | 18.6 | 25.2 |
| 1984 | 14.7 | 12.4 | 19.2 | 21.2 |

*Data not available.

Source: Calculated from data in the following: U.S. Bureau of the Census, Current Population Reports, Series P-60, No. 147, Characteristics of the Population Below the Poverty Level: 1983, U.S. Government Printing Office, Washington, DC, 1985, pp. 5 and 9, for 1959 to 1983; U.S. Bureau of the Census, Current Population Reports, Series P-60, No. 149, Money Income and Poverty Status of Families and Persons in the United States: 1984, U.S. Government Printing Office, Washington, DC, 1985, pp. 21 and 24, for 1984 data.

years of age increased from about 15.5 million to 27 million, their numbers in poverty declined from 5.5 million to 3.3 million.[34] The extraordinarily large reductions in poverty among the aged was primarily a result of the expansion and indexation of Social Security, which accounted for most of the increased transfer payments by the government over the past two decades.[35]

Friedman concludes his discussion of Social Security in *Free to Choose* with the following opinion: "All in all, Social Security is an excellent example of Director's Law in operation, namely, 'Public expenditures are made for the primary benefit of the middle class, and financed with taxes which are borne in considerable part by the poor and the rich.'"[36] Thus, again we see the triumph of simplistic ideology and polemics over careful analysis.

## A "RAGBAG" OF PROGRAMS

When Friedman discusses the role of government and social programs, he presents data to indicate their substantial growth. In his attack on government programs, however, he does not limit his use of statistics to expenditures and taxation. The number of hours the total population spends in preparing personal income tax returns (300 million man hours in 1970),[37] the total number of pages in the several federal budget documents (2,089 pages),[38] and the number of inches of shelf space taken up by the Federal Register (127 inches),[39] all are grist for his ideological mill.

Friedman's passion for arcane statistics when mounting an assault on government programs disappears when he turns to a discussion of income distribution. He then presents no statistics, but instead concentrates on a philosophical and economic justification of income inequality. Although Friedman devotes much of his popular writing to income distribution issues, a reader would learn nothing of the extent of income inequality in the United States. The reader would have no idea, for example, that the share of money income of the top 20 percent of the families was 30 percent more than the share for the bottom 60 percent of families or that the income share of the top 5 percent of families was equal to that of the bottom 40 percent of families (see Table 8.3). Neither would the reader get any clear idea of the number and characteristics of those living in poverty (see Table 8.4), nor would he or she get an accurate picture of the impact of the various antipoverty programs on the

## TABLE 8.3
## Money Income of Families: Percent of Aggregate Income Received by Each Fifth, 1983

|  | *Percent of Aggregate Income* | *Upper Limit of Each Fifth* |
|---|---|---|
| Lowest fifth | 4.7 | $11,629 |
| Second fifth | 11.1 | 20,060 |
| Third fifth | 17.1 | 29,204 |
| Fourth fifth | 24.4 | 41,824 |
| Highest fifth | 42.7 | — * |
| Top 5 percent | 15.8 | — |

*Data not available.

*Source:* U.S. Department of Commerce, Bureau of the Census, *Money Income and Poverty Status of Families and Persons in the United States: 1983,* Series P-60, no. 145 (Washington, D.C.: Government Printing Office, 1984), p. 10.

extent of poverty. Instead, what he or she would find is an unqualified assault on almost all aspects of those programs.

Friedman has a long list of criticisms of welfare programs that involve a means test for the receipt of benefits.

The actual outcome of almost all programs that are sold in the name of helping the poor . . . is to make the poor worse off.[40]

The paternalistic programs weaken the family.[41]

In setting up programs such as Aid to Dependent Children and all other welfare programs we have created . . . a system that not only induces people to seek its benefits but forces them to stay on the program once they're involved.[42]

Welfare . . . discourages job seeking.[43]

The present setup has encouraged fathers, even responsible fathers, to leave their families. . . . If a deserted woman is going to be immediately eligible for welfare, the incentive for the family to stick together is not increased, to put it mildly.[44]

Medicine is the latest welfare field in which the role of the government has been exploding. . . . The inevitable result has been sharp increases in the price of medical care and in the incomes of physicians.[45]

The rapid growth of the paternal state threatens . . . national security by absorbing the taxable capacity of the nation, leaving little margin for a rapid expansion of military strength should international developments so require . . . a fact other countries cannot fail to notice.[46]

Clearly, this money is not going primarily to the poor. Some is siphoned off by administrative expenditures, supporting a massive bureaucracy at attractive pay scales.[47]

Let us look at the four largest programs directed at low-income persons: Aid to Families with Dependent Children (AFDC), Food Stamps, Medicaid, and Supplementary Security Income (SSI). Expenditures on these programs in 1983 amounted to $74 billion, or about two-thirds of the expenditures on programs aimed at persons with limited incomes.[48] We will first summarize briefly the main features of those programs and then examine them in relation to Friedman's criticisms.

Aid to Families with Dependent Children is the largest of the means-tested welfare programs. It provides cash assistance for families with dependent children and a parent who is absent, incapacitated, or, in some states, unemployed. States determine eligibility criteria and benefit levels under broad federal guidelines. Expenditures on AFDC amounted to $15.4 billion in 1983, with the cost being borne about equally between the federal and state governments. In the 3.7 million families receiving assistance under the program, there were 10.9 million individuals, of whom 7.1 million were children. The average monthly benefit was $320 per family and $109 per recipient, ranging from a low of $89 in Mississippi to a high of $516 in Alaska.[49]

The Food Stamp program is federally financed and administered by the states. Aid is based upon need, but unlike AFDC, assistance is provided without regard to other family or individual characteristics. Food coupons are dispensed by state agencies and redeemed by recipients at retail stores. The maximum monthly food stamp allotment is automatically adjusted each year for increases in food costs. Actual benefits are determined by subtracting from the maximum 30 percent of a household's countable income (gross income minus certain allowable deductions). The average monthly benefit received by 21.6 million participants in 1983 was $43, and the total federal cost $13.3 billion.[50]

Medicaid is a state-administered entitlement program. It is financed jointly by the federal and state governments and insures persons actually or potentially eligible for welfare benefits against the costs of medical and long-term care. Of the total expenditure on the program in 1983 of $35 billion, the share of the federal government was approximately $19

# TABLE 8.4
## Persons below the Poverty Level by Family Status, 1959–84

|  | Number Below Poverty Level | | | | Poverty Rate | | | |
|---|---|---|---|---|---|---|---|---|
|  | Total All Persons | In Families | Children under 18 | Unrelated Individuals | Total All Persons | In Families | Children under 18 | Unrelated Individuals |
| 1984 | 33,700 | 26,458 | 12,929 | 6,609 | 14.4 | 13.1 | 21.0 | 21.8 |
| 1983 | 35,515 | 28,025 | 13,449 | 6,861 | 15.3 | 13.9 | 21.8 | 23.5 |
| 1982 | 34,398 | 27,349 | 13,139 | 6,458 | 15.0 | 13.6 | 21.3 | 23.1 |
| 1981 | 31,822 | 24,850 | 12,068 | 6,490 | 14.0 | 12.5 | 19.5 | 23.4 |
| 1980 | 29,272 | 22,601 | 11,114 | 6,227 | 13.0 | 11.5 | 17.9 | 22.9 |
| 1979 | 26,072 | 19,964 | 9,993 | 5,743 | 11.7 | 10.2 | 16.0 | 21.9 |
| 1978 | 24,497 | 19,062 | 9,722 | 5,435 | 11.4 | 10.0 | 15.7 | 22.1 |
| 1977 | 24,720 | 19,505 | 10,028 | 5,216 | 11.6 | 10.2 | 16.0 | 22.6 |
| 1976 | 24,975 | 19,632 | 10,081 | 5,344 | 11.8 | 10.3 | 15.8 | 24.9 |
| 1975 | 25,877 | 20,789 | 10,882 | 5,088 | 12.3 | 10.9 | 16.8 | 25.1 |
| 1974 | 23,370 | 18,817 | 9,967 | 4,553 | 11.2 | 9.9 | 15.1 | 24.1 |
| 1973 | 22,973 | 18,299 | 9,453 | 4,674 | 11.1 | 9.7 | 14.2 | 25.6 |
| 1972 | 24,460 | 19,577 | 10,082 | 4,883 | 11.9 | 10.3 | 14.9 | 29.0 |
| 1971 | 25,559 | 20,405 | 10,344 | 5,154 | 12.5 | 10.8 | 15.1 | 31.6 |
| 1970 | 25,420 | 20,330 | 10,235 | 5,090 | 12.6 | 10.9 | 14.9 | 32.9 |

| 1969 | 24,147 | 19,175 | 9,501 | 4,972 | 12.1 | 10.4 | 13.8 | 34.0 |
| 1966 | 28,510 | 23,809 | 12,146 | 4,701 | 14.7 | 13.1 | 17.4 | 38.3 |
| 1965 | 33,185 | 28,358 | 14,388 | 4,827 | 17.3 | 15.8 | 20.7 | 39.8 |
| 1960 | 39,851 | 34,925 | 17,288 | 4,926 | 22.2 | 20.7 | 26.5 | 45.2 |
| 1959 | 39,490 | 34,562 | 17,208 | 4,928 | 22.4 | 20.8 | 26.9 | 46.1 |

*Source:* U.S., Department of Commerce, Bureau of the Census, *Money Income and Poverty Status of Families and Persons in the United States: 1984,* Series P-60, no. 149 (Washington, D.C.: Government Printing Office, 1985), p. 21

billion. Of the 34.4 million people below the poverty level in 1982, 12.6 million, or about 36 percent, received assistance under Medicaid.[51]

Supplementary Security Income provides cash assistance to low-income aged, blind, and disabled persons. It is a federally funded and means-tested program. Maximum benefit levels are $314 per month for single individuals and $472 for a couple, and benefits are automatically adjusted for inflation. About half the states supplement the federal program at their own expense. Total expenditures in 1983 amounted to $10.1 billion.[52]

One of the charges frequently made by Friedman is that bureaucrats lobby for welfare programs because they can then "press for better pay and perquisites for themselves — an outcome that larger programs will facilitate."[53] Some of the money intended for the poor, he states, "is siphoned off" by a "massive bureaucracy."[54] Contrary to the implication by Friedman, the administrative costs, given the size of the programs, tend to be relatively low. For AFDC, Medicaid, and SSI, they were 8 percent of total expenditures and for the Food Stamp program, 16 percent (see Table 8.5). From the viewpoint of the beneficiaries, they received as benefits about 91 percent of the total expenditures on the programs, a record that surely compares more than favorably with private philanthropic efforts.

What of Friedman's claims that AFDC and all other welfare programs not only induce people to seek the benefits and discourage job seeking but force them to stay on the program once they are involved. The best evidence on these issues is in a comprehensive study that summarizes

## TABLE 8.5
### Administrative Expenditures as a Percent of Total Expenditures in Four Major Social Programs, 1983

| Program | Percentage |
|---|---|
| Aid to Families with Dependent Children | 8 |
| Food Stamps | 16 |
| Medicaid | 8 |
| Supplementary Security Income | 8 |

*Source:* For AFDC, Food Stamps, and Medicaid, calculated from benefit and total expenditure data in U.S. Bureau of the Census, *Statistical Abstract of the United States: 1985* (105th edition), pp. 123, 357, 373, and 379, Washington, D.C., 1984. For SSI, *Budget of the United States Government, FY 1985, Appendix,* U.S. Government Printing Office, Washington, D.C., pp. I-K31 and I-K32.

over ten years of findings based on a Panel Study of Income Dynamics conducted by the Unversity of Michigan's Survey Research Center. The Panel Study collected data on family economic status through repeated annual interviews over a ten-year period with a single, continuing sample of over 5,000 U.S. families. With the data it was possible to construct a statistical picture of changing family and individual economic circumstances.[55]

The set of welfare programs in the study included AFDC, SSI, Food Stamps, and income from state-administered General Assistance payments. The data analyzed are of a national scope and cover a ten-year time span for analysis of patterns of welfare use. Table 8.6, reproduced from the study, summarizes the findings.

Between 1969 and 1978 more than one-quarter of the United States population lived in families where some form of welfare was received in at least one year. For many of those families, food stamps were the only form of welfare; if those are excluded, the fraction receiving welfare income drops from one-fourth to one-sixth.[56]

The data indicate considerable turnover in the welfare rolls. That is, contrary to Friedman's claim, most of those families getting welfare

## TABLE 8.6
## Incidence of Short- and Long-run Welfare Receipt and Dependence, 1969–78

|  | *Percent U.S. Population* | |
|---|---|---|
|  | *Receiving Any Welfare Income* | *Dependent on Welfare for More than 50% of Family Income* |
| Welfare in 1978 | 8.1 | 3.5 |
| Welfare in 1 or more years, 1969–78 | 25.2 | 8.7 |
| Welfare in 5 or more years, 1969–78 | 8.3 | 3.5 |
| Welfare in all 10 years, 1969–78 | 2.0 | 0.7 |
| Persistent welfare (welfare in 8 or more years, 1969–78) | 4.4 | 2.0 |

*Note: Welfare* is defined as AFDC, General Assistance and other welfare, Supplemental Security Income, and food stamps received by the head of household or wife. *Welfare dependence* is defined as welfare income received by the head or wife amounting to more than half of their combined incomes. Table reads, "In 1978, 8.1% of the U.S. population lived in families that received some welfare income."

*Source:* Greg J. Duncan, *Years of Poverty, Years of Plenty* (Ann Arbor: University of Michigan Press, 1984), p. 75.

benefits are not forced to stay in the program. Turnover is indicated by the fact that while more than 25 percent of the population received some welfare during the ten-year period, much smaller proportions of the population received welfare for several of the ten years. Only about 8 percent received welfare in at least five of the ten years, and only 2 percent received some for all ten years.

Furthermore, families rarely rely solely on welfare income. "Instead, welfare appears to be used to supplement income from labor market earnings and other sources or as an alternative source of income when other sources dry up."[57] As a comparison of the two columns in Table 8.6 makes clear, less than half of the welfare recipients in each category depended on welfare for more than half of their annual income. Thus, although 25 percent of the population lived in families that received some welfare income in at least one of the ten years, only 8.7 percent were dependent on it for at least one of those years. In addition, long-term dependency (that is, when families were dependent on welfare for more than 50 percent of their income) was even less frequent. Only 3.5 percent of the population was dependent on welfare income for at least five of the ten years, and only 0.7 percent was dependent for all ten years.

As Duncan observed in summarizing the findings,

> The fact that over a ten-year period the number of people who receive any welfare is considerably larger than over a one-year span indicates that the current system does not foster large-scale dependency . . . the greater share of welfare recipients clearly did not come to rely on welfare as a long-term means of support. . . . No broad demographic group in our society appears immune from shocks to their usual standard of living, shocks resulting from rapidly changing economic or personal conditions. . . . Few people are immune to occasional misfortune, and when it strikes, welfare serves as a kind of insurance for them, providing temporary assistance until they are able to regain their more customary levels of living. That the welfare system does not foster extensive dependency is also reflected in the fact that, even in the year they receive it, most welfare recipients are not *dependent* on welfare income. Since much of the other income comes from work, work and welfare appear to go together in most cases. . . . Thus *dependency* is the exception rather than the rule among welfare recipients.[58]

Charles Murray, also using the panel data of the University of Michigan's Survey Research Center, broke the data down by age groups. Focusing on women who were less than 25 years old when they first receive welfare, he found that 70 percent of these women received welfare for at least five years, and more than one-third stayed on the rolls for at least a decade. Only 3 percent received assistance for less than a year. On the other hand, he found that older women who became eligible for welfare after the break-up of a marriage, stayed on the rolls for much shorter periods. "Among women who show up on the rolls when they are 40 years or older, 50 percent are off the rolls within two years," he said (New York *Times,* September 10, 1986, p. A28).

A 1984 statistical study by the U.S. General Accounting Office (GAO) of the labor-market behavior of welfare recipients resulted in findings consistent with those of the University of Michigan's Panel Study. The GAO study was conducted in order to evaluate the impact on welfare recipients of the passage of the Omnibus Budget Reconciliation Act of 1981 (OBRA). The act made some significant changes in AFDC, particularly with respect to the working poor. Prior to the passage of OBRA, AFDC recipients with earned income could disregard the first $30 plus one-third of the rest of their monthly earnings when their benefits were calculated. Under the new rules, this may be done only for four months. In addition, work-related expenses, such as child care and transportation, may no longer be deducted (as was possible prior to OBRA) from the income that is considered in determining a family's initial eligibility for benefits. The GAO estimated that as a result of these changes, 493,000 families, including about 1 million children, were dropped from the AFDC rolls. The average monthly AFDC dollar losses for those dropped from the program were substantial, ranging from $71 to $74 in Dallas and Memphis and $156 to $198 in Boston, Milwaukee, and Syracuse. For many, the loss of AFDC benefits also meant they were dropped from the Food Stamp program and Medicaid. The loss of Medicaid meant that many found themselves without either public or private health insurance. The income from any earnings, plus AFDC and food stamp grants, was significantly lower — $115 to $229 a month lower in constant dollars across the five sites in the GAO survey.[59]

Despite these very substantial losses, the GAO found that "in general, most earners who lost AFDC benefits [and the other benefits noted] did not quit their jobs and return to the rolls. Twelve months after OBRA's implementation, only 7–18 percent of these cases were back on the AFDC rolls in our five localities."[60]

As the studies just discussed clearly indicate, the commonly held stereotype of the welfare family, long-term dependency on welfare with little commitment to the labor market and welfare "queens" driving around in Cadillacs bought with multiple relief checks, a stereotype fostered by Friedman, is a gross distortion of reality.[61]

Friedman argues that AFDC contributes to a breakdown of the nuclear family by encouraging fathers, even responsible fathers, to leave their homes. Furthermore, he states, since a deserted woman becomes immediately eligible for welfare, there is little incentive for the family to stay together. The argument he makes is based on the fact that many states do not recognize child dependency resulting from parental unemployment as grounds for AFDC benefits. In those states, an unemployed father has an incentive to desert his family to make it eligible for AFDC benefits and thereby increase its income. These views expressed by Friedman are widely held. How and why those views evolved and came to be a popular concern is described by George Steiner.

> Of all the specific criticisms leveled against the federal-state public assistance system since World War II, the most persistently voiced is the allegation that it fosters famly instability. No such allegation was heard in its earlier years ... because it seemed to fit so well the family-stabilizing model envisioned by its sponsors: permanent or long-term loss of a father by death, disability, or institutionalization leaves a mother unable to maintain a family; public support at the level suitable for her particular circumstances sustains the family.... The philosophical goal of the AFDC system was the same in 1980 as what it was when it was invented in 1935: to help the miner's widow or her industrial equivalent care for her children. Since social insurance and union pensions have taken over much of the protection of miners' orphaned children, most welfare cases now involve children outside the protection of social insurance.... Whereas public assistance once compensated for irreversible, involuntary, tragic dependency, that situation ceased to fit most of the customers by the early 1950's, when only one in five AFDC cases involved death of the father.[62]

As Table 8.7 indicates, by 1971 only 1 in 20 AFDC cases involved death of the father, and by 1982, less than 1 in 100. Overwhelmingly, and increasingly since the 1950s, the AFDC caseload consists of families headed by divorced and legally and nonlegally separated women and unwed mothers. It is this kind of data that lends support to Friedman's claim that welfare programs encourage the breakup of families. But are the conditions reflected in the caseload data a product of AFDC, or are other forces at work? Let us look at the available evidence.

In response to the change in the composition of the AFDC caseload, Congress in 1961 made available to the states an unemployed-father component of Aid to Dependent Children (AFDC-U). Since then there have been several studies of the relationship of AFDC to family stability.

## TABLE 8.7
## Aid to Families with Dependent Children: Percent Distribution of Recipients by Basis for Eligibility, 1971, 1975, and 1982

|  | 1971 | 1975 | 1982 |
|---|---|---|---|
| Father is: |  |  |  |
| Deceased | 4.3 | 3.7 | .9 |
| Incapacitated | 9.8 | 7.7 | 3.5 |
| Unemployed | 6.1 | 3.7 | 6.0 |
| Father is absent from home: | 78.9 | — * | — |
| Divorced | — | 19.4 | 20.6 [a] |
| Separated | — | 28.6 [a] | 19.0 [b] |
| Not married to mother | — | 31.0 | 46.5 |
| Other | — | 4.3 | 2.2 |
| Mother is absent, not father | — | 1.6 | 1.3 |

Data not available.
[a]Legally separated included with divorced.
[b]Nonlegally separated only.

*Source:* U.S. Bureau of the Census, *Statistical Abstract of the United States: 1985* (105th edition) Washington, DC, 1984, p. 382, for 1975 and 1982 data; for 1971 data, the 96th edition (1975) of the *Statistical Abstract of the United States,* p. 309.

A study of New York City welfare rolls found that most separated families were on the rolls before they reportedly separated, that is, the families did not break up to qualify for benefits. Furthermore, since in New York families could qualify for benefits without breaking up, other factors must have produced the high desertion rate. In another study of desertion, in 19 states with AFDC-U programs, 9 of the states had a higher percentage of AFDC cases caused by desertion after the program was in place than before AFDC-U was permissible. The percentage of cases attributable to desertion declined in the other ten states. That is, there was no consistent change in stability patterns as a result of removing the need to desert in order to qualify. In reviewing these studies, Steiner concluded, "The presumed connection between welfare rules and family instability must be viewed as not proved."[63]

Studies of the impact of AFDC on family stability were also conducted at the University of Michigan using the Panel Study data described previously. Reviewing those studies and others, Greg Duncan concluded, "Further research is clearly needed in this area, but the work thus far supports the tentative conclusion that there are no major effects of

AFDC on family composition decisions."[64] Clearly, there is much more involved in decisions concerning marriage, divorce, separation, or desertion than the simplistic economic calculus suggested by Friedman.

"The actual outcome of almost all programs that are sold in the name of helping the poor," states Friedman, "is to make the poor worse off." The Great Society programs such as President Johnson's War on Poverty, he asserts, "spent a lot of money but accomplished very little except to create employment for a lot of high priced poverty fighters."[65] Let us first look at the pattern of growth in welfare expenditures and then examine the evidence with respect to their impact on the poor.

Between 1965 and 1982, the combined sum of means-tested cash assistance and means-tested noncash benefits increased 223 percent in constant dollars, from $22.6 billion to $72.8 billion (see Table 8.8). While cash assistance rose by 50 percent, noncash benefits increased almost ninefold. As a result, noncash benefits, which were only one-third the size of cash benefits in 1965, by 1982 was the larger of the two by 80 percent. Virtually all of the total increase in means-tested benefits took place between 1969 and 1979; after 1979 the increase in noncash benefits was offset by a decline in cash assistance.

**TABLE 8.8**
**Means-tested Cash Assistance and the Market Value of Means-tested Noncash Benefits: 1965, 1970, 1975, 1979, 1980, and 1982**

(in millions of 1982 constant dollars)

| Type of Benefit | 1965 | 1970 | 1975 | 1979 | 1980 | 1982 |
|---|---|---|---|---|---|---|
| Means-tested cash assistance[a] | 17,218 | 17,719 | 32,090 | 28,594 | 27,643 | 25,907 |
| Means-tested noncash benefits | | | | | | |
| Total | 5,342 | 19,688 | 35,451 | 43,791 | 45,750 | 46,896 |
| Food stamps | 98 | 1,370 | 7,886 | 8,624 | 10,175 | 10,206 |
| School lunches | N.A. | 306 | 1,481 | 1,755 | 1,793 | 1,770 |
| Public housing | 1,074 | 4,077 | 4,059 | 5,561 | 5,275 | 5,014 |
| Medicaid | 4,170 | 13,935 | 22,045 | 27,859 | 28,507 | 29,906 |

[a]Includes AFDC, SSI, General Assistance and means-tested veterans' pensions.

*Source:* U.S., Department of Commerce, Bureau of the Census, *Estimates of Poverty Including the Value of Noncash Benefits: 1979 to 1982,* Technical Paper 51, (Washington, D.C.: Government Printing Office, 1984), p. XI.

Did the poverty programs make the poor worse off, as Friedman contends? An indicator of the extent to which market forces leave some households in poverty is the pretransfer poverty rate. If the poverty programs were making the poor worse off, we would expect the pretransfer poverty rate to vary directly with changes in the level of means-tested benefits.[66] The data indicate, however, that there is no consistent relationship between pretransfer poverty rates and means-tested benefits. Between 1965 and 1970, real means-tested benefits per household rose 50 percent with the institution of President Johnson's Great Society programs. Over the same period, the pretransfer poverty rate declined about 12 percent. From 1970 to 1975, real benefits again grew greatly (by 61 percent), but during those years the pretransfer poverty rate increased 17 percent. Between 1975 and 1980, while real benefits declined, the pretransfer poverty rate remained stable. From 1980 to 1983, while real benefits continued to decline, the pretransfer poverty rate again increased sharply (see Table 8.9).

There is, however, a much closer relationship between the pretransfer poverty rate and the unemployment rate. That is, the data are consistent with the view that the level of poverty is a function of labor demand. As Danziger and Gottschalk observed,

> As unemployment dropped between 1965 and 1969, pre-transfer poverty declined. Since then, unemployment and pre-transfer have tended upward. Throughout the 1970's, the poverty-increasing impact of rising unemployment was offset by rising transfers. When transfers stopped growing and unemployment continued to rise, the official poverty rate rose. By 1983, it reached the level of the late 1960's.[67]

With respect to Friedman's claim that the social programs make the poor worse off and his challenge to his readers "to name a government social program that has achieved the results promised,"[68] one can quote Friedman against Friedman. In the context of a discussion in which he attempts to demonstrate that unemployment-rate statistics tend to exaggerate the gravity of unemployment (see p. 130, this volume), he states, "The growth of government transfer payments in the form of unemployment insurance, food stamps, welfare, social security, and so on, *has reduced drastically the suffering associated with involuntary unemployment*" (emphasis added). When Friedman wants to attack the welfare programs, he finds they accomplish little and make the poor worse off; when he wants to demonstrate that a rise in the unemployment rate is not so serious, in a remarkable switch, he then finds that those

# TABLE 8.9
## Pre- and Posttransfer Poverty Rates, Real Means-tested Transfers per Household, and Unemployment Rates, 1965–83

|  | Pretransfer Poverty (in percent) | Official (Posttransfer) Poverty (in percent) | Real Means-tested Benefits per Household (in constant 1982 dollars) | Unemployment Rate (in percent) |
|---|---|---|---|---|
| 1965 | 21.3 | 17.3 | 393 | 4.5 |
| 1966 | — * | 15.7 | — | 3.8 |
| 1967 | 19.4 | 14.3 | — | 3.8 |
| 1968 | 18.2 | 12.8 | — | 3.6 |
| 1969 | 17.7 | 12.1 | — | 3.5 |
| 1970 | 18.8 | 12.6 | 590 | 4.9 |
| 1971 | 19.6 | 12.5 | — | 5.9 |
| 1972 | 19.2 | 11.9 | — | 5.6 |
| 1973 | 19.0 | 11.1 | — | 4.9 |
| 1974 | 20.3 | 11.2 | — | 5.6 |
| 1975 | 22.0 | 12.3 | 949 | 8.5 |
| 1976 | 21.0 | 11.8 | — | 7.7 |
| 1977 | 21.0 | 11.6 | — | 7.1 |
| 1978 | 20.2 | 11.4 | — | 6.1 |
| 1979 | 20.5 | 11.7 | 936 | 5.8 |
| 1980 | 21.9 | 13.0 | 908 | 7.1 |
| 1981 | 23.1 | 14.0 | — | 7.6 |
| 1982 | 24.0 | 15.0 | 871 | 9.7 |
| 1983 | 24.2 | 15.2 | — | 9.6 |

*Data not available.

*Note:* Benefits divided by all households, not by recipient households.

*Source:* For pre-transfer poverty, Sheldon Danziger and Peter Gottschalk, "The Poverty of Losing Ground," *Challenge,* May/June 1985, p. 34. The data were computed by the authors from March Current Population Survey data tapes. For official poverty percentages, U.S. Bureau of the Census, Current Population Reports, Series P-60, *Consumer Income.* For real means-tested benefits per household, computed from benefits shown in Table 8.7, and households from U.S. Bureau of the Census, *Statistical Abstract of the United States: 1981,* p. 42 for 1965 and 1979 data, and 1985 *Statistical Abstract,* for 1970, 1975, 1980, and 1982 data. Unemployment rates from U.S. Bureau of Labor Statistics, *Monthly Labor Review,* various issues.

same programs aimed at the poor "drastically reduce the suffering associated with involuntary unemployment."

In another peculiar twist in logic, Friedman argues that the census poverty figure is a "gross overestimate because it classifies families solely by money income, neglecting entirely any income in kind — from an owned home, a garden, *food stamps, Medicaid, public housing* (emphasis added)."[69] Inclusion of welfare benefits does drastically reduce the poverty rate, as Friedman states.

Using alternative income concepts and valuation techniques, the U.S. Bureau of the Census, in an exploratory study, estimated that if the noncash welfare benefits cited by Friedman are included as part of income, the poverty rates for 1979 and 1982 are reduced by 15.3 percent or as much as 41.9 percent, depending upon the approach used for estimating noncash benefits (see Table 8.10). But note the anomalous position in which Friedman has again placed himself. On the one hand, when denigrating the welfare programs, he asserts they make the poor worse off; on the other hand, when arguing that the census data overstate

## TABLE 8.10
## Comparison of Number of Poor and Poverty Rates Using Alternative Income Concepts and Valuation Techniques, 1982 and 1979

| Income Concept | Market Value Approach | | Cash Equivalent Value Approach | | Poverty Budget Share Value Approach | |
|---|---|---|---|---|---|---|
| | 1982 | 1979 | 1982 | 1979 | 1982 | 1979 |
| Money income alone: | | | | | | |
|   Number of poor | 34,398 | 26,072 | 34,398 | 26,072 | 34,398 | 26,072 |
|   Poverty rate (%) | 15.0 | 11.7 | 15.0 | 11.7 | 15.0 | 11.7 |
| Money income plus food, housing, and medical care[a] | | | | | | |
|   Number of poor | 22,885 | 15,099 | 29,058 | 20,152 | 28,713 | 20,184 |
|   Poverty rate (%) | 10.0 | 6.8 | 12.7 | 9.0 | 12.5 | 9.1 |
|   Percent reduction [b] | −33.3 | −41.9 | −15.3 | −23.1 | −16.7 | −22.1 |

[a]Including institutional care expenditures.

[b]Percent reduction in the poverty rate from the current poverty estimate based on money income alone.

*Source:* U.S., Department of Commerce, Bureau of the Census, *Estimates of Poverty Including the Value of Noncash Benefits: 1979 to 1982,* Technical Paper 51, (Washington, D.C.: Government Printing Office, 1984), p. XI.

the poverty rate, he points to the noncash welfare benefits received by the poor that bring literally millions of them above the government defined poverty level.

Commenting on the growth in the government's share of total health spending as a result of Medicare and Medicaid, Friedman states,

> To judge from the continuing complaints, the quality of medical care has shown no comparable rise. Higher government spending has mostly gone to raise the incomes of physicians and other health personnel, pay for the duplication of expensive equipment, and support other forms of waste.[70]

In the preface to *Free to Choose,* he quotes from his earlier book, *Capitalism and Freedom*: "In any particular case of proposed [government] intervention, we must make up a balance sheet, listing separately the advantages and disadvantages."[71] In his comments on Medicare and Medicaid, he issues a blanket indictment of the programs, ignoring his own prescription with respect to the need to weigh the advantages and disadvantages.

Medicare and Medicaid came into existence in 1965. They undoubtedly raised the incomes of physicians and other health personnel, as Friedman notes. Contrary to his assertion, however, those increased costs did much more than line the pockets of those providing medical care. The services rendered as a result of incurring those costs gave the poor and aged much greater access to needed medical care than was available to them in the past. No attempt is made by Friedman to weigh the significance of those benefits or even to consider the possibility of their existence.

By almost any measure, as Table 8.11 clearly indicates, the programs have increased the access of the poor to health care. In fiscal year 1984, of the 21.4 million persons who received health care under Medicaid, 15.4 million were in the AFDC category, of whom 9.8 million were children.[72] About 38 percent of Medicaid expenditures are for elderly people who become poor in old age. Most (75 percent) of these funds provide nursing-home care for people who were productive members of financially independent families for most of thier lives but are now 70, widowed, and unable to live alone. The blind, mentally retarded, and physically disabled receive about 27 percent of all Medicaid expenditures, including nursing-home services for those with severe disabilities and higher-than-average needs for medical care.[73]

# TABLE 8.11

## Access to Health Care by Race and Economic Status, 1964 and 1973

|  | 1964 | 1973 |
|---|---|---|
| *Short-stay hospital discharges per 100 population per year* | | |
| Total | | |
|     Poor | 13.8 | 19.0 |
|     Nonpoor | 12.6 | 12.5 |
| White | | |
|     Poor | 15.3 | 20.2 |
|     Nonpoor | 12.9 | 12.6 |
| All other | | |
|     Poor | 9.9 | 15.3 |
|     Nonpoor | 9.6 | 11.6 |
| *Percent of population with no doctor visits in past two years* | | |
| Total | | |
|     Poor | 27.7 | 17.2 |
|     Nonpoor | 17.7 | 13.4 |
| White | | |
|     Poor | 25.7 | 16.8 |
|     Nonpoor | 17.1 | 13.2 |
| All other | | |
|     Poor | 33.2 | 18.5 |
|     Nonpoor | 24.7 | 15.3 |
| *Number of doctor visits per person per year* | | |
| Total | | |
|     Poor | 4.3 | 5.6 |
|     Nonpoor | 4.6 | 4.9 |
| White | | |
|     Poor | 4.7 | 5.7 |
|     Nonpoor | 4.7 | 5.0 |
| All other | | |
|     Poor | 3.1 | 5.0 |
|     Nonpoor | 3.6 | 4.3 |
| *Number of dental visits per person per year* | | |
| Total | | |
|     Poor | 0.8 | 1.1 |
|     Nonpoor | 1.8 | 1.8 |
| White | | |
|     Poor | 0.9 | 1.2 |
|     Nonpoor | 1.8 | 1.9 |
| All other | | |
|     Poor | 0.6 | 0.7 |
|     Nonpoor | 1.2 | 1.1 |

*Source:* Ronald W. Wilson and Elijah L. White, "Changes in Morbidity, Disability, and Utilization Differentials Between the Poor and the Nonpoor; Data from the Health Interview Survey, 1964: 1964 and 1973," table reprinted in *Journal of Health Politics, Policy and Law*, Vol. 1, No. 2 (Summer 1976), p. 160.

Uwe E. Reinhardt, a prominent authority on health economics, has commented on Medicaid as follows:

> During the past two decades, there has been a notable increase in the utilization of health services by low-income groups. There has also been a dramatic increase in the health status of the poor. Surely, the Medicaid program can claim partial credit for this achievement. Furthermore, the average cost of health care per Medicaid recipient is about the same as that of roughly comparable age groups not in the program. The program does not appear to be less efficient than the private system, occasional incidents of fraud notwithstanding.[74]

Benefits under Medicare are provided as a matter of right, unlike Medicaid, which is a means-tested program. Medicare covers persons age 65 and over who receive Social Security or Railroad Retirement cash benefits. About 95 percent of all elderly are covered by the program. In 1973, Medicare coverage was extended to persons with end-stage renal disease and to persons totally disabled for two years or more. Medicare has two parts. Part A covers hospital, nursing-home, and home health services and is financed by a payroll tax on employers and employees. Coverage under Part A is extended to all eligible persons. Those covered by Part A may voluntarily enroll in Part B coverage by paying a premium. Part B is financed by those premium contributions and general revenues and covers the services of physicians. Both parts have limitations on the kinds and amounts of coverage and have deductible provisions whereby the beneficiaries pay some of the initial costs of services.[75]

There is considerable evidence that Medicare has improved the quality of life for the aged. In 1963, just before Medicare, only 56 percent of persons over 65 years of age had hospital insurance. Studies of the impact of Medicare found that it had a major impact on utilization of services, particularly with respect to those elderly traditionally identified as most in need of care — individuals living alone with low incomes, minorities, residents of the South and nonmetropolitan areas. Cataract operations doubled in the first ten years of the program and arthroplasty tripled, surgical procedures of considerable benefit to the quality of life of the aged.[76] After the enactment of Medicare, between 1968 and 1977, death rates for the elderly took a pronounced downward turn, a decline much more dramatic than those that occurred in Canada and Europe over the same period.[77]

Professor Karen Davis of Johns Hopkins University's School of Hygiene and Health made the following assessment of Medicare's accomplishments:

> In the last fifteen years, Medicare has established itself as a highly successful program. It has been run well for the most part, has filled a gap in private health insurance coverage existing prior to the program, and has achieved its goals of ensuring access to health care services and reducing the severe financial burden of health care bills for the elderly. Death rates of the elderly have plummeted, and the health of the elderly has improved markedly since it began.[78]

Both Medicare and Medicaid have some serious problems, particularly with respect to controlling costs and the continued lack of adequate medical care for many poor. But to damn those programs with simplistic polemics without considering their substantial benefits is intellectually and socially irresponsible.

## THE NEGATIVE INCOME TAX ALTERNATIVE

Friedman has recommended a drastic transformation of the present welfare system. While living up to present obligations, he would gradually wind down the Social Security system and ultimately eliminate it along with the "ragbag" of other welfare programs. He would replace the entire welfare system with a single program — the negative income tax (NIT). A number of noted liberal economists have followed Friedman's lead in recommending NIT, but not necessarily as a substitute for all welfare programs as he suggests.

Let us look at a simple example that will illustrate the basic principles underlying NIT. A family of four might, for example, receive a basic allowance of $4,000. In addition, the family would pay a tax on each dollar of income earned. Table 8.12 shows how the system would work. The family of four with no income would qualify for a basic allowance (subsidy) of $4,000 and not pay any taxes. Assuming an income tax rate of 50 percent, with an income of $2,000, the family would pay $1,000 in taxes, which, with the basic allowance, would leave it with a disposable income of $5,000. If the family had an income of $8,000, it would break even since the tax of $4,000 would equal the basic allowance, and its disposable income would be $8,000. The subsidy, in effect, would be

**TABLE 8.12**
**The Negative Income Tax**
**(in U.S. dollars)**

| Income before Basic Allowance and Tax | Basic Allowance | Tax (50% Income) | Income After Allowance and Tax |
|---|---|---|---|
| 0 | 4,000 | 0 | 4,000 |
| 2,000 | 4,000 | 1,000 | 5,000 |
| 4,000 | 4,000 | 2,000 | 6,000 |
| 6,000 | 4,000 | 3,000 | 7,000 |
| 8,000 | 4,000 | 4,000 | 8,000 |

*Source:* Constructed by the author.

zero. As earnings rose above $8,000, the family would start paying taxes.

Friedman argues that NIT would

> end the present division of the nation into two classes, reduce both government spending and the massive bureaucracy, and at the same time assume a safety net for everyone in the country, so that no one need suffer dire distress. . . . It gives help in the form most useful to the recipient, namely cash. . . . It makes explicit the tax borne by taxpayers. . . . Like any other measure to alleviate poverty, it reduces the incentive of people who are helped to help themselves. However, if the subsidy is kept at a reasonable level, it does not eliminate the incentive entirely. An extra dollar earned always means more money available for spending.[79]

A negative income tax could be a good substitute for some of the nation's welfare programs, but even if it were politically acceptable, there are needs for which it would be inadequate, like nursing-home care for the aged, the special costs of the disabled, and unusual and high medical costs for those of any age.

Two difficult but fundamental questions must be dealt with in establishing NIT: (1) at what level should the basic allowance be set and (2) how high should the tax rate be? A low basic allowance may provide inadequate support, while a high allowance will add to costs and may lessen incentives. High tax rates will also lessen incentives, but low tax rates will increase costs by raising the break-even point. For example, if the tax in Table 8.12 were lowered to 25 percent, the break-even point would rise from $8,000 of earned income to $16,000, dramatically increasing the number of families subsidized.

How much income support would a Friedman-constructed negative income tax provide? Probably considerably less than most people receive under existing programs. In an interview in which he discussed NIT, he said, "Let me stress one thing. If we were starting with a clean slate — if we had no government welfare programs, no Social Security, etc. — I'm not sure I would be in favor of a negative income tax. But unfortunately, we don't have a *tabula rasa*."[80] Clearly, Friedman would prefer to rely on private charity to assist the poor. In that same interview, Friedman comments, "Everyone does take the line that laissez-faire is heartless. But when do you suppose we had the highest level of private charitable activity in this country? In the nineteenth century. . . . Obviously, it bothers me, as it bothers anyone else, to see people destitute, whether through their own fault or not. That's why I'm strongly in favor of charitable activities."[81]

## NOTES

1.   *Newsweek,* October 25, 1982, p. 111.

2.   Milton Friedman and Rose Friedman, *Free to Choose* (New York: Avon, 1981), p. 98.

3.   U.S., Department of Commerce, Bureau of the Census, *Statistical Abstract of the United States, 1985,* 105th ed. (Washington, D.C.: Government Printing Office, 1985), p. 365.

4.   *Newsweek,* April 3, 1967, p. 81; June 14, 1971, p. 88; Wilbur J. Cohen and Milton Friedman, *Social Security: Universal or Selective* (Washington, D.C.: American Enterprise Institute for Public Policy Research, 1972), pp. 93–98.

5.   Friedman and Friedman, *Free to Choose,* pp. 94–95.

6.   Ibid., p. 93.

7.   U.S., Department of Commerce, *Statistical Abstract, 1985,* p. 363.

8.   Bruno Stein, *Social Security and Pensions in Transition* (New York: Free Press, 1983), pp. 191–92.

9.   Friedman and Friedman, *Free to Choose,* p. 93.

10.   Ibid., pp. 96–97.

11.   Stein, *Social Security,* p. 204.

12.   Ibid.

13.   Ibid.

14.   Friedman and Friedman, *Free to Choose,* pp. 95, 97.

15.   Kenneth Arrow, "Book Review," *New Republic,* 186 (March 22, 1980), p. 27.

16.   Friedman and Friedman, *Free to Choose,* p. 97.

17.   *Newsweek,* October 8, 1973, p. 90.

18.   Robert B. Avery, et al., "Survey of Consumer Finances, 1983," *Federal Reserve Bulletin* (1984): 685–87. Total financial assets include checking accounts,

savings accounts, money market accounts, certificates of deposits, IRA Keogh accounts, savings bonds, stocks, other bonds, nontaxable holdings (municipal bonds and shares in certain mutual funds), and trusts.

19.   Friedman and Friedman, *Free to Choose*, p. 99.

20.   Ibid.

21.   *Newsweek*, October 8, 1973, p. 90.

22.   Cohen and Friedman, *Social Security*, pp. 94, 95.

23.   *The Gallup Report*, Report No. 208, February 1983, p. 20.

24.   Friedman states that Social Security "is a sacred cow that no politician can question — as Barry Goldwater discovered in 1964." Friedman and Friedman, *Free to Choose*, p. 93.

25.   Cohen and Friedman, *Social Security*, p. 22.

26.   Ibid., p. 76.

27.   Ibid., pp. 76–77.

28.   Milton Friedman, *Bright Promises, Dismal Performance: An Economist's Protest*, ed. William R. Allen (New York: Harcourt, Brace, Jovanovich, 1983), p. 33.

29.   Friedman and Friedman, *Free to Choose*, pp. 97–98.

30.   Joseph A. Pechman, *Federal Tax Policy* (Washington, D.C.: Brookings Institution, 1983), p. 213.

31.   Henry J. Aaron, *Economic Effects of Social Security* (Washington, D.C.: Brookings Institution, 1982), p. 80.

32.   U.S., Department of Commerce, *Statistical Abstract, 1985*, pp. 429, 454.

33.   Aaron, *Economic Effects*, p. 70.

34.   U.S., Department of Commerce, Bureau of the Census, *Money Income and Poverty Status of Families in the United States, 1984*, Series P-60, no. 149 (Washington, D.C.: Government Printing Office, 1985), p. 21.

35.   Sheldon Danziger and Peter Gottschalk, "The Poverty of Losing Ground," *Challenge* 28 (1985): 35.

36.   Friedman and Friedman, *Free to Choose*, p. 98.

37.   Milton Friedman and Rose Friedman, *Tyranny of the Status Quo* (New York: Harcourt, Brace, Jovanovich, 1984), pp. 13, 14.

38.   Ibid., pp. 19, 20.

39.   Friedman and Friedman, *Free to Choose*, p. 181.

40.   Friedman, *Bright Promises*, p. 19.

41.   Friedman and Friedman, *Free to Choose*, p. 118.

42.   Friedman, *Bright Promises*, p. 44.

43.   Ibid., p. 45.

44.   Ibid.

45.   Friedman and Friedman, *Free to Choose*, p. 103.

46.   *Newsweek*, January 22, 1979, p. 39.

47.   Friedman and Friedman, *Free to Choose*, p. 99.

48.   U.S., Department of Commerce, *Statistical Abstract, 1985*, p. 357.

49.   Ibid., pp. 357, 379, 381; John L. Palmer and Isabel V. Sawhill, *The Reagan Record* (Cambridge, Mass.: Ballinger, 1984), p. 363.

50.   U.S., Department of Commerce, *Statistical Abstract, 1985*, pp. 123, 357; Palmer and Sawhill, *The Reagan Record*, p. 367.

51.  U.S., Department of Commerce, *Statistical Abstract, 1985*, pp. 100, 357.

52.  Ibid., p. 357; Palmer and Sawhill, *The Reagan Record*, p. 378.

53.  Friedman and Friedman, *Free to Choose*, p. 108.

54.  Ibid., p. 99. See also pp. 87, 88, 109, 233.

55.  Greg J. Duncan, *Years of Poverty, Years of Plenty* (Ann Arbor: University of Michigan Press, 1984), pp. 1, 2.

56.  Ibid., pp. 75, 76.

57.  Ibid., p. 76.

58.  Ibid., p. 90.

59.  U.S., Congress, House, *GAO Analysis of the 1981 AFDC Reductions,* Hearing before the Subcommittee on Public Assistance and Unemployment Compensator, 98th Cong. 2d sess. (Washington, D.C.: Government Printing Office, 1985), pp. 8–11, 20.

60.  Ibid., p. 10.

61.  Friedman and Friedman, *Free to Choose*, p. 98.

62.  George Steiner, *The Futility of Family Policy* (Washington, D.C.: Brookings Institution, 1981), pp. 96, 97.

63.  Ibid., pp. 103, 104.

64.  Duncan, *Years of Poverty*, p. 84.

65.  Friedman, *Bright Promises*, pp. 19, 20.

66.  Danziger and Gottschalk, "The Poverty of Losing Ground," pp. 33, 34.

67.  Ibid., p. 34.

68.  *Newsweek*, October 5, 1982, p. 111.

69.  Friedman and Friedman, *Free to Choose*, p. 99.

70.  *Newsweek*, April 21, 1975, p. 84; Friedman and Friedman, *Free to Choose,* pp. 87, 103.

71.  Friedman and Friedman, *Free to Choose*, p. ix.

72.  U.S., Department of Health and Human Services, Health Care Financing Administration, *Health Care Financing Review, 1985 Annual Supplement* (Baltimore: Office of Research and Demonstrations, December, 1985), p. 25.

73.  David E. Rogers, "Providing Medicine to the Elderly and Poor: A Serious Problem for the Downsizing 1980s," in *Health Care for the Poor and Elderly: Meeting the Challenge*, ed. Duncan Yaggy (Durham, N.C.: Duke University Press, 1984), p. 6.

74.  U.S., Department of Health and Human Services, *Health Care Financing Review*, p. 107.

75.  Karen Davis, "Medicine Reconsidered," in *Health Care for the Poor and Elderly: Meeting the Challenge,* ed. Duncan Yaggy (Durham, N.C.: Duke University Press, 1984), pp. 77, 78.

76.  Ibid., p. 83.

77.  Ibid.

78.  Ibid., p. 93.

79.  Friedman and Friedman, *Free to Choose*, pp. 110–13.

80.  Friedman, *Bright Promises*, p. 43.

81.  Ibid., pp. 19, 43.

# 9

# FRIEDMAN, REAGAN, AND REALITY

We have already seen the striking similarity in free-market ideology and rhetoric between the popular writings of Friedman and the statements by President Reagan in his first (1982) *Economic Report* (see Chapter 1). His 1986 *Economic Report* reiterated those principles:

> The Federal government cannot provide prosperity or generate economic growth; it can only encourage private initiative, innovation, and entrepreneurial activity that produce economic opportunities. An overly active government hinders economic progress. The Federal government has several definite responsibilities. . . . The first is provide an adequate national defense. . . . Furthermore, we will . . . provide an appropriate safety net to aid those individuals who need help. Finally, even though we believe that markets generally allocate resources most efficiently, there are a few special cases, such as air and water pollution, in which the market mechanism alone may be inadequate. In these instances, government intervention is necessary, but it should be based on market principles.[1]

How closely have the president's policy proposals conformed to his and Friedman's ideology? How successful has the president been in achieving goals consistent with that ideology? Are the president's stated goals his real goals? More specifically, what has happened under President Reagan with respect to such issues of concern to both the president and Friedman as taxation, defense, social programs, government deficits, the federal bureaucracy, free trade, Social Security, and the balanced budget? Let us look at the Reagan record.

In March 1981, President Reagan proposed a budget and economic program based on the following five principles:

172

First, we must cut the growth of Government spending. Second, we must cut tax rates so that once again work will be rewarded and saving encouraged. Third, we must carefully remove the tentacles of excessive government regulation which are strangling our economy. Fourth, while recognizing the independence of the institution, we must work with the Federal Reserve Board to develop a monetary policy that will rationally control the money supply. Fifth, we must move, surely and predictably, toward a balanced budget.[2]

All five of these principles are clearly in harmony with Friedman's ideological framework.

As a result of being largely successful in getting Congress to accept his spending and tax program in 1981, President Reagan was euphoric in his first State of the Union Address to a joint session of Congress in January 1982:

The record is clear, and I believe history will remember this as an era of American renewal; remember this administration as an administration of change, and remember this Congress as a Congress of destiny. Together, we not only cut the increase in Government spending nearly in half, we brought about the largest tax reductions and the most sweeping changes in our tax structure since the beginning of this century. . . . Together, after 50 years of taking power away from the hands of people in their States and local communities, we have started returning power and resources to them. . . . Together, we have cut the growth of new Federal regulations nearly in half. . . . Together, we have created an effective strike force to combat waste and fraud in government. . . . Together, we have begun to mobilize the private sector . . . to bring thousands of Americans into a volunteer effort to help solve many of America's social problems. . . . Together, we have begun to restore that margin of military safety that insures peace. . . . Together, we have made a New Beginning, but we have only begun.[3]

In that same address, he cited some $44 billion in cuts already obtained in social programs and announced that he would propose additional savings in entitlement programs of $63 billion over the next four years. He also attacked what he referred to as a jungle of federal categorical grants, including programs for social services, education, and pollution control. Characterizing them as wasteful and inefficient, he proposed to solve the problem with a "single broad stroke" that would "return some $47 billion in Federal grants-in-aid programs to state and local governments, along with the means to finance them." He said he would continue in his efforts to reduce the number of employees in the federal work force by 75,000. The president expressed his confidence that "the economic programs we have put into operation will protect the needy while it triggers a recovery that will benefit all Americans."[4] President Reagan's euphoria was justified; Congress had given him much of what he had asked for in taxation, defense spending, and deep cuts in the social programs. Let us examine the president's principal achievements and how they relate to Friedman's views.

## TAXATION

Personal income tax rates were cut 5, 10, and 10 percent, or 15 percent over a three-year period, and the top bracket was slashed from 70 percent to 50 percent. Business taxes were reduced substantially in 1981 through accelerated depreciation and increases in the investment tax credit. However, in response to the fears of large projected deficits, about half the 1981 business tax reductions were eliminated in 1982. Nevertheless, the net effect, despite the partial reversal, added significantly to corporate cash flow. Additional tax changes included lowering the maximum rate on long-term capital gains from 28 to 20 percent, increasing the exemptions from estate and gift taxes from $175,000 to $600,000, and lowering the maximum tax rate from 70 to 50 percent.[5]

The reduction in personal and corporate tax rates was the heart and soul of "supply-side" economics. It was that view of how the world works that was most novel in what came to be known as Reaganomics during the first couple of years of the Reagan administration.

When Reagan, during the 1980 presidential campaign, promised to increase defense spending, cut taxes, and balance the budget all at the same time, he was repeatedly taunted by presidential candidates John Anderson and George Bush with the question, "How could this all be achieved simultaneously?"[6] Unanswered during the campaign, supply-side theory provided the answer after President Reagan assumed office.

The supply-side answer was marvelously simple. A dramatic reduction in personal and business tax rates and deregulation would awaken the sleeping giant of U.S. capitalism and painlessly free it from the twin aggravations of high inflation and stagnant growth. A centerpiece of the theory was the so-called Laffer Curve (see Figure 9.1).

If tax rates are zero, obviously there will be no government revenue. At a tax rate of 100 percent, revenues will again be zero, as no one will have the incentive to work. Somewhere in between, revenues will reach a maximum. If the rates are at A, reducing them to B will actually increase

**FIGURE 9.1**
**The Laffer Curve**

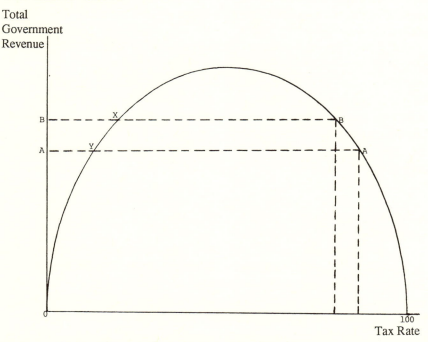

revenue. How will such a miraculous development be achieved? With lower tax rates, workers will have the incentive to work more since they will be left with greater income. People will save more out of their higher income, and the saving would be made available to investors, who in turn will have the incentive because of lower tax rates to buy more machinery and equipment and produce more. Because of greater output, inflation will be cured. And, for the pièce de résistance, the federal budget will be balanced as the greatly increased growth in output and income will generate much greater revenue for the government, even with lower tax rates.

But what if the rates were at X? Lowering the rates to Y would then reduce federal revenue and increase the deficits. Where was the U.S. economy on the curve? No one really knew. In fact, no one had any idea of the shape of the curve. The supply-siders simply assumed the U.S. economy was at a position similar to A, as did President Reagan. As late as 1984, in the debates with Mondale, despite having accumulated massive deficits in 1983 and 1984, he still talked of eliminating the deficits by economic growth.

Few economists swallowed the supply-side mythology. Neither did Milton Friedman. Commenting on the tax cut argument made by the supply-siders, he wrote,

> An across-the-board cut such as they propose would, as they recognize, be unlikely to generate enough extra revenue from this source alone to compensate for the reduction in revenue from lower rates on currently taxed income. They count on a different free lunch — a large tax base from the higher output stimulated by lower tax rates. Here, however, argument falters . . . without a simultaneous reduction in government spending, the deficit would, at least initially go up.[7]

Nevertheless, Friedman supported the tax cuts. We'll discuss why later.

## DEFENSE

Expenditures on defense increased enormously, from $158 billion in 1981 to $253 billion in 1985, an increase of 60 percent as compared with a 40 percent growth in total federal expenditures. As a result, outlays on defense as a share of total federal expenditures rose from 23 to 27 percent.

The Reagan budget for research and development (R & D) programs tells us a great deal about the president's priorities. For fiscal year 1987, the president is asking for authority to spend $41.8 billion on R & D for defense, 68 percent of the R & D budget. If the National Aeronautics and Space Administration (NASA) proposal and the $2 billion of R & D for nuclear weapons research in the Energy Department are added to the defense figure, then expenditures for the military make up 79 percent of the budget proposal for R & D, eight times more than the proposal for Health and Human Services. Almost 100 percent of the $11 billion increase in R & D between the amount authorized in 1985 and the amount proposed in 1987 is scheduled for the military (see Table 9.1).

For Friedman, defense is one of the few legitimate activities of government. The little that Friedman has written on defense and foreign policy clearly indicates that he would support the Reagan military posture. As we noted previously, although there are 55 page references to the bureaucracy in *Free to Choose,* with all the references dealing with social or regulatory activities of the government, there is not a single reference to the largest bureaucracy of all, the immense civilian

**TABLE 9.1**
**Research and Development by Major Agencies**
**(in millions of U.S. dollars)**

| | Budget Authority | | |
| --- | --- | --- | --- |
| | 1985 | 1986 | 1987 |
| Department or Agency | Actual | Estimate | Estimate |
| Defense-military function | 31,099 | 33,485 | 41,823 |
| Health and Human Services | 5,444 | 5,524 | 5,471 |
|    National Institutes of Health[a] | (4,824) | (4,905) | (4,672) |
| Energy | 4,901 | 4,785 | 4,886 |
| National Aeronautics and Space Administration | 3,235 | 3,594 | 4,051 |
| National Science Foundation | 1,346 | 1,334 | 1,508 |
| Agriculture | 941 | 922 | 907 |
| Transportation | 430 | 364 | 277 |
| Interior | 389 | 381 | 345 |
| Environmental Protection Agency | 320 | 334 | 310 |
| Commerce | 399 | 380 | 297 |
| Agency for International Development | 210 | 206 | 203 |
| Veterans Administration | 227 | 186 | 194 |
| All other [b] | 550 | 531 | 531 |
| Total | 49,491 | 52,024 | 60,803 |

[a]These are part of Health and Human Services. Their funding is included in the HHS totals.

[b]Includes the Departments of Education, Justice, Labor, Housing and Urban Development and Treasury, the Tennessee Valley Authority, the Smithsonian Institution, the Army Corps of Engineers, the Nuclear Regulatory Commission, and the Federal Emergency Management Agency.

*Source: Weekly Report* (Washington, D.C.: Congressional Quarterly Inc.) 44, February 8, 1986, p. 244.

bureaucracy in the Defense Department (see page 121, this volume). In his *Tyranny of the Status Quo,* in a chapter entitled "Defense," the main thrust and thesis of the chapter is an attack on the welfare state (see page 123 of this volume).

Several columns he devoted to South Africa and Zimbabwe (then Rhodesia) in 1976 and 1977 are indicative of his general outlook. After discussing some of the deplorable conditions for blacks in South Africa, he writes,

In the absence of a threat from the outside, there would be no immediate crisis. There is vigorous discussion of alternative policies within the white community, there are many responsible leaders in the black community, and there is some, though clearly inadequate, communications between the whites and blacks. But of course there is a threat from the outside, which brings me to my second topic — our national interest. . . . South Africa and the Soviet Union are the major sources of a number of critical minerals. [He then goes on to mention platinum, vanadium, chromium, asbestos, uranium, and fluorspar.] The stakes are high. Little wonder that the Soviet Union is making every effort to stir the pot of race discord in southern Africa. . . . For us, South Africa and Rhodesia are natural allies. . . . Their economic system is, like ours, organized on the basis of private enterprise though with much government intervention [see his relationship with Pinochet's Chile, Chapter 5]. . . . We are no match for the Soviet Union in deviousness and ruthlessness. . . . Have we learned nothing from either Vietnam or Angola?[8]

Friedman's columns were written shortly after he had visited South Africa. Less than a month after writing the words just quoted, there was a demonstration by 15,000 high school students in Soweto protesting a recent order by the education authorities that arithmetic and social studies be taught in Afrikaans. They were confronted by a police detachment that, when tear gas failed to disperse the students, fired into the crowd, killing two and injuring several others. Demonstrations continued throughout the summer months. By the time the Soweto uprising subsided, it left in its wake 575 dead and 2,389 wounded, according to "the highly conservative official estimates."[9] Our "natural" ally, with which we share a "common culture," according to Friedman, was again victorious.

In a year after the Soweto slaughter of school children, Friedman wrote that he had a "nightmare vision." Was it a vision born of compassion for children? No! Friedman wrote,

History is full of surprises and every now and then I have the nightmare vision of a modern Nazi-Soviet pact — an entente between the Soviet Union and the present government of South Africa, possibly including Rhodesia as well. . . . To white South Africa . . . an entente with Russia could enhance the return from its mineral resources, assure protection against the United Nations sanctions, and most important of all, enable the whites to preserve their separate way of life against effective attack, internal or external. . . . I am by no means predicting a Boer-Soviet pact. But can we afford to neglect this possibility completely?[10]

Again, there seems little doubt that Friedman would be supportive of President Reagan's defense buildup.

## SOCIAL PROGRAMS

Table 9.2 presents the impact, by fiscal year 1985, of the spending cuts achieved by President Reagan relative to the spending levels that would have prevailed had the policies inherited by the president been continued. The "pre-Reagan policy baseline" in the table is a projection of the spending that would have occurred in fiscal year 1985 under the policies in effect when President Reagan came into office. The "enacted changes" show the combined effect on spending, relative to the baseline projections, of the Reagan proposals and congressional action.

Bawden and Palmer, of the highly respected Urban Institute, summarized the president's achievements with respect to social spending as follows:

> Congress granted the President (in the Omnibus Budget Reconciliation Act of 1981) most of the social spending cuts he requested in his FY 1982 budget. Except for action on Social Security, however, few further cuts were taken in the FY 1983 and 1984 budgets. As a result, the enacted reductions by FY 1985 will total a little under 10 percent from prior policy levels — about half what the President requested. The pattern of reductions across the broad types of programs is similar to what he sought, with the greatest relative reductions by far in the discretionary grant programs, and the smallest in the social insurance programs. Purely in terms of his aims, however, the President was least successful in cutting the programs providing benefit payments to low-income individuals, ending up with less than one-third of the reduction he sought (in contrast to more than half and nearly three-quarters of what he sought in the social insurance and discretionary grant programs, respectively). Despite his FY 1983 and 1984 budget proposal for additional deep cuts in the lower tier of the social safety net, these programs were left entirely alone, as a consensus seemed to emerge in Congress and the country that the 1982 budgetary actions went as far as was warranted in reducing aid to the poor.[11]

Commenting on the Reagan record, Friedman observed that "President Reagan had remarkable initial success in persuading Congress to adopt his proposals for taxes and spending, even if somewhat revised form." However, contrary to the list of reductions in Table 9.2 and the comments by Bawden and Palmer, Friedman claims welfare for the poor has not been cut. He argues that a "fascinating aspect" of the reductions is that they do not include welfare programs for the poor, that they do not include

> Aid to Families with Dependent Children, *not* SSI (Supplementary Security Income), *not* food stamps, *not* housing subsidies, *not* Medicaid, *not* social

**TABLE 9.2**

**Estimated Outlay Changes in FY 1985 Resulting from Reagan Administration Proposals and Congressional Actions through FY 1984**

| | Projected Outlays under Pre-Reagan Policy Baseline (in billions of U.S. dollars) | Enacted Changes (percentage of baseline) |
|---|---|---|
| Retirement and disability | | |
|   Social Security | 200.6 | −4.6 |
|   Veterans' Compensation | 10.7 | −.9 |
|   Veterans' Pensions | 3.8 | −2.6 |
|   Supplemental Security Income (SSI) | 8.1 | +8.6 |
| Other income security | | |
|   Unemployment Insurance | 29.8 | −17.4 |
|   Aid to Families with Dependent Children (AFDC) | 9.8 | −14.3 |
|   Food Stamps | 14.5 | −13.8 |
|   Child Nutrition | 5.0 | −28.0 |
|   Women, Infants, and Children (WIC) | 1.1 | +9.1 |
|   Housing Assistance | 12.3 | −11.4 |
|   Low-Income Energy Assistance | 2.4 | −8.3 |
| Health | | |
|   Medicare | 80.4 | −6.8 |
|   Medicaid | 24.9 | −2.8 |
|   Other health services | 1.8 | −33.3 |
| Education and social services | | |
|   Compensatory Education | 4.1 | −19.5 |
|   Head Start | 1.0 | [a] |
|   Vocational Education | .8 | −12.5 |
|   Guaranteed Student Loans | 4.1 | −39.0 |
|   Other Student Financial Assistance | 4.5 | −15.6 |
|   Veterans' Readjustment Benefits | 1.1 | −9.1 |
|   Social Services Block Grant | 3.4 | −23.5 |
|   Community Services Block Grant | .7 | −37.1 |
| Employment and training | | |
|   General Employment and Training | 5.7 | −38.6 |
|   Public Service Employment | 4.8 | −100.0 |
|   Job Corps | .7 | −7.7 |
|   Work Incentive Program | .5 | −35.1 |
|     Total | 436.6 | −8.8 |

[a]Total reductions amount to less than $50 million.

*Source:* D. Lee Bawden and John L. Palmer, "Social Policy," in *The Reagan Record,* ed. John L. Palmer and Isabel V. Sawhill (Cambridge, Mass.: Ballinger, 1984), pp. 185, 186.

services. Some of these items went down, some went up, but both the increases and decreases were slight. Taken as a whole, the best description is that *welfare programs for the poor were held constant as a fraction of income*. These facts paint a very different picture from that drawn by either President Reagan's supporters or his opponents. Welfare for the poor has not been cut. To that extent, the charge that President Reagan has destroyed the safety net for the poor is not correct.[12]

When Friedman claims that some of the programs for the poor have increased and some have decreased and that, taken as a whole, "welfare for the poor has not been cut," he is hiding the truth by playing with statistics. That "welfare programs for the poor were held constant as a fraction of income" does not indicate that the programs were not cut. They were cut, and cut substantially, as Table 9.2 indicates. Despite the reductions, the actual expenditures held constant as a fraction of income because of the deep recession of 1982 and 1983 and the automatic rise in spending on entitlement programs for the poor in response to higher unemployment and lower incomes. Unemployment during each of those years averaged 9.5 percent, the highest levels since the depression of the 1930s; in 1982 and 1983 there were 5 and 6 million more persons living in poverty than in 1980. Had the entitlement programs for the poor not been cut, expenditures would have been significantly higher. That Friedman is aware that a depressed economy will increase expenditures for many entitlement programs is evident from the fact that only two pages prior to the above quotation he notes that "the long and sharp recession increased both unemployment compensation and subsidies to agriculture . . . consistently and markedly from 1980 to 1983."[13]

The combined effects of the Reagan tax and benefit changes increased the inequality in the distribution of income. On the tax side, the equal percentage reduction in tax rates was much more beneficial for the rich than for the poor, since personal income taxes are a higher proportion of the income of rich families than it is of poor families. The reductions in cash and in-kind benefits, as estimated by the Congressional Budget Office, lowered the incomes of households with less than $10,000 of income by 7.5 percent, of those between $10,000 and $20,000 by 1.6 percent, of those between $20,000 and $40,000 by 0.4 percent, of those between $40,000 and $80,000 by 0.2 percent, and for those above $80,000 by less than 0.1 percent.[14] The combined effects of the tax and benefit changes in dollars are shown in Table 9.3.

Moon and Sawhill, of the Urban Institute, also estimated the contribution of the Reagan policies to changes in the distribution of

**TABLE 9.3**
**Effects on 1984 Household Incomes of Tax and Benefit
Changes in 1981–83**

| Household Income (1982 U.S. dollars) | Tax Reduction | Benefit Reductions (dollars per household) | Total Change |
|---|---|---|---|
| Less than 10,000 | 20 | –410 | –390 |
| 10,000–20,000 | 330 | –300 | 30 |
| 20,000–40,000 | 1,200 | –190 | 1,010 |
| 40,000–80,000 | 3,080 | –170 | 2,910 |
| 80,000 and over | 8,390 | –130 | 8,260 |

*Source:* Congressional Budget Office, "The Combined Effects of Major Changes in Federal Tax and Spending Programs Since 1981," Staff Memorandum, April 1984, in U.S., Congress, House, Committee on the Budget, *A Review of President Reagan's Budget,* Congressional Budget Office Staff Memorandum, 98th Cong. 2d sess. (Washington, D.C.: Government Printing Office, 1984), p. 40.

income (see Table 9.4). These estimates did not measure the effects of every policy change. For example, they did not measure changes in unemployment benefits, health care, and stricter review of disability benefits. They concluded that

> a fuller accounting of changes in family economic welfare would show that over the 1980–1984 period, Reagan policies have increased the degree of inequality in family economic well-being — broadly defined to include services as well as money incomes — by more than we have been able to capture.[15]

## BIG GOVERNMENT, DEFICITS, AND THE FEDERAL BUREAUCRACY

Although the president was successful in reducing expenditures on many social programs, government expenditures, deficits, and the federal bureaucracy all continued to grow. The initial Reagan budget proposals combined with a slower growth in the money supply and reduced regulations were supposed to promote a buoyant economy and a balanced budget by 1984. Instead, under his administration, the nation has seen unprecedented peacetime deficits (see Table 9.5), resulting in a $2 trillion national debt, a debt twice the size of that when he took office.

## TABLE 9.4
## Contribution of Reagan Policies to Changes in the Distribution of Real Disposable Family Income, 1980–84 (in millions of 1982 U.S. dollars)

| | | Quintile | | |
|---|---|---|---|---|
| Bottom | Second | Third | Fourth | Top |
| −4.1 | −3.0 | −1.7 | −0.6 | 1.6 |

Source: Marilyn Moon and Isabel V. Sawhill, "Family Income, Gainers and Losers," in *The Reagan Record,* ed. John L. Palmer and Isabel V. Sawhill (Cambridge, Mass.: Ballinger, 1984), p. 329.

## TABLE 9.5
## Federal Receipts and Expenditures, 1981–85

| | Receipts | Expenditures | Deficits | Receipts as percent of GNP | Expenditures as percent of GNP |
|---|---|---|---|---|---|
| 1981 | 639.5 | 703.3 | 63.8 | 20.9 | 23.0 |
| 1982 | 635.3 | 781.2 | 149.9 | 20.1 | 24.7 |
| 1983 | 658.1 | 837.5 | 179.4 | 19.3 | 24.6 |
| 1984 | 725.1 | 898.0 | 172.9 | 19.2 | 23.7 |
| 1985[a] | 785.7 | 983.0 | 197.3 | 19.7 | 24.7 |

[a]Preliminary.

Source: *Economic Report of the President, February 1986* (Washington, D.C.: Government Printing Office, 1986), pp. 252, 343.

Friedman and Reagan called for reduced government expenditures. The president in 1981 proposed to reduce federal outlays to 19.4 percent of gross national product (GNP) by 1985 from the pre-Reagan 1981 level of 23 percent.[16] Rather than declining, federal expenditures rose about 40 percent, so that by 1985 they were about 25 percent of the GNP (see Table 9.5). Three components accounted for more than three-fourths of the increase in outlays: national defense, 36 percent of the increase; net interest, 23 percent; and Social Security, 18 percent (see Table 9.6).

Both Friedman and Reagan have been sharp critics of the federal bureaucracy. In his 1984 *Economic Report,* President Reagan proudly announced,

## TABLE 9.6
## Federal Expenditures, Fiscal Years 1981 and 1985
### (in millions of dollars)

|  | 1981 | 1985 | Percent Increase |
|---|---|---|---|
| Total outlays | 678,209 | 946,323 | 39.5 |
| National defense | 157,513 | 252,748 | 60.5 |
| International affairs | 13,104 | 16,176 | 23.4 |
| General science, space | 6,469 | 8,627 | 33.3 |
| Net interest | 68,734 | 129,436 | 88.3 |
| Social Security | 139,584 | 188,623 | 35.1 |
| Medicare | 39,149 | 65,822 | 68.1 |
| Income security | 99,723 | 128,200 | 28.6 |
| Education, training, employment, and social science | 33,709 | 29,342 | −29.5 |
| Health | 26,866 | 33,542 | 24.8 |
| Community and regional development | 10,568 | 7,680 | −27.3 |
| Natural resource and environment | 13,568 | 13,357 | −1.6 |
| General purpose fiscal assistance | 6,854 | 6,353 | −7.3 |
| Agriculture | 15,944 | 25,565 | 60.3 |
| Commerce and housing credit | 8,206 | 4,229 | −48.5 |
| Transportation | 23,379 | 25,838 | 10.5 |
| Energy | 15,166 | 5,685 | −62.5 |
| Veterans' benefits and services | 22,991 | 26,352 | 14.6 |
| General government | 4,582 | 5,228 | 14.1 |
| Administration of justice | 4,762 | 6,277 | 31.8 |

Source: *Economic Report of the President, February 1986* (Washington, D.C.: Government Printing Office, 1986), pp. 340, 341.

> Many wasteful bureaucratic activities have been eliminated and the number of nondefense employees on the Federal payrolls has been reduced by 71,000. We have examined every area of Federal Government spending, and sought to eliminate unnecessary and wasteful spending while protecting the benefits needed by the poor and aged.[17]

As did Friedman in his *Free to Choose,* where the federal bureaucracy was pilloried unmercifully, President Reagan "forgot" to mention the massive bureaucracy in the Department of Defense. While noting that the nondefense bureaucracy had decreased by 71,000, he says nothing of the steady increase in civilian employment in the Defense Department. Between 1980 and 1985, the number of civilian employees in the military establishment increased by 147,000 (a 15 percent increase), more than double the president's decrease in the nondefense bureaucracy.[18]

## FREE TRADE

In his rhetoric, Reagan has been a strong proponent of free international trade, as has Friedman.[19] However, although Friedman has invariably been consistent on this issue, Reagan has a number of times, in key cases, pursued a vigorous protectionist program.

Soon after taking office, the president pressured Japanese auto manufacturers to accept a voluntary quota on the export of Japanese cars to the United States. Each year the "voluntary restraints" have been renewed to protect the U.S. automobile industry from competition.[20] In what may be the strongest protectionist measure by an administration in recent years, the president ordered a tenfold increase in tariffs on heavyweight motorcycles to protect the sole-surviving U.S. manufacturer, the Harley-Davidson Motor Company.[21]

In the 1980 presidential campaign, Reagan promised the textile industry that he would work to protect it from imports. In December 1983, the administration put into effect a series of trade-tightening measures that went far beyond what even the textile industry had thought possible. The action was taken despite the fact that textile makers were already one of the most protected sectors of the U.S. economy and were in a relative boom period. When some of his advisers complained that the industry was not really hurting that badly, the president was reported to have replied, "It's what *they're* saying" (emphasis added).[22]

The steel industry, in September 1984, was promised by the president that there would be negotiated "voluntary restraints" on steel imports to lower the foreign share of the U.S. market from 26 percent to 18.5 percent.[23] Tariffs on stainless steel products were increased by an additional 10 percent in July 1983. At the same time, much tighter import quotas were imposed on stainless steel bar and rod and alloy tool steel products.[24]

Under a system of quotas established in May 1982, sugar imports into the United States were slashed about 40 percent. The quotas protected U.S. growers and kept domestic sugar prices at more than three times world levels.[25] In 1983, the Reagan administration subsidized the exports of wheat, butter, and cheese to Egypt.[26]

Friedman vigorously attacked these protectionist measures, stating, "Recent protectionist measures by the Reagan Administration have severely disappointed those of us who expected this Administration to display a higher threshold than earlier administrations before it sacrificed principle on the alter of political expediency."[27]

President Reagan has exhibited considerably greater compassion for the welfare of powerful industry representatives than he has for the poor. For industry he has often provided protection; for the poor he offers to lift them out of poverty through the economic growth provided by free markets.

## SOCIAL SECURITY

President Reagan's sharpest departure from Friedman's political economy came on the issue of Social Security. As we have discussed in some detail, Friedman is a harsh critic of Social Security and has called for its gradual elimination. Although it was not always thus, Reagan, during the 1984 presidential campaign, became a defender of Social Security. Let us see what brought about the president's change.

During Senator Goldwater's campaign in 1964, Reagan questioned both the soundness and the compulsory nature of Social Security: "Now are we so lacking in business sense that we cannot put this program on a sound actuarial basis . . . and at the same time can't we introduce voluntary features so that those who can make better provisions for themselves can be allowed to do so?"[28]

In 1981, the Reagan administration sent to Congress a bill that would reduce Social Security benefits by $46 billion over a five-year period. The proposal created such a tremendous uproar that it was rejected by the Republican-controlled Senate by a 96 to zero vote. The administration quickly retreated and the president appointed a bipartisan commission to study the system's problems and report after the 1982 election. Early in 1983, Congress adopted most of the commission's recommendations, and Reagan signed the legislation.[29]

Reagan did make one more significant move against the Social Security program. The administration in 1981–82 cut off benefits to 500,000 recipients of Social Security disability benefits, some of whom had serious mental and physical handicaps. Many sued to retain their benefits, and the federal courts restored 200,000 to the rolls. At least two judges threatened to sue Reagan's Secretary of Health and Human

Services after the government refused to apply the rulings of some courts to similar cases in other courts. Even some prominent Republicans attacked the administration, so it suspended the effort to cut off disability benefits.[30]

In the 1984 campaign, President Reagan became a "true believer" in Social Security. Under attack from Democrats who claimed the president wanted to cut Social Security benefits, he proposed that Social Security recipients be given a cost-of-living increase even if current law does not require it.[31] Having learned from the reaction to attacks on Social Security in the Goldwater campaign and from the severe rebuffs in Congress and in the courts, he has, at least temporarily, abandoned Friedman's ideology on this issue, announcing that he would not "pull the rug" from under people receiving Social Security benefits.[32]

## BALANCED BUDGETS: A REAGAN GOAL?

President Reagan has pounded a persistent drumbeat against spending, demanding that Congress produce a balanced budget. Friedman is a long-time advocate of a constitutional amendment that would mandate a balanced budget and the president has given strong verbal support to that path to nirvana.[33] But are an end to deficit spending and a balanced budget real goals of the president and Friedman? The answer to that question is a clear and unequivocal no.

The real goal of the Reagan administration, behind its deficit-spending and balanced-budget rhetoric, is to force a decline in government expenditures and, more specifically, a decline in spending on the social programs. To see that this is so, it is first necessary to explain why, according to Friedman and the Reagan administration, government expenditures grow.

The Reagan administration and Friedman have precisely the same explanation for the growth in government expenditures. Following are two passages, one from Friedman's *Free to Choose* and a second from President Reagan's 1986 *Economic Report*. Note the striking similarity between the two passages in logic and even in language. It is as if both passages were written by Friedman. From *Free to Choose*,

> Government budgets are determined by adding together expenditures that are authorized for a host of separate programs. The small number of people who have a special interest in each specific program spend money and work hard to

get it passed; the large number of people, each of whom will be assessed a few dollars to pay for the program, will not find it worthwhile to spend money or work to oppose it, even if they manage to find out about it. The majority does rule. But it is a special kind of majority. It consists of special interest minorities. The way to get elected to Congress is to collect groups of say, two or three percent of your constituents, each of which is strongly interested in one special issue that hardly concerns the rest of your constituents. Each group will be willing to vote for you if you promise to back its issue regardless of what you do about other issues. Put together enough such groups and you will have a 51 percent majority that rules the country.[34]

From the president's 1986 *Economic Report,*

One basic force explaining such growth is that the benefits of individual government spending programs are typically concentrated among a relatively small number of beneficiaries whereas the cost of individual programs are widely dispersed among millions of taxpayers. The beneficiaries of government spending programs, including the suppliers of inputs to such spending and government employees who administer such programs, have incentives to support and muster forces for lobbying efforts that may influence the final outcome of spending legislation. Moreover, because benefits are concentrated among a few, beneficiaries can easily join forces with one another to form coalitions endorsing spending programs. . . . Government spending continues to grow, therefore, not because the private sector fails to provide desired goods and services, but because of weaknesses in the political decisionmaking process.[35]

If the weakness in the political decision-making process fosters government spending, how can expenditures be reduced? The approach taken by President Reagan and recommended by Friedman is to resist tax increases, even if the result is huge deficits. If huge deficits emerge, as they have under Reagan, holding the line on taxes, given the political appeal of balancing the budget, can force cutbacks in government spending.

Almost two decades ago, Friedman made clear the underlying rationale for the Reagan administration's acceptance (creation?) of huge deficits.

For the twelve months ending June 30, 1967, the Federal government ran a deficit of about $10 billion. . . . What does fiscal policy call for in the face of these staggering deficits?

At first glance, the answer seems straightforward: restraint in spending and higher taxes. . . . In my opinion, this is a shortsighted answer. *The deficit in the Federal budget is only a symptom of a more deep-seated malady: the size of the government spending.*

Most of us regard high military spending as a necessary evil. But even many proponents of big government are having second thoughts about numerous civilian programs — from the agricultural subsidies of the New Deal to the zooming welfare measures of the Great Society. Time and time again, extravagant promises have been made that this or that expensive program will solve this or that social problem. And time and again, the result is that both costs and problems multiply.

But what relevance does this have to taxes? ... The answer is that postwar experience has demonstrated two things. First, Congress will spend whatever the tax system will raise — plus a little (and recently, a lot) more. Second, that surprising as it seems, it has proved difficult to get taxes down once they are raised. The special interests created by government spending have proved more potent than the general interest in tax reduction.

*Those of us who believe that government has reached a size at which it threatens to become our master rather than our servant should therefore (1) oppose any tax increase; (2) press for expenditure cuts; (3) accept larger deficits as the lesser of evils. ... In the long view, that is the course of true fiscal responsibility.*[36] [Emphasis added]

More recently, in February 1981, while President Reagan was preparing his first budget, a budget that was to generate the largest deficit in U.S. history up to that time, Friedman wrote,

The political appeal of a "balanced budget" has often been counterproductive. Big spenders have pushed through government programs leading to higher deficits. Fiscal conservatives, having lost that battle, have responded by supporting an increase in taxes to narrow the deficit. The fiscal conservatives have been turned out of office, partly for having the courage to raise taxes. The big spenders have been re-elected partly for their irresponsibility in raising spending. They have then set off on another spending spree and launched yet another cycle of higher spending, bigger deficits, higher taxes. *That scenario persuaded me, years ago, to be in favor of tax reductions under almost any circumstances. Cutting taxes reverses the cycle. If the tax cut threatens bigger deficits, the political appeal of balancing the budget is harnessed to reducing government spending rather than to raising taxes. That is the right way to achieve a balanced budget. It is the way that President Reagan proposes to follow. Much hinges on his success.*[37] [Emphasis added]

In an interview in a Viennese journal in the spring of 1985, Nobel Prize-winning economist, Friedrich von Hayek stated,

One of Reagan's advisors told me ... Reagan thinks it is impossible to persuade Congress that expenditures must be reduced, unless one creates deficits so large that absolutely everyone becomes convinced that no more money can be spent. Thus, he hoped to persuade Congress of the necessity of spending reductions by means of an immense deficit.[38]

And in this country, Norman J. Ornstein, a prominent political scientist with the American Enterprise Institute, wrote,

The deep tax cut did compound the deficit. And behind the scenes the people around Reagan clearly knew that it would. In the middle of the tax-cut war, a key Reagan lieutenant candidly assessed the situation: We're well aware that tax cuts at the level we're discussing will add tremendously to future deficits. Most of us, to be frank, don't buy the supply-side line. Regardless, Reagan's main goal is not to balance the budget — it is to reduce the role of government. How do we best do this? In our view, if we don't cut taxes and generate big deficits, spending will never come down. Congress will just spend the revenues and more. . . . But with huge deficits, their choices are tougher . . . they'll have to cut spending.[39]

With military expenditures scheduled for substantial increases, interest on the debt impossible to reduce significantly, and Social Security declared untouchable by the president and Congress — and with those three items comprising 65 percent of the budget — the major significant areas left for cutbacks in spending are the social programs. And so we arrive at the hidden agenda behind the Reagan rhetoric on balanced budgets: his assault on deficit spending is in essence a covert assault on social spending, an assault largely directed at the poor and disadvantaged, an assault on those who are not so free to choose.

The attack on the social programs that provide transfer payments by the government to individuals (Social Security, unemployment benefits, welfare payments, food stamps, Medicare, and Medicaid) is particularly significant because of its implications for the distribution of income. In a study of 1980 data, Joseph Pechman, a prominent authority on taxation, concluded that the tax system as a whole (federal, state, and local) had very little effect on the distribution of income. He also found that transfer payments, because they are highly progressive, had a major effect on income distribution.

Families in the lowest three deciles of market incomes received substantially more transfers than they paid in taxes, those in the fourth decile received about the same amount as they paid in taxes, and families in the six highest deciles paid more in taxes than they received in transfers. For the distribution of income as a whole, incomes after taxes and transfers were distributed 7 to 10 percent more equally than market incomes. The greater equality, Pechman concluded, "was almost entirely the result of the transfer system."[40] Cutbacks in the social programs, in line with the Reagan agenda, would reduce transfer payments and hence aggravate the already substantial inequality in the distribution of income.

## MONETARISM

A new "Age of Friedman" has replaced the Keynesian consensus that reigned since the 1930's. . . . This new "Age of Friedman" expresses a broad consensus that curbing inflation is the top economic priority. . . . Monetarism and the free-market views of Milton Friedman are becoming so institutionalized that this philosophy will remain dominant for decades, as did the ideas of Keynes previously.[41]

Thus spake futurologist Herman Kahn in September of 1982 as he gazed into what must have been an extremely murky crystal ball. Only six months later *Business Week* was writing of "The failure of monetarism."[42] And exactly three years after Kahn's prediction that Friedman's monetarism would remain dominant for decades, *Newsweek*, in a story entitled "The Monetarists on the Run," observed that

few have come so far and then fallen so fast as the monetarists. . . . Traditional opponents, such as Keynesians in academia, have been joined in monetarist bashing by the U.S. Chamber of Commerce, Wall Street, Congress and a number of Federal Reserve and Reagan Administration economists.[43]

Why the precipitous decline in the status of monetarism?

In testimony before the Joint Economic Committee of Congress in 1959, Friedman stated:

The urgent need . . . is to keep monetary changes from being a destabilizing force, as they have been through much of history. In my view, this can best be done by assigning the monetary authorities the task of keeping the stock of money growing at a regular and steady rate, month in and month out. This would at one and the same time provide a stable monetary background for the short-term adjustments and assure long-run stability in the purchasing power of the dollar.[44]

It took 20 years and the severe inflationary conditions of the late 1970s before the Federal Reserve monetary authorities adopted an essentially monetarist policy. On October 6, 1979, the Federal Reserve announced that it would support the objective of containing growth in the monetary aggregates by placing greater emphasis on the supply of bank reserves and less emphasis on controlling short-term fluctuations in interest rates. The goal was to achieve slower and steadier monetary growth even if it meant greater variability in short-term interest rates.

As it was in accord with basic monetarist principles, Friedman found the objective excellent. And so did the Reagan administration. As the *Wall Street Journal* reported in 1981,

> Unlike previous administrations, President Reagan and his advisers advocate a strict "monetarist" approach to fighting inflation. They blame inflation on one cause: the Fed's tendency over the past 15 years to let the money supply grow faster than the national output. . . . Mr. Reagan is the first President to appoint outspoken monetarists such as Mr. [Beryl] Sprinkel and Jerry Jordan of the Council of Economic Advisers, to high policy-making positions. To maintain pressure on the central bank, Mr. Sprinkel has installed a group of monetarists in a new Treasury Office of Domestic Monetary Policy to keep watch on the Fed's performance and to suggest improvements.[45]

Since then Beryl Sprinkel, a protégé of Milton Friedman, has moved from the Treasury to chairmanship of the Council of Economic Advisers.[46]

In line with its new objective, and with the strong support of the Reagan administration, the Federal Reserve brought down the rate of growth in the money supply from about 8 percent in 1979 to almost 5 percent in 1981. The tight money policy slashed the inflation rate from 18 percent in 1979 to 4 percent in 1983. The victory over inflation, however, was bought at a heavy cost in terms of record high interest rates and the worst recession in post-World War II history. The unemployment rate rose steadily and sharply from 7.2 percent in April 1981 to a high of 10.7 percent in November 1982. The severity of the recession was undoubtedly the major factor in bringing about the strong reaction against monetarism.[47]

In the summer of 1982, in order to check the deepening recession and to promote economic recovery, the Federal Reserve retreated significantly from strict adherence to monetarism. Rather than concentrating solely on achieving a slow, steady increase in the money supply, Chairman Volcker announced that growth in the money supply above targeted ranges would be tolerated and that "we will look to a variety of factors . . . including . . . the growth of credit, the behavior of banking and financial markets, and more broadly, the behavior of velocity and interest rates."[48] In essence, Volcker was rejecting the rigid monetarist rule of focusing on the single variable of monetary growth in favor of discretionary monetary policy that would have the Federal Reserve responding to a number of changing conditions in financial markets.

In the year following Volcker's announcement, the money supply grew substantially, by 13 percent. The Reagan administration's expansionary fiscal policy, along with the Federal Reserve's switch to an accommodative monetary policy, turned the economy around in the second quarter of 1983 — GNP rose sharply and unemployment fell.

In an essay written in 1985 for the Joint Economic Committee of Congress, Friedman vigorously denied that the Federal Reserve ever followed a monetarist program.

> It is widely believed that monetarism was tried in the United States from 1979 to 1984 and that it did not work in practice. That is very far from the truth. In October 1979, the Federal Reserve in desperation adopted monetarist rhetoric. It did not then and has not since adopted a monetarist policy.
>
> A monetarist policy consists of two essential items: First, the acceptance of a monetary aggregate by the monetary authorities as their primary target; second, the adoption of policies directed at producing a stable and predictable rate of growth in that monetary aggregate. . . . Every variety of monetarist, whatever his specific formula, has regarded relatively stable and relatively predictable growth in a specific monetary aggregate as an essential feature of a monetarist policy.[49]

While the Federal Reserve's 1979 announced objective of containing growth in the money supply was applauded by Friedman, he found the execution of the policy a failure. Although the average monetary growth was lower after the 1979 change in policy and, says Friedman, accounts for the subsequent decline in inflation, the cost of the adjustment was too high because of the extreme variability in monetary growth. "Monetary growth," he observed, "became much more variable after the change rather than steadier." As a result, he argues,

> Interest rates and economic activity followed suit, fluctuating more violently and over shorter periods than earlier. In addition, the lag between changes in monetary growth and subsequent changes in interest rates, economic activity, and inflation shortened. . . . To the best of my knowledge, no earlier three year period since the Fed was established shows such wide fluctuations in either monetary growth or economic activity as the three years from the fourth quarter of 1979 to the third quarter of 1982.[50]

Friedman concludes that "if a monetarist policy had in fact been followed from the third quarter of 1979 to the third quarter of 1982 not only in the sense that a monetary target was aimed at, but that it was reasonably effectively achieved . . . unemployment would never have risen as it did. Output would never have fallen as low."[51]

In a sharply worded attack on the behavior of the Federal Reserve, Friedman states: "I have repeatedly noted that it is far easier to predict the consequence of the monetary growth produced by the Fed than it is to predict what monetary growth the Fed will produce. The former is a question of economic analysis; the latter often appears to be a question of psychoanalysis."[52]

Contrary to Friedman's claim, he has had considerable difficulty in predicting the consequences of monetary growth produced by the Federal Reserve. In fact, his erroneous predictions, along with those of other monetarists, with respect to the impact of monetary growth during the 1980s probably did as much to discredit monetarism as did the Federal Reserve's role in the severe recession of 1981–82. Friedman, in discussing economic methodology, has argued quite vigorously that the validity of any theory must be judged primarily by how well it predicts.[53] Let us examine how successful Friedman has been in employing his monetarist model to predict economic developments in the 1980s.

In December 1982 Friedman predicted that the explosive growth in the money supply that had started in July 1982 was almost certain to bring on a recovery within the next few months and, as the recovery gathered steam, interest rates would erupt. The explosion in the money supply would likely end with a bang, followed by a contraction in monetary growth that would "produce a renewed recession early in 1984." He concluded that "luck" was about all we could count on to avoid a recession.[54]

A recovery did occur in the second quarter of 1983. Contrary to his forecasts, however, interest rates did not erupt, the explosive growth in the money supply did not end with a bang, and most important of all, his prediction of a recession in early 1984 never materialized.[55]

In September of 1983, in a *Wall Street Journal* column, Friedman wrote the following:

Excessive monetary growth over the past year means that we are facing the near-certainty of an overheated economy for the next few quarters at least, which will almost certainly mean a subsequent acceleration of inflation, probably in middle or late 1984.

Unfortunately, the damage has now been done, and there is no easy, or for that matter, difficult way out. Continuation of present levels of monetary growth would mean reduced nominal GNP growth next year. Combined with the delayed impact on inflation of the recent monetary explosion, the result would be a recession — a replay of the downturn in 1981 after a replay of the rapid expansion from late 1980 to early 1981. There is no middle course that at this point will avoid both higher inflation and at least a decided slowing if not premature termination of the expansion.[56]

He was wrong again. Evidently there was a middle course. The overheated economy did not materialize, nor was there any acceleration of inflation in middle or late 1984. On the contrary, the rate of inflation was remarkably stable: from December to December the consumer price index increased 3.8 percent in 1983, 4 percent in 1984, and 3.8 percent in 1985.[57]

In April and June of 1984 Friedman was again predicting an inevitable inflationary movement.

Friedman says that the nation would be "fortunate" to escape inflation of 7 to 10 percent by the fourth quarter.[58]

In a speech to institutional clients of Oppenheimer & Company, Mr. Friedman said that by the end of this year, prices would be rising at an 8 or 9 percent rate, with some double digit inflation likely during 1985. The most optimistic scenario, he said, is for inflation to peak in 1985 at 10 percent or 11 percent.[59]

For Mr. Friedman and for the small group of strict "monetarists" who share his views, rapid inflation was predetermined two years ago when the Federal Reserve decided to pump up the nation's money supply in an effort to bring the economy out of a recession.

"Money growth was very rapid from the second quarter of 1982 to the second quarter of 1983," notes Mr. Friedman. The first effect of that surge of money was a rapid rise in the economy's growth. But historical experience, as interpreted by Mr. Friedman, suggests that a wave of inflation should follow approximately two years after such a monetary surge. Those forecasters who predict otherwise are "extremely shortsighted," he says. [Friedman] sees prices rising at nearly 10 percent by year end — nearly twice the current inflation rate.[60]

And yet again, at no time during 1984 and 1985 did the inflation rate come close to approximating Friedman's predictions in the above three reports. From July 1984 to December 1984 the compounded rate of change in the consumer price index was 3.7 percent, and in the October 1984 to December 1984 rate only 2.7 percent — about one-fourth the inflation rate predicted by Friedman.[61]

In August 1985 in a *Wall Street Journal* column, Friedman wrote,

> The substantial rise in monetary growth since the fourth quarter of 1984 will almost surely be followed by a substantial acceleration in the growth of nominal GNP, perhaps already in its early stages, perhaps not beginning until the third or fourth quarter. Whenever it does begin, it will be some months before the Fed recognizes that such an acceleration is underway. It will then step on the monetary break, setting the stage for a subsequent deceleration — and so on, ad nauseum.[62]

Rather than Friedman's predicted substantial acceleration in the growth of nominal GNP, the annual growth rate in the fourth quarter was the same as in the second quarter during which Friedman had made his prediction — 4.5 percent.[63]

The *Wall Street Journal* in December 1984 commented on Friedman's predictions.

> Monetarism is suffering from self-inflicted wounds. . . . Late last year, Milton Friedman predicted a recession in the first half of 1984 and soaring inflation in the second half. He was dead wrong. The economy boomed in the first half, and there aren't any indications of a major resurgence of inflation in the second. His recession forecast was based on a sharp slowdown of M1 [money supply] growth in late 1983; inflation would surge as a result of sharp growth in the money supply from mid-1982 to mid-1983, he said.[64]

Friedman, in a *Newsweek* column in May 1983, cited predictions by three chairmen of the Federal Reserve Board, Arthur F. Burns, G. William Miller, and Paul A. Volcker. Finding all three predictions wrong, Friedman commented, "Times at bat, 3; hits, 0; runs, 0; errors, 3." Assessing Friedman's record of predictions concerning inflation, the money supply, interest rates, and economic growth, and employing his odd scorekeeping techniques, we similarly calculate, "Times at bat, 8; hits, 1; runs, 0; errors, 7." A batting average of .125 and seven errors may satisfy compassionate parents of little leaguers, but it clearly won't get their kids into the majors.

The failure of monetarism to explain developments in the economy over the past four years is, in essence, admitted in the 1986 *Economic Report of the President*. In that report, the President's Council of

Economic Advisers, under the chairmanship of staunch monetarist Beryl
Sprinkel, states,

> Growth of M1 has been very strong in this expansion, yet the rise of
> inflation that would be inferred from the historical relationship between M1
> growth and inflation has not occurred. Over the past twelve quarters of this
> expansion, M1 growth has been about 9 percent and has exceeded the rates
> associated with the rise in inflation in the 1970's. In addition, M1 growth
> was more than 11 percent in 1985, but the rebound in the real economy
> recorded through the fourth quarter has not been as strong as would be
> expected from the historical relationship between the short-term changes in
> money growth and economic activity.[65]

We are not aware that Friedman has modified his position in any way
whatsoever with respect to monetarism. For the ideologue, if reality is
inconsistent with his theory, so much the worse for reality.

## SUMMARY AND CONCLUSIONS

In the introductory chapter, we quoted an assessment of Friedman's
popular writings by one of his editors. He stated that Friedman's essays
"responsibly provide genuine economic analysis" for a diverse audience,
that although "one cannot look to such essays for definitive scientific
treatments," nevertheless the reader "will be impressed that he is
observing an economist — not an ideologue or a poet — employing his
craft."

Contrary to that laudatory appraisal, our analysis in this volume
reveals Friedman the ideologue, employing his craft as an economist in
defense of laissez-faire markets and his own conception of economic and
political freedom. Rather than responsibly providing genuine economic
analysis, his popular writings are often simplistic and frequently cavalier
in their treatment of social, political, and economic history. Friedman
exhibits a pronounced tendency to cite data that tend to confirm a position
he is defending, while he conveniently ignores readily available data that
are obviously inconsistent with his analysis.

With respect to the role of government in society, Friedman states in
*Capitalism and Freedom* and again in *Free to Choose,*

> In any particular case of proposed intervention, we must make up a balance
> sheet, listing separately the advantages and disadvantages. Our principles tell

us what items to put on the one side and what items to put on the other and they given us some basis for attaching importance to the different items.[66]

No one could argue with such a laudable approach to an analysis of the role of government intervention. However, in reading all of Friedman's popular writings, one is hard pressed to find any weighing of the advantages and disadvantages when a government action is under discussion. Rather than any careful weighing of the costs and benefits, Friedman's ideological blinders invariably lead him to present an accounting anomaly, a one-sided balance sheet. For any government action, aside from national defense, the maintenance of law and order, and perhaps in dealing with externalities, he sees no benefits — only costs.

Despite his rhetoric in defense of freedom, his passion for capitalism and free markets has led him to produce apologetics for the repressive regimes of South Africa and Pinochet's Chile, while at the same time attacking "socialist" planning in democratic India and the welfare states of the United Kingdom and Sweden. The preservation of market capitalism seems to have a higher priority for Friedman than the violation of human rights.

Our review of his widely disseminated popular writing and the *Economic Reports* of the president indicate that Friedman has had a significant influence on the ideology, rhetoric, and policies of the Reagan administration. So closely do the *Reports* adhere to Friedman's free-market ideological framework, even with respect to rhetoric, it is almost as if they were ghostwritten by Friedman himself.

In his persistent and often successful attempts to cut back sharply on the social programs of the New Deal and the Great Society, President Reagan has moved in the general direction pointed by Friedman, with one major exception — Social Security. After an initial attempt to make substantial reductions in Social Security was met with a unanimous rebuff by a Republican-controlled Senate, the president pulled back from his previous criticisms of Social Security. In the 1984 presidential campaign, obviously in recognition of the power of the broad-based, middle-class voting block behind the program, Reagan announced he would never "pull out the rug" from under Social Security beneficiaries. Friedman, on the other hand, would eliminate Social Security. From his criticisms of Social Security prior to becoming a presidential candidate, it seems safe to conjecture that Reagan would not be unhappy with its elimination. Fortunately, political reality sometimes does make a difference.

President Reagan has broken sharply with Friedman on the issue of free trade. Whereas Friedman has been a consistent proponent of free international trade, President Reagan has, on a number of occasions, taken protectionist measures to defend U.S. industry from foreign competition. The president's passionate free-market rhetoric becomes muted when U.S. industries are threatened by competition that might have an adverse effect on their welfare. When the issue is welfare for the poor and disadvantaged, on the other hand, he offers those living in poverty free-market capitalism and the promise that they will rise out of poverty with the economic growth of the economy.

Despite the massive deficits accumulated under his administration, President Reagan, following the line laid down by Friedman, has been rigid in his opposition to tax increases. The rationale is clear. By holding the line on taxes, given the political appeal of balanced budgets and the fear of huge deficits, the president believes that he can force a reduction in government expenditures. With the commitment to rising military expenditures, the high interest burden, and the political untouchability of Social Security, the only places left for significant cuts in expenditures are in the social programs that provide transfer payments. Since transfer payments represent the basic means for reducing the inequality in the distribution of income, an attack on the social programs will leave the poor in a position where they are not so free to choose.

It may be argued that this volume has been excessively critical of Friedman's popular writings. One might ask if it is fair to demand professional standards in essays and books intended for popular consumption. Kenneth Arrow, a Nobel laureate in economics, in a review of Friedman's *Free to Choose,* gave an excellent answer to that question.

> As Friedman himself is so fond of quoting, there is no such thing as a free lunch. In policy terms, this means that every policy change is bound to do some harm somewhere. Yet in his popular writings there is little sense of qualification. In this book, as in the earlier *Capitalism and Freedom,* both written jointly with Rose Friedman, there is very little suggestion that their very large redirections of policy could possibly have any negative consequences. Government regulations of all sorts — occupational licensing, social security, public education — are all to be committed to the bonfire. There is no sense that there may be any real losses as well as possible gains to these drastic changes.

It may be said that I am demanding professional standards of a book intended for popular consumption. . . . But in my view, the responsibilities of the economist (or any other scholar) for fairness, "two handedness," are greater when writing for the general public than when writing for his colleagues, who are knowledgeable and can notice omissions.[67]

In presenting his long one-sided balance sheet on important social problems, Friedman has attempted to deny his reader the opportunity to be truly free to choose.

## NOTES

1. *Economic Report of the President, February 1986* (Washington, D.C.: Government Printing Office, 1986), p. 6.

2. U.S., Congress, House, Committee on the Budget, *A Review of President Reagan's Budget Recommendations, 1981–1985,* 98th Cong., 2d sess. (Washington, D.C.: Government Printing Office, 1984), p. 3.

3. *Congressional Quarterly Almanac,* 23 (Washington, D.C.: Congressional Quarterly Inc, 1982), p. 3-E.

4. Ibid., p. 4-E.

5. Joseph A. Pechman, *Federal Tax Policy,* (Washington, D.C.: Brookings Institution, 1983), pp. 110, 152–58, 310.

6. William Greider, "The Education of David Stockman," *Atlantic Monthly,* (1981): 29.

7. *Newsweek,* August 7, 1978, p. 39.

8. *Newsweek,* May 24, 1976, p. 78.

9. Tom Lodge, *Black Politics in South Africa Since 1945,* (London and New York: Longman, 1983), pp. 328–30.

10. *Newsweek,* November 28, 1977, p. 94.

11. D. L. Bawden and John L. Palmer, "Social Policy," in *The Reagan Record,* ed. John L. Palmer and Isabel V. Sawhill (Cambridge, Mass.: Ballinger, 1984), p. 187.

12. Milton Friedman and Rose Friedman, *Tyranny of the Status Quo* (New York: Harcourt, Brace, Jovanovich, 1984), p. 32.

13. Ibid., p. 30.

14. Marilyn Moon and Isabel V. Sawhill, "Family Income, Gainers and Losers," in *The Reagan Record,* ed. John L. Palmer and Isabel V. Sawhill (Cambridge, Mass.: Ballinger, 1984), p. 325.

15. Ibid., p. 331.

16. Gregory B. Mills, "The Budget," in *The Reagan Record,* ed. John L. Palmer and Isabel V. Sawhill (Cambridge, Mass.: Ballinger, 1984).

17. *Economic Report of the President, February 1984* (Washington, D.C.: Government Printing Office, 1984), p. 7.

18. U.S., Department of Commerce, Bureau of the Census, *Statistical Abstract of the United States, 1985* (Washington, D.C.: Government Printing Office, 1985), p. 325; *Federal Civilian Workforce Statistics, Monthly Release,* August 1985, p. 10.

19. New York *Times,* February 5, 1986, p. A20; September 26, 1984, p. D5.

20. Ibid., October 23, 1984, p. A26.

21. Ibid.

22. *Wall Street Journal,* January 6, 1984, p. 1.

23. New York *Times,* September 20, 1984, p. D1; May 17, 1985, p. D2.

24. *Wall Street Journal,* July 6, 1983, p. 3.

25. Ibid., March 12, 1984, p. 38.

26. Ibid., July 25, 1983, p. 15.

27. *Newsweek,* November 15, 1982, p. 90.

28. Jack W. Germond and Jules Witcover, *Wake Us Up When It's Over* (New York: Macmillan, 1985), p. 18.

29. Ibid., p. 32; Bruno Stein, *Social Security and Pensions in Transition* (New York: Free Press, 1983), p. xiii.

30. New York *Times,* October 25, 1984, p. B20.

31. *Wall Street Journal,* July 26, 1984, p 54.

32. New York *Times,* July 8, 1984, p. 1.

33. *Economic Report, 1986,* p. 7.

34. Milton Friedman and Rose Friedman, *Free to Choose* (New York: Avon, 1981), pp. 290–91.

35. *Economic Report, 1986,* pp. 62–63.

36. *Newsweek,* August 7, 1967, p. 68.

37. *Newsweek,* February 23, 1981, p. 70.

38. *Wall Street Journal,* August 16, 1985, p. 19.

39. Ibid. The quotes of Hayek and Ornstein are in a letter to the *Wall Street Journal* from Senator Daniel Patrick Moynihan of New York.

40. Joseph A. Pechman, *Who Paid the Taxes, 1966–1985* (Washington, D.C.: Brookings Institution, 1985), pp. 3–6, 51–53.

41. Peter Brimelow, "Talking Money with Milton Friedman," *Barron's,* October 25, 1982, p. 6.

42. *Business Week,* April 4, 1983, p. 64.

43. *Newsweek,* September 23, 1985, p. 48.

44. U.S., Congress, *Employment, Growth, and Price Levels,* Hearings before the Joint Economic Committee, 86th Cong., 1st sess. (Washington, D.C.: Government Printing Office, 1959), p. 611.

45. *Wall Street Journal,* August 4, 1981, p. 1.

46. Ibid., August 21, 1983, p. 4.

47. *Business Week,* April 4, 1983, p. 64.

48. Andrew F. Brimmer, "Monetary Policy and Economic Activity: Benefits and Costs of Monetarism," *American Economic Review,* May 1983, p. 4.

49. Milton Friedman, "How to Give Monetarism a Bad Name," essay prepared for the Joint Economic Committee, 99th Cong., 1st sess., 1985, p. 51.

50. Ibid., p. 54.

51.    Ibid., pp. 57–58.

52.    Ibid., p. 60.

53.    Milton Friedman, *Essays in Positive Economics* (Chicago: University of Chicago Press, 1953), p. 4.

54.    *Newsweek,* December 27, 1982, p. 58.

55.    *Economic Report of the President, February 1985* (Washington, D.C.: Government Printing Office, 1985), pp. 239, 303, 311.

56.    *Wall Street Journal,* September 1, 1983, p. 24.

57.    *Economic Report, 1986,* pp. 252, 319.

58.    New York *Times,* April 9, 1984, p. D1.

59.    New York *Times,* April 30, 1984, p. D7.

60.    *Wall Street Journal,* June 13, 1984, p. 4.

61.    *National Economic Trends,* March 1986 (Federal Reserve Bank of St. Louis), p. 4.

62.    *Wall Street Journal,* August 20, 1985, p. 28.

63.    *National Economic Trends,* p. 12.

64.    *Wall Street Journal,* December 10, 1984, p. 1.

65.    *Economic Report, 1986,* pp. 54–55.

66.    Milton Friedman, *Capitalism and Freedom* (Chicago: University of Chicago Press, 1962), p. 32; Friedman and Friedman, *Free to Choose,* p. ix.

67.    Kenneth Arrow, "Book Review," *New Republic,* 186 (March 22, 1980), pp. 25–26.

# BIBLIOGRAPHY

Aaron, Henry J. *Economic Effects of Social Security*. Washington, D.C.: Brookings Institution, 1982.

Alexander, Robert J. *The Tragedy of Chile*. Westport, Conn.: Greenwood Press, 1978.

Ascher, William. *Scheming for the Poor*. Cambridge: Harvard University Press, 1984.

Banks, Arthur S., ed. *Political Handbook of the World, 1979*. New York: McGraw-Hill, 1979.

Bawden, D. L., and J. L. Palmer, "Social Policy." In *The Reagan Record*, edited by John L. Palmer and Isabel V. Sawhill, pp. 177–215. Cambridge, Mass.: Ballinger, 1984.

Beard, Charles A., and M. Beard. *The Rise of American Civilization*. New York: Macmillan, 1930.

Blum, John M. et al. *The National Experience*. New York: Harcourt, Brace, and World, 1963.

Brantingham, Paul, and Barbara Brantingham. *Patterns in Crime*. New York: Macmillan, 1984.

Brinton, Crane. *A History of Civilization*. New York: Prentice-Hall, 1955.

Brittan, Samuel. "How British is the British Sickness," *Journal of Law and Economics* 21 (1978): 245–68.

Cohen, Wilbur J., and Milton Friedman. *Social Security: Universal or Selective*. Washington, D.C.: American Enterprise Institute for Public Policy Research, 1972.

Danziger, Sheldon, and Peter Gottschalk. "The Poverty of Losing Ground." *Challenge* 28 (1985): 32–38.

Davidson, Basil. *Africa in History*. New York: Collier Books, 1974.

Duncan, Greg J. *Panel Study of Income Dynamics*. Ann Arbor: University of Michigan, 1981.

_____. *Years of Poverty, Years of Plenty*. Ann Arbor: University of Michigan Press, 1984.

*Economic Report of the President, February 1982.* Washington, D.C.: Government Printing Office, 1982.

*Economic Report of the President, February 1984.* Washington, D.C.: Government Printing Office, 1984.

*Economic Report of the President, February 1986.* Washington, D.C.: Government Printing Office, 1986.

Faulkner, Harold U. *American Economic History.* 7th rev. ed. New York: Harper & Brothers, 1954.

Feinberg, Richard E. *The Triumph of Allende.* New York: New American Library, 1976.

Foxley, Alejandro. *Latin American Experiments in Neoconservative Economics.* Berkeley: University of California Press, 1983.

Freeman, Richard B. *Labor Economics.* 2d ed. Englewood Cliffs, N.J.: Prentice-Hall, 1979.

_____. *Changes in the Labor Market for Black Americans, 1948–1972.* Brookings Papers on Economic Activity, pp. 67–120. Washington, D.C.: Brookings Institution, 1973.

Friedman, Milton. *Capitalism and Freedom.* Chicago: University of Chicago Press, 1962.

_____. *Dollars and Deficits.* Englewood Cliffs, N.J.: Prentice-Hall, 1968.

_____. *Bright Promises, Dismal Performance: An Economist's Protest,* edited by William R. Allen. New York: Harcourt, Brace, Jovanovich, 1983.

Friedman, Milton, and Rose Friedman. *Free to Choose.* New York: Avon, 1981.

_____. *Tyranny of the Status Quo.* New York: Harcourt, Brace, Jovanovich, 1984.

Friedman, Milton, and Walter W. Heller. *Monetary vs. Fiscal Policy.* New York: W. W. Norton, 1969.

Friedman, Milton, and Simon Kuznets. *Income from Independent Professional Practices.* New York: National Bureau of Economic Research, 1945.

Germond, Jack W., and Jules Witcover. *Wake Us Up When It's Over.* New York: Macmillan, 1985.

Gordon, Robert J. *Macroeconomics.* Boston: Little, Brown, 1981.

Greider, William. "The Education of David Stockman," *Atlantic Monthly* (1981): 27–54.

Heller, Walter W. *New Dimensions of Political Economy.* New York: W. W. Norton, 1967.

Hellman, Daryl A. *The Economics of Crime.* New York: St. Martin's Press, 1980.

Hersh, Seymour M. *The Price of Power.* New York: Summit Books, 1983.

Higgins, Benjamin, and Jean Downing Higgins. *Economic Development of a Small Planet.* New York: W. W. Norton, 1979.

Hobsbawm, E. J. *The Age of Revolution, 1789–1848.* New York: New American Library, 1964.

____. *Industry and Empire.* New York: Pantheon Books, 1968.

Keynes, John Maynard. *The General Theory of Employment, Interest, and Money.* New York: Harcourt, Brace, 1936.

Knight, Frank. *Freedom and Reform.* Port Washington: Kennikat Press, 1947.

Kublin, Hyman. *Japan.* Boston: Houghton Mifflin, 1969.

Kurien, C. T. *India's Economic Crisis.* Bombay: Asia, 1969.

Langer, Walter, ed. *An Encyclopedia of World History.* Boston: Houghton Mifflin, 1948.

Lindblom, Charles E. *Politics and Markets.* New York: Basic Books, 1977.

Loeher, William, and John P. Powelson. *The Economics of Development and Distribution.* New York: Harcourt, Brace, Jovanovich, 1981.

Maddison, Angus. *Economic Progress and Policy in Developing Countries.* New York: W. W. Norton, 1970.

Manchester, William. *The Glory and the Dream.* Boston: Little, Brown, 1973.

McCord, William. "The Japanese Model." In *The Political Economy of Development and Underdevelopment,* edited by Charles K. Wilbur, pp. 278–83. New York: Random House, 1973.

McElvaine, Robert S. *The Great Depression.* New York: Times Books, 1984.

Meier, August, and Elliot Rudwick. *From Plantation to Ghetto.* New York: Hill and Wang, 1970.

Mill, John Stuart, *Principles of Political Economy.* New York: Augustus Kelley, 1969.

_____. *Autobiography.* New York: Columbia University Press, 1944.

Mills, Gregory B. "The Budget." In *The Reagan Record,* edited by John L. Palmer and Isabel V. Sawhill, pp. 107–39. Cambridge, Mass.: Ballinger, 1984.

Mitchell, J. Paul, ed. *Race Riots in Black and White.* Englewood Cliffs, N.J.: Prentice-Hall, 1970.

Moon, Marilyn and Isabel V. Sawhill. "Family Income, Gainers and Losers." In *The Reagan Record,* edited by John L. Palmer and Isabel V. Sawhill, pp. 317–46. Cambridge, Mass.: Ballinger, 1984.

Myrdal, Gunnar. *Asian Drama.* New York: Pantheon, 1968.

Nove, Alec. "The Political Economy of Allende Regime." In *Allende's Chile,* edited by Phillip J. O'Brien, pp. 51–77. New York: Praeger, 1976.

O'Brien, Phillip J. "The New Leviathan: The Chicago School and the Chilean Regime." *IDS Sussex Bulletin* 13 (1981): 38–50.

Ohkawa, Kajushi, and Henry Rosovsky. "Capital Formation in Japan." In *The Cambridge Economic History of Europe,* Vol. III., Part 2. Cambridge: Cambridge University Press, 1978.

Pechman, Joseph A. *Federal Tax Policy.* Washington, D.C.: Brookings Institution, 1983.

_____. *Who Paid the Taxes, 1966–1985.* Washington, D.C.: Brookings Institution, 1985.

Peffer, Nathaniel. *The Far East.* Ann Arbor: University of Michigan Press, 1958.

Polyani, Karl. *The Great Transformation.* New York: Rinehart, 1944.

Rogers, David E. "Providing Medicine to the Elderly and Poor: A Serious Problem for the Downsizing 1980s." In *Health Care for the Poor and Elderly: Meeting the Challenge,* edited by Duncan Yaggy, pp. 3–12. Durham, N.C.: Duke University Press, 1984.

Rude, George. *Revolutionary Europe, 1783–1815.* London: Collins, 1967.

Samuelson, Paul. *Economics.* New York: McGraw-Hill, 1961.

____. "Personal Freedom and Economic Freedoms in the Mixed Economy." In *The Business Establishment,* edited by Earl Chest, pp. 193–227. New York: Wiley, 1964.

Schumpeter, Joseph. *History of Economic Analysis.* New York: Oxford University Press, 1954.

Shonfield, Andrew. *Modern Capitalism.* New York: Oxford University Press, 1965.

Sigmund, Paul E. *The Overthrow of Allende and the Politics of Chile, 1964–1976.* Pittsburgh: University of Pittsburgh Press, 1977.

Smith, Adam. *The Wealth of Nations.* New York: Random House, 1937.

Smith, James Morton, and Paul L. Murphy, eds. *Liberty and Justice.* New York: Alfred A. Knopf, 1958.

Stallings, Barbara. *Economic Development in Chile, 1958–1973.* Stanford, Calif.: Stanford University Press, 1978.

Stein, Bruno. *Social Security and Pensions in Transition.* New York: Free Press, 1983.

Taussig, F. W. *The Tariff History of the United States.* New York: G. P. Putnam's Sons, 1892.

Tuttle, William M., Jr. *Race Riots.* New York: Atheneum, 1972.

U.S., Congress, House. *GAO Analysis of the 1981 AFDC Reductions.* Hearing before the Subcommittee on Public Assistance and Unemployment Compensation, 98th Cong., 2d sess. Washington, D.C.: Government Printing Office, 1985.

U.S., Congress, House, Committee on the Budget. *A Review of President Reagan's Budget Recommendations, 1981–1985.* 98th Cong., 2d sess. Washington, D.C.: Government Printing Office, 1984.

U.S., Congress, Senate. Select Committee to Study Governmental Operations with Respect to Intelligence Activities. *Covert Action in Chile.* 94th Cong., 1st sess. Washington, D.C.: Government Printing Office, 1975.

U.S., Department of Commerce, International Trade Administration. *Foreign*

*Economic Trends and Their Implications for the United States, Chile.* Washington, D.C.: Government Printing Office, 1984.

U.S., Department of Health and Human Services, Health Care Financing Administration, *Health Care Financing Review, 1985 Annual Supplement,* Baltimore: December 1985.

Valenzuela, Arturo. "Eight Years of Military Rule in Chile." *Current History* 81 (1982): 64.

Viet, Lawrence A. *India's Second Revolution.* New York: McGraw-Hill, 1976.

Whitehead, Lawrence. "Inflation and Stabilization in Chile, 1970–77." In *Inflation and Stabilization in Latin America,* edited by Rosemary Thorp and Lawrence Whitehead, pp. 65–109. New York: Holmes and Meier, 1979.

Wilcox, Clair, et al. *Economies of the World Today,* 3rd ed. New York: Harcourt, Brace, Jovanovich, 1976.

World Bank. *World Development Report, 1980.* Washington, D.C.: World Bank, 1980.

Zahler, Roberto. "Recent Southern Cone Liberalization Reforms and Stabilization Policies." *Journal of Interamerican Studies and World Affairs* 25 (1983): 509–63.

# INDEX

# ABOUT THE AUTHOR

Elton Rayack received his doctorate in economics at the University of Chicago in 1957. He has published in a number of journals in the fields of labor economics and the economics of medical care, and has been a consultant for various state and federal agencies and professional organizations. He is presently a professor of economics at the University of Rhode Island where he is also associated with the university's Labor Research Center.